Praise for *When Presidents Fight the Last War*

"Bryan N. Groves peels back the veil that shrouds Oval Office decision-making during major conflicts. Keen analysis, supported by those who helped make policy, reveals the rationale and connective tissue behind the decisions of commanders in chief since Vietnam."

—Admiral James G. Stavridis, US Navy (Ret.),
former NATO commander

"Groves takes on an ambitious task: comparing the impact of two historic inflection points on presidential decision-making, Vietnam and 9/11. The strategic lessons he draws are thought-provoking and should inform policymakers as they contend with the most recent tectonic shift in global affairs: the war in Ukraine."

—Lieutenant General Douglas Lute, US Army (Ret.),
former US ambassador to NATO

"Superbly written! Groves's account describes presidents' rationale for conflict decision-making, illustrating common themes among very different commanders in chief. His policy recommendations hit the mark, highlighting the strategic importance of policy adjustments and how to win wars again."

—General Barry McCaffrey, US Army (Ret.), MSNBC security
expert and former SOUTHCOM commander

"A thoughtful study of an understudied aspect of war leadership: how leaders think through pivot points once war has started. The book uses insights from behavioral economics and political psychology to shed light on the decision-making calculus—and does so in a way that will ring true to the participants in war councils."

—Peter D. Feaver, author of *Thanks for Your Service: The Causes and Consequences of Public Confidence in the US Military*

"A very important contribution to a vital subject of great value to both scholars and policy professionals. The product of extensive research and insights of someone who has both intensive academic training and wide-ranging policy experience."

—Bruce W. Jentleson, William Preston Few Distinguished
Professor of Public Policy at Duke University

"Groves provides an insightful and compelling answer to a question that has tormented US presidents for over half a century: whether to 'double down' or 'cut one's losses' when engaged in an open-ended conflict. A must-read for scholars and practitioners alike."

—Andrew F. Krepinevich Jr., founder and former director of the Center for Strategic and Budgetary Assessments and author of *The Origins of Victory: How Disruptive Military Innovation Determines the Fates of Great Powers*

"All strategic thinkers know that history teaches lessons, but very few can discern those lessons in clear, compelling prose supported by extensive research. Groves has done just that. With a scholar's insight and a soldier's instinct, Groves identifies decisive factors behind five critical presidential wartime decisions to expand or contract military involvement. . . . A superb book for everyone studying and practicing national security."

—Brigadier General Michael Meese, US Army (Ret.), former West Point social sciences department chair

"Why do presidents choose to escalate or de-escalate ongoing military conflicts? In this important and carefully argued book, Groves highlights the role of salient historical analogies and how they shape the types of risks that capture leaders' attention. Comparing cases in the post-Vietnam and post-9/11 periods, Groves offers a compelling explanation for why Reagan and Clinton chose de-escalation while George W. Bush and Obama chose escalation. A great example of interdisciplinary social science, this book will be of interest to scholars and practitioners alike."

—Christopher Johnston, coauthor of *The Ambivalent Partisan: How Critical Loyalty Promotes Democracy*

When Presidents Fight *the* Last War

AUSA Books

Series Editor: Joseph Craig

When Presidents Fight *the* Last War

THE OVAL OFFICE, SUNK COSTS, AND WARTIME DECISION-MAKING SINCE VIETNAM

BRYAN N. GROVES

Scholarly publisher for the Commonwealth,
serving Bellarmine University, Berea College, Centre
College of Kentucky, Eastern Kentucky University,
The Filson Historical Society, Georgetown College,
Kentucky Historical Society, Kentucky State University,
Morehead State University, Murray State University,
Northern Kentucky University, Spalding University,
Transylvania University, University of Kentucky,
University of Louisville, University of Pikeville,
and Western Kentucky University.

Editorial and Sales Offices: The University Press of Kentucky
663 South Limestone Street, Lexington, Kentucky 40508–4008
www.kentuckypress.com

The views expressed in this book do not necessarily represent the views of the United States Army, the Department of Defense, or any agency of the United States government.

Unless otherwise noted, all figures and tables are from the author's collection.

Cataloging-in-Publication data available from the Library of Congress

ISBN 978-1-9859-0278-7 (hardcover)
ISBN 978-1-9859-0277-0 (paperback)
ISBN 978-1-9859-0275-6 (pdf)
ISBN 978-1-9859-0274-9 (epub)

This book will be made open access within three years of publication thanks to Path to Open, a program developed in partnership between JSTOR, the American Council of Learned Societies (ACLS), University of Michigan Press, and The University of North Carolina Press to bring about equitable access and impact for the entire scholarly community, including authors, researchers, libraries, and university presses around the world. Learn more at https://about.jstor.org/path-to-open/

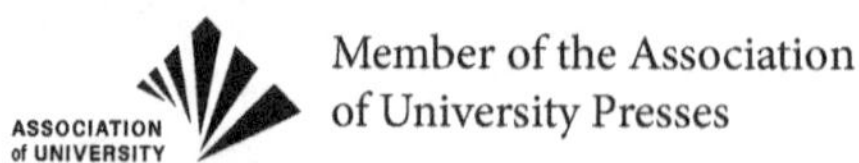

Member of the Association
of University Presses

For God and my family,
who make it all possible and worthwhile

Contents

Presidential Option and Response Legend

- Reduce or Withdraw Entirely
- When at Intersection, Keep Force Level Constant
- When Elsewhere, Add Small # of Forces
- Add Medium # of Forces; *Conditions-Based Withdrawal*
- Add Med-Lg # of Forces; *Time-Based Withdrawal*
- "[President's Name] Strategy"—Policy Implemented

1

Wartime Sunk Cost Dilemmas in Vietnam's Shadow

Vietnam looms over every major U.S. foreign policy decision.

—M. B. Young

INTRODUCTION

In his first major foreign policy move, President Joseph Biden made a controversial decision in April 2021 to withdraw the military from Afghanistan after nearly twenty years. Despite being the longest war in American history and what some refer to as a forever war, it is not the first time the commander in chief has had to make such a decision after a significant investment of lives, treasure, and effort—without the level of success desired.[1]

American presidents during the Vietnam War faced multiple inflection points where they had to deal with costs already invested and decide how to move forward. President Lyndon Baines Johnson felt trapped by bad options during these pivot points, expressing: "I can't get out, I can't finish it with what I have got. So what the hell do I do?"[2] Despite Johnson's frustration, the fear of jeopardizing his Great Society domestic agenda by appearing weak on communism persisted, and he repeatedly escalated in these situations.[3] As the one most responsible for military escalation over several years in the mid-1960s, Johnson grew US involvement from sixteen thousand military advisers to more than a half million troops.

Presidents since then have responded to similar situations during military operations in various ways. Some cut losses after reevaluating intervention policy while others doubled down, trying to obtain a clear victory. Presidents Ronald Reagan and William (Bill) Clinton de-escalated the Lebanon (1982–84) and Somalia (1992–93) peacekeeping and humanitarian interventions, respectively. Their reactions stand in starkest contrast to Johnson's escalatory policies. Clinton rapidly cut losses following the loss of eighteen soldiers in Somalia in early October 1993.[4] Reagan took a bit longer to decide following the Beirut bombing, but he eventually withdrew the US Marines and abandoned the US military intervention in Lebanon in early 1984. Presidents George W. Bush and Barack Obama, on the other hand, made escalation decisions for wars in Iraq (2007) and Afghanistan (2009), respectively.

In each set of de-escalations and escalations, quite different presidents—a Republican and a Democrat—pursued each basic approach. What led presidents since Johnson to respond to their own midcourse military dilemmas in disparate ways? One motivation for presidents' responses was "to exorcize the ghosts of Vietnam and therefore bring that chapter of American history to a close."[5] Before examining that in future chapters, it is useful to first understand those "ghosts."

VIETNAM'S IMPACT ON AMERICA AND ITS FOREIGN POLICY

Vietnam War ghosts had a searing emotional and psychological impact on America.[6] Before the war in Afghanistan, the Vietnam War was the longest in American history. Historian Brian VanDeMark characterizes the Vietnam War and its lasting impact on America this way:

> The American war in Vietnam ground on for eight long years, from 1965 to 1973. It notoriously and voraciously consumed both lives and reputations on its way to becoming an iconic cautionary tale: hubris—arrogance and pride that ancient Greeks warned against twenty-five hundred years ago—led the United States at the height of its power into the quagmire of Vietnam. The resulting war grew into a disastrous and divisive conflict that devastated the land of Indochina, killed an estimated 3 million Vietnamese and more than 58,000 Americans, exposed the limits of America's massive military power, sapped American treasure, polarized American politics, shook Americans' faith in their country and themselves, and cast a shadow that persists to this day.[7]

The resulting multifaceted Vietnam syndrome boils down to the fear of a future war turning into another such quagmire. It entails fears of an indecisive outcome or a political defeat. Symptoms can involve a long war, the military not having the resources it needs to accomplish policy aims, micromanagement from the White House reflective of distrust between civilian policymakers and military leaders, the loss of popular support, or mission creep leading to incremental escalation and a seemingly endless war.[8] Another key result was that "the American political establishment and public were more cautious in committing the American military to foreign engagements and interventions."[9] In this way, the war increased recognition of public opinion's importance, and its role in shaping the environment in which policy is made, as well as defining the parameters of the possible.[10]

Vietnam ghosts have long affected the American identity, the way the country saw itself, and became "baked into" the American psyche after the war.[11] The country no longer saw its power as unlimited and exceptional.[12] Nor did Americans blindly trust their leaders anymore. Americans no longer took it for granted that commanders in chief would only enter a war on a congressional declaration of war and would make the best decisions regarding how to prosecute a war after having entered it.[13] This "shadow" of the Vietnam War affected future presidents' use-of-force decisions—both before deployment and during employment.[14]

Some saw future military interventions as opportunities to overcome a crippling inability to use power to pursue their interests. President Reagan spoke about this as a presidential candidate and then acted on it as commander in chief.[15] Les Janka, White House deputy press secretary in 1983, reflected in 1985 on the impact of military involvement in Vietnam on Reagan's intervention in Lebanon. "There was a sense in the White House that we wanted to overcome the Vietnam Syndrome. It was specifically discussed on a number of occasions. . . . It [the Lebanon intervention] was an attempt to show the American people that we had overcome it, as well as [to show] not just the Middle East, but the rest of the world that America was back, . . . that we were ready to use force for our interests and for the good of Western civilization."[16]

As Janka indicates, the Vietnam syndrome entailed caution about utilizing military force in the war's aftermath that administrations sometimes heeded and sometimes sought to overcome. Indeed, "every president since Lyndon Johnson has lived with the legacies of the war and this has severely limited their freedom of action in foreign policymaking."[17] What was it about American conduct in the Vietnam War, not just its outcome, that gave rise to these ghosts?

DECISION-MAKING DURING THE VIETNAM WAR

> Our current policy can lead only to disastrous defeat.
>
> —National Security Adviser McGeorge Bundy

> We cannot turn our back on all we fought for.
>
> —President Lyndon B. Johnson

These top-line citations provide a glimpse into President Johnson and his national security adviser's tension, persistence, and despair while evaluating options for US policy during the Vietnam War. Vietnam War historian Brian VanDeMark provides further insight into Johnson's perception of being trapped with no good options for conducting or concluding the war. "Like [Secretary of Defense Robert] McNamara, he [President Lyndon Johnson] felt caught in a terrible dilemma of his own making with no discernible exit. . . . Like McNamara, rather than cut his losses, Johnson plunged in deeper in a desperate effort not to nullify the choices and sacrifices already made."[18]

When faced with other options, Johnson escalated multiple times instead of de-escalating or otherwise changing his strategy or narrowing his aims. Prior to these decisions, Johnson's advisers did attempt to offer other options and explain the risks of escalation to him, though it occurred infrequently because they were often boxed out by McNamara, Bundy, or chairman of the Joint Chiefs of Staff, General Maxwell Taylor.[19] Some argued against escalating in favor of another course. Some even pointed out the slippery slope that would likely ensue.[20] Yet "Johnson's mindset was rooted in his assumption that the loss of South Vietnam *would entail greater risks and costs* than would the introduction of U.S. combat forces."[21] So he repeatedly deployed large numbers of US forces to Vietnam. The result was a seemingly endless commitment that extended beyond anything imagined when he first assumed the presidency.

President Johnson and Secretary McNamara found themselves locked in a civil-military debate with General William Westmoreland and the Joint Chiefs of Staff regarding the efficacy of continued escalations. As civilian policymakers began to question their own policy and the prospects for success in Vietnam, the generals dug in. A sunk cost effect led to ever greater escalations of commitment to justify earlier intervention decisions and achieve initial objectives. "Once the first American combat troops splashed ashore, the initiative implicitly but ineluctably shifted toward the military. The long-standing taboo against committing American ground forces [not just military advisers] to South Vietnam, once breached—however slightly—broke an important psychological barrier and began generating powerful pressures for more troops. . . . Approving the first troop request created a subtle but powerful psychological dynamic that made it harder for Johnson to deny subsequent approaches in order to remain consistent with his initial approval."[22]

Another problem was that Johnson and his advisers' "goal [with all these troops] was not to win the war as quickly (and ruthlessly) as possible."[23] Rather, according to a State Department document—later known as the "McNaughton

Percentage Memo" when embraced by the assistant secretary of defense under McNamara, John McNaughton—there were three main reasons for US intervention in Vietnam. None of them specified winning. The memo characterized the effort as "70%—To avoid a humiliating US defeat (to our reputation as a guarantor). 20%—To keep SVN [South Vietnam] (and then adjacent) territory from Chinese hands. 10%—To permit the people of SVN to enjoy a better, freer way of life."[24] Ninety percent of this rationale was negative in orientation. The 10 percent that was focused on achieving a positive aim had the least direct relation to imperative US national security interests. Nonetheless, the longer American military involvement dragged on, and with each successive troop escalation, Johnson and his officials' perverse incentive to continue became more entrenched.

As scholars and policymakers reflected on the Vietnam War decision-making and related it to the psychology of decision-making on projects and investments in the private sector, or of a personal nature, the message became clear. "People who face very bad options take desperate gambles, accepting a high probability of making things worse in exchange for a small hope of avoiding a large loss. . . . The thought of accepting the large sure loss is too painful and the hope of relief too enticing to make the sensible decision that it is time to cut losses."[25] "Johnson and his advisors fell into this trap. Frustrated by setbacks and burdened by mounting American casualties, they responded . . . by reaching for future results. Like gamblers desperate to recoup their losses—in this case, the precious cost of human lives—they pressed onward."[26]

Despite the immense effort, America failed to achieve its political objectives, leaving a bitter sense across the country that the cost was not worth it. Seen as the first time that the nation had failed to win a war, that assessment struck at Americans' identity and diminished perceptions of the nation's strength.[27] This, in turn, caused intense reflection about—and reaction to—decision-making during the war, giving rise to "ghosts" that haunted future endeavors.[28] The decisions for repeated escalation, in spite of some advice, evidence, and even decision-makers' consciences suggesting it was unwise, contributed—along with the outcome—to Vietnam's ghosts, casting a long, dark shadow.[29]

The war's shadow is long, lasting to the present day, almost fifty years since the end of American military involvement. It is dark in that it demonstrated the limits of US power and cast a negative hue over future military ventures. Foreign policy endeavors have become even more politicized.[30] The irony reinforcing Vietnam's shadow is the recognition that "America's role in the Vietnam War could have been averted. . . . We adopted that [no combat troop] policy in 1961; we could have kept it in later years; we did not, to our great cost."[31] Johnson and key advisers included sunk costs in their assessments and did not know when to cut losses. Escalation decisions were made despite low prospects of victory and not always for the best interests of the country. One fateful decision followed another, gradually sucking America farther and farther into the growing quagmire.[32]

THE CAUSE OF FAILURE IN VIETNAM

Many scholars and practitioners agree that the American military intervention in Vietnam was a policy and societal disaster. However, they have drawn different conclusions about the cause of failure.[33] Three major camps offer differing explanations of the type of failure the Vietnam War represents. One argues that the war was winnable if US leaders had properly understood the nature of the war on which they were embarking and employed the appropriate corresponding strategy and sufficient resources. Escalation "was neither sinister nor self-seeking; rather it was mechanistic, incremental, and sanguine. The rationale was that of always pursuing 'the next logical step.' . . . 'The best and the brightest' that the nation had to offer believed unflaggingly that commitment and will would bring success."[34] So the political loss of the war—eventually losing South Vietnam to the communist North—was an epic failure of misunderstanding.

A second camp holds that the war could not have been won because the North Vietnamese political and social will to fight far exceeded that of the United States. There were no feasible options America could have utilized that would have brought political success. US advisers did not recommend dropping nuclear bombs on North Vietnam, for instance.[35] Hence, intervention itself—and subsequent escalations—was a mistake.[36] Policymakers should have determined earlier that the war was unwinnable at the price the United States was willing to pay. A related argument fits into both of the first two groups and is known as the quagmire thesis. It holds that policymakers regarded each escalatory step as the last that would be necessary to secure victory.[37] Eventually those steps—based on faulty assumptions of friend and foe alike—embroiled the United States in a quagmire.[38]

The third camp claims that American decision-makers understood the unreliable nature of the South Vietnamese government, recognized that the odds of success were low, and yet deliberately deceived the public about them, making participation a deception or a crime.[39] Whether a misunderstanding, a mistake, a deception, or a crime, the Vietnam War's legacy is etched into the American psyche. Both for people who fought in Vietnam and for those who did not, the war has affected beliefs about when military force should be utilized and when it should not.[40] Frances FitzGerald, backed by many of the critics in all of these groups, proffered that "the lesson to be drawn from this debacle was that the United States ought to pursue a more discriminating foreign policy that took account of the limits of American power."[41] Whatever your belief about the cause of America's Vietnam War debacle, the United States spent too long, too much treasure, and too much human sacrifice there without a full or proper understanding of our foe or the nature of the war. Before building on how that impacted future presidential decision-making, defining terms and context is central to understanding my argument.

KEY TERMS AND THE MAIN ARGUMENT

Lessons are indelibly strong impressions learned from past tragedies and shared across many of the relevant actors. In these cases, relevant actors include civilian policymakers and military leaders, with the commander in chief as the ultimate decider. Lessons from the past lead presidents and other key players to favor certain options when they see what appears to be a similar threat. In Vietnam's shadow, fear of another Vietnam-like quagmire, or, after 9/11, another spectacular attack at home, shaped midcourse responses to hard-to-win military interventions.

The operations in these cases have long stalemated or are experiencing shocking outcomes. Presidents face criticism whether they withdraw, continue the status quo, reinforce the troops, or conduct a hybrid approach. These wartime dilemmas occur after a significant investment of lives, financial treasure, time, and effort, making them even tougher to abandon. There are no easy answers; there are costs associated with any feasible option. Therefore, *sunk cost trap* is an apt term for these situations.

Because previous work focuses on war initiation or war termination rather than on midcourse policy adjustments, little is known about how or why presidents change policy *during* conflicts. Drawing on behavioral economics, political psychology, and other literature provides some insights from the private sector about leaders making risky decisions after significant investments. One body of literature from the rational camp offers an economic logic that argues for ignoring sunk costs. Other scholarship argues that influential political or psychological factors often cause leaders to include sunk costs in their decision-making. Yet there is a lack of empirical research on major military policy adjustments midcourse. The puzzle, then, is why American presidents decide to make the policy changes they do during military conflicts. Narrowed further, the puzzle explored in this book is how US presidents have decided what to do when major military interventions in Vietnam's shadow are not going well. Chapter two describes the lesson-based framework, including 9/11's displacement of the Vietnam lesson as dominant during major war policy adjustments. The argument in response to the puzzle is that pre-9/11 presidents believed that the risks of entrapment (via escalation) were worse than the risks of de-escalation. After 9/11, the logic flipped due to a new lesson. Before detailing the argument in chapter 2 (the "theory" chapter), the rest of this chapter explains the military sunk cost dilemmas presidents face, how they differ from other use-of-force and private sector decisions, and my case selection.

WHAT ARE SUNK COST TRAPS AND SUNK COST OPPORTUNITIES?

Sunk costs are expenses that have already been spent, are not recoverable, and are independent from future costs and benefits.[42] Wartime sunk costs can be significant influencers due to the lives lost (i.e., human sunk costs). The time, money, and effort already invested are other sunk costs. A leader's responsibility for the war's initiation is a sunk cost related to his personal credibility. The change in support for the president's handling of the conflict from initiation to the time of decision is a proxy measure for the president's credibility. A change of 25 percent approval for the president's leadership of the military operation, for instance, reflects an estimated 25 percent change in the personal credibility, or political capital and operating freedom, he has to manage the war.

Changes in national prestige are another sunk cost related to the war's progress or lack thereof. They can be understood through proxy factors that gauge the impact on the country's credibility if American military participation were to stop immediately. For instance, in a sunk cost trap in which the military is fighting nonstate actors, a withdrawal decision could mean that America would lose prestige by pulling out at a low point, appearing to "lose" to less powerful elements (or at least not "win"—i.e., not fully accomplish its objectives). That drop in national prestige may influence the country's future credibility, affecting its ability to deter enemies and assure allies. Admittedly, unlike time, money, and effort, prestige can be recovered. However, that will not happen without significant effort and time. Further, decision-makers sometimes think they can get a return on their investment for all of these sunk costs. In that sense, their perception is that even money, time, and effort can be recovered or redeemed.

Sunk cost traps can require a presidential strategy change during armed conflict. The "trap" occurs when there appears to be no good way out of the conflict. Battlefield developments have made it unclear whether the achievement of political objectives is possible, especially at the cost the nation is willing to pay. A decision to escalate may require incremental investments of soldiers, money, and time, all the while staking ever more national prestige on an uncertain outcome and making withdrawal short of victory ever more difficult.[43] On the other hand, abandoning the effort means the costs that have already been incurred will have been in vain. Instead of the potential for them to be the price of victory, they may become the price of defeat. It is unclear, therefore, how much value should be placed, and effort undertaken, to accomplish the goals sought. The sunk costs already incurred trap presidents who recognize these dynamics and yet have strong pulls to win, reestablish American credibility, gain a better bargaining position, or justify prior decisions for war. The presidential challenge with sunk cost traps is to determine whether it is worthwhile to apply greater or modified effort against a failing endeavor, but one in which victory, though elusive, seems within reach.

A sunk cost opportunity is the opposite of a sunk cost trap. Instead of a tragic failure or lengthy stalemate that limits presidential decision space, rapid or unexpected success can open additional policy options. The intersection of military success and policy opportunity makes sunk cost opportunities tantalizing and difficult to turn down. Having already sent troops halfway around the world and accomplished a major military objective, why would a president eschew the opportunity to achieve another important policy aim that now appears to be within reach and may have been long sought? Within the same military intervention, moreover, a commander in chief might face both a sunk cost opportunity and a sunk cost trap. He might seize an opportunity after heavy investment, for example, then add a policy aim and see operations backfire, leaving him in a sunk cost trap.

HOW SUNK COST DILEMMAS ARISE

Sunk cost opportunities arise when the American military devastates its enemy and achieves its objectives more rapidly than anticipated. Major failures, however, or a prolonged stalemate, can awaken presidents to a sunk cost trap, both of which could be compounded by an election cycle. Shocking failure is usually the most effectual alarm, alerting presidents that they must make major war policy changes. Shocking failures can include the tragic loss of life on a larger scale than the recent trend; defeat at the hands of an enemy heretofore considered unsophisticated, incompetent, or without advanced weaponry; use of weapons of mass destruction; or a surprise invasion. A protracted stalemate can have a similar effect, just requiring a longer trip wire to trigger presidential action.[44] This presents presidents with a predicament: Should they escalate, hopefully increasing their odds of success? The challenge is the intrinsic uncertainty associated with these decisions. The president may escalate and find the situation no better several months or years later but having cost more.

Finally, elections can energize calls for change, especially if they occur in conjunction with widespread perceptions of failure or stalemate. Candidates debate the pros and cons of war and the related strategies for dealing with the strategic decision point. Campaign rhetoric then follows elected presidents into office, potentially limiting their flexibility or requiring more political capital if circumstances change their minds about the best policy. In either case, the campaign trail calls much attention to the war and the strategy used to accomplish national objectives. Once elected (or reelected), presidents face the leadership challenge of implementing their proposed policy changes, pursuing a satisfactory conclusion to the war, as well as measuring and touting successes, while also balancing resources and the political capital necessary for other foreign and domestic initiatives.

WHY SUNK COST DILEMMAS ARE IMPORTANT

Midwar adjustments are often necessary. Changing course represents the ability to learn from what has gone wrong and what has gone well and adjust midstream. The side that makes the best course corrections the fastest gains an advantage.[45] During World War II, the German U-boat attacks were highly effective in destroying American ships carrying supplies across the Atlantic for the British and other Allied forces. Once America devised an effective strategy of convoy escorts using naval and air assets, as well as breaking the German Enigma machine's code so that leaders could decipher from intercepted communications what the enemy was planning, the results changed dramatically.[46]

During the recent wars in Iraq and Afghanistan, al-Qaeda, the Taliban, and other enemy elements utilized improvised explosive devices (IEDs) to great success against US vehicles. Secretary of Defense Robert (Bob) Gates worked with defense contractors to rapidly develop a solution. The result was the Mine-Resistant Ambush Protected vehicle. Fielded first in 2007–08, the vehicle's V-shaped hull provided better protection against IEDs' explosive power. That change, along with a faster medical evacuation time, complemented troop surges and a new counterinsurgency strategy in Iraq and Afghanistan. These changes did not facilitate a clear victory but did save many lives.[47]

Policy adjustments like these can involve technical and operational-level solutions. They can also involve diplomatic, political, economic, and human components. They may involve increasing lethality, changing target types, removing enemy sanctuary, or changing the rules of engagement. They may involve actions to increase popular support at home and to gain more international resources for the fight. The ability to adjust midcourse often means the difference between winning and losing. Like the Vietnam escalations (and later de-escalations), they may also influence popular perceptions of the government, military, and country.

These factors illustrate the gravity of presidents' sunk cost responses and why they are worth studying. Over the course of an armed conflict, more information becomes available about the enemy, its intentions, and its capabilities, as assessed on the battlefield. Public opinion and congressional support levels fluctuate, as do presidents' urgency for political survival, raising or lowering the domestic costs of pursuing particular war policies. As with the Vietnam War, presidential policy changes at these critical moments focus on the outcomes they shape and the missed opportunities (resource trade-offs).

PRESIDENTIAL SUNK COST DILEMMAS DIFFER FROM THOSE IN THE PRIVATE SECTOR

Sunk cost traps are even more difficult dilemmas for commanders in chief than for business leaders. Presidents weigh factors beyond profit maximization. The ability to accurately forecast future costs and benefits is even less predictable on the battlefield than in economic markets. The stakes are higher; life and death are in the balance. Wars and their outcomes matter for national prestige, resource allocation, economic strength, and regional/global influence. Corporate leaders contend with an equivalent of bureaucratic politics, but not with domestic politics, an important presidential decision factor.

Congruence between civilian principals (bosses) and military agents (executors) can strengthen the president's hand in dealing with Congress or in articulating his decision to the American people. For instance, it was helpful to President George W. Bush, when he announced his surge decision, to be able to say that his military leadership supported his decision.[48] Generals whose preferences differ from the president occasionally cause principal-agent problems or increased risk when they insist on a particular course of action or express public dissent.[49] These extra dimensions make the sunk cost problem more fraught than in the traditional economic and business literature that gave rise to the sunk cost trap concept.

SUNK COST TRAP DILEMMAS DIFFER FROM OTHER USE-OF-FORCE DECISIONS

War initiation and termination are the two common categories of international conflict. The logic of responding to sunk cost dilemmas midconflict is distinct from both but more closely resembles war termination logic. Like war termination, sunk cost traps occur after the shooting has begun, when the country already has skin in the game. In questions of war initiation, there are no sunk costs because fighting has not yet begun. There might be sunk diplomatic costs prior to war initiation, such as alliances lost or the like. Additionally, during training exercises, mobilization, and deployment, money and time are spent, and accidents can occur, causing injuries or death. These are of a limited nature and are not sunk costs actually caused by war, however. A new reality sets in as the president and the public recalibrate prewar expectations. The country's breakpoint—the number of casualties the public is willing to sustain before giving up on the war—might be different as seen from the middle of the conflict than at its outset.[50] The human toll and national prestige at stake during the middle of a war change calculations from those at the outset.

During the initial decision, all relevant considerations about the use of force are hypothetical. This includes estimates of the cost to achieve aims; of the enemy's capabilities, will, and intentions, and of US resolve and means versus those of the enemy. War reveals which side's will is superior and who has the technological edge. The president knows how much the war has already cost, how many lives have been lost, and what the nation has already achieved. Knowing the price tag with greater certainty can alter his decision calculus. The cases this book examines and explanations for why they met the criteria (while others did not) follow.

CASE SELECTION

Multiple criteria guided case selection based on what constitutes a major sunk cost dilemma in the post-Vietnam era. While adapted to the foreign policy realm and wartime environment, these criteria rhyme with those that characterize sunk cost traps in the business sector. First, the intervention was at least a month long; was a recognized, significant element of American foreign policy; and was led by the US military. Second, America had officially recognized military forces on the ground. Third, the United States suffered casualties. Fourth, sunk cost traps/opportunities had experienced a shocking failure/success recently (in the last few months) or a prolonged stalemate lasting longer than six months. Shocking failure could involve either a negative shock that impacted the prospects of mission accomplishment or inflicted casualties that seemed—in the administration's view and that of the American public—disproportionate to the number deployed and the apparent mission type. Shocking success could entail rapid operational success at a much lower-than-expected casualty rate or the possibility of fulfilling additional policy goals. Fifth, there was general recognition by the administration and the national security community that a major policy shift was necessary. Finally, this awareness culminated in a presidential decision to implement a major policy shift—not simply a minor, day-to-day tweak. My final criterion was a practical requirement. Researching a negative (i.e., a nondecision) was not practical. A decision was needed to facilitate definitive primary and secondary research.

The case studies of policy reevaluations midconflict include four of the most notable sunk cost traps in the Vietnam War's shadow and one sunk cost opportunity. The first case is President Reagan's decision to withdraw marines from the Lebanon peacekeeping mission following the Beirut barracks bombing and the collapse of the Lebanese government, announced on February 7, 1984. The second is President Clinton's decision to withdraw from Somalia following the tragic losses incurred during the Battle of Mogadishu, announced on October 7, 1993. The third is President George W. Bush's decision to surge troops to Iraq and change strategy in a desperate bid to salvage a favorable outcome, announced on January 10, 2007. The fourth is President Barack Obama's similar decision for a third surge of troops to Afghanistan within his first year in office and to conduct a limited counterinsurgency campaign, announced on December 1, 2009. The only sunk cost opportunity and thus the last case explored is President George H. W. Bush's decision on February 27, 1991, to end the Gulf War despite tremendous, rapid success.

These conflicts meet all the case selection criteria. The operations were US-led, had officially recognized American military forces on the ground, were significant endeavors, and were important elements of American foreign policy. They lasted longer than six months from deployment to redeployment. Some lasted multiple years, and one became the longest war in American history (Afghanistan). The nation suffered casualties in all of them. The presidents' decisions for policy change were distinct from the routine, minor revisions that characterize daily policymaking during conflicts. They involved major shifts made after the nation incurred substantive sunk costs, painting a stark contrast between the available options. In the sunk cost traps, America seemed to be losing, was in a stalemate, or had recently suffered a shocking loss, and it was widely acknowledged that a major change was needed. The question was whether to cut losses or escalate in an attempt to recoup the sunk costs. In the sunk cost opportunity, US-led forces realized success more quickly than expected, presenting the prospect of going after a bigger prize (removing Iraqi president Saddam Hussein from power). After considering the feasible options, all the presidents made key policy decisions that changed the course of American military intervention.

Although the policies implemented involve more nuance (which is discussed in the case study chapters), in general terms, three of the five presidents de-escalated; two escalated. Other US military interventions since the Vietnam War do not fit one or more of the selection criteria. The lack of a prolonged stalemate, shocking failure, or unexpected success disqualifies multiple operations from inclusion in this group. This includes the 1983 Grenada invasion, Operation Just Cause in Panama in 1989, Operations Provide Comfort I/II and Northern Watch in Iraq in the 1990s, Bosnia in the mid- to late 1990s, and Kosovo in 1999. It also excludes smaller operations, such as the 1986 bombing of Libya. Grenada and Panama also do not fit the criteria, as they did not last a month or were over too fast for a strategic reevaluation point. The same is true of the military operation in Libya in the mid-1980s.

Bosnia (1995–2004) lasted long enough but progressed reasonably well and resulted in only one combat death, thereby averting such an introspective reexamination. The Kosovo operation lasted a lot longer than expected, and there were debates in April and May 1999 about whether to redouble efforts, including whether to use ground troops. Yet there were only four combat deaths in Kosovo, barely meeting the casualty requirement, and no shocking failure. The situation also did not reach the level or duration of deadlock required to precipitate consensus among the administration and the national security community that a major change was critical. Nor did the dilemma culminate in a presidential policy shift.

European leadership of the 2011 operation in Libya and the lack of officially recognized American military personnel on the ground eliminates that intervention. The lack of a recent shocking failure, combined with several years of successes in reducing violence across Iraq following that withdrawal, prevents the US military departure from Iraq in 2011 from making the list. The war on terrorism efforts outside of Iraq and Afghanistan, including the campaign to defeat the Islamic State, do not meet these criteria. They do not include shocking failure or clear decision points for notable policy pivots during active US involvement. The withdrawal from Afghanistan in August 2021 also does not meet the criteria. The operation was rushed and received significant criticism. Though the withdrawal itself and the war effort writ large were widely perceived as a failure, the period leading up to the decision was *not* marked by the same type of sunk cost dynamics that characterized the other cases and are required by my criteria. Even if it did meet the selection criteria, this case is too recent. There is not yet the quality nor quantity of reputable analysis (in either secondary, or especially primary, sources), necessary to draw definitive casual assessments. Finally, Russia's ongoing war against Ukraine (as of this writing) does not involve American military forces on the ground, in the air, or on the waters around that country. Thus, it also does not qualify.

CONCLUSION

The selected cases occurred both in the shadow of the Vietnam War and in the shadow of the subsequent cases that took place in the intervening years. For instance, when President Clinton decided how to respond to the tragedy in Somalia, he did so in the shadow of both the Vietnam and Lebanon failures and the Desert Storm success. When contemplating the Iraq surge, President George W. Bush was affected by all of that as well as the lessons of Mogadishu and the early part of the Iraq War. And President Obama, of course, was operating in the shadow of all these military operations as well as the Iraq surge when deciding whether to escalate in Afghanistan. The following chapter lays out the lesson- and fear-based historical framework used in chapters three through seven to evaluate the rationale for presidential decision making.

2

Historical Lessons Drive Fear

Vietnam and 9/11's Impact on Future War Policy

INTRODUCTION

Major military sunk cost traps have no easy answers. Even more than with business projects, the investment of financial treasure, time, effort—and lives—already sunk makes them difficult to abandon. In such moments, the choice involves not only calculations of success and failure but also an assessment of whether a larger-than-expected investment can be recouped. Whatever their choice (de-escalation, status quo, escalation, or hybrid approach), presidents walk away having lost something of value. If they cut losses, they will not accomplish all the aims they had hoped to achieve. If they double down or change strategy, other policy agenda items will suffer from the unexpected additional financial and temporal investment in the conflict, or the debt will go up—affecting future generations—with no guarantee that America will achieve its goals.

As explained in chapter 1, President Lyndon Johnson's escalation decisions during the Vietnam War were classic sunk cost traps. Ever since, presidents have confronted their decision points in Vietnam's shadow. Two trends emerge from major military sunk cost dilemmas during this period.

Trend 1: In the first three major sunk cost dilemmas after the Vietnam War, presidents de-escalated commitment in Lebanon (1984), the Persian Gulf (1991), and Somalia (1993).

Trend 2: In the next two major sunk cost dilemmas, presidents escalated their commitments in Iraq (2006–2007) and Afghanistan (2009).

The change in sunk cost dilemma responses presents a puzzle: What caused the shift in responses from de-escalation to escalation? No theoretical expectation exists for how US presidents will respond to military sunk cost traps and why. In establishing an explanation that does just that, this chapter argues that fear drives presidents' sunk cost dilemma decisions during conflicts. Fear of escalation's or de-escalation's potential hazards, activated by the relevance of different historical shadows (or lessons), explains the individual cases as well as the shift to escalation from de-escalation.

After the Vietnam War, presidents were initially most influenced by Vietnam's lesson to avoid long, "messy" wars in states of debatable national security interests. Many believed that the Vietnam War proved the wisdom of avoiding extended involvement in wars with limited prospects for success, such as those that depended on unreliable local actors. Presidents anticipated that escalating to address their sunk cost traps would have worse policy implications and thus be more regrettable than de-escalating.

The terrorist attacks of September 11, 2001, defined a new era, causing Vietnam lessons to decrease in relative importance. September 11 was a lesson in "how to think about risks, about what weight America's leaders should now attach to certain kinds of risks."[1] It taught presidents that they must prosecute counterterrorism as a war rather than a crime—or face another massive attack on the homeland. Following 9/11, the failed stabilization effort in Iraq from 2003 to 2006 further taught presidents that a counterinsurgency strategy was necessary to achieve lasting success in wars against international terrorists. Presidents believed that the threat warranted escalating commitment and that they might pull out a victory with additional resources. The Iraq surge's success in reducing violence reinforced this belief. Presidents feared that de-escalating would have worse policy implications and thus would be more regrettable than escalating. In other words, pre-9/11, presidents believed that the risks of entrapment were worse than the risks of de-escalation. After 9/11, the logic flipped.

The rest of this chapter briefly summarizes the existing explanations for similar business decisions. It then adds literature about political psychology and learning from history to build an expectation for presidential decisions during conflict-related sunk cost traps.

OTHER EXPLANATIONS—A BRIEF SUMMARY

Rationalist economic literature states that leaders (should) make hyperrational decisions based on future cost-benefit calculations. Behavioral economics and the sunk cost fallacy say decision-makers will pay attention to past (i.e., sunk) costs. This group of literature offers a mixed prediction for what leaders will do. Rationalists argue for de-escalation as sunk cost traps are moments with low prospects of success. Behavioralists predict escalation, especially if the sunk cost decider was responsible for the initial decision. Prospect theory says that how leaders weigh the costs depends on their risk propensity, which can be shaped by sunk costs. If their sunk costs have landed them in a domain of gains (sunk cost opportunities), they will de-escalate. However, by definition, those in a sunk cost trap are in a domain of losses and will escalate. Thus, prospect theory and other explanations are unsatisfying when trying to understand the reasoning behind presidents' midcourse decisions during major military operations. My "theory" explains how historical lessons or analogies, coupled with fear, *actually* shape these decisions.

HISTORICAL "LEARNING"

> Analogies and paradigms play a powerful role in shaping the perspectives of policymakers.
>
> —James B. Steinberg

> Historical analogies did play a role in policy making. They were an element of every decision.
>
> —H. R. McMaster

Learning from the past provides a "historical sensibility" that helps busy presidents and their advisers make sense of an uncertain world.[2] "Analogies [from history] . . . help policymakers define which aspects of a phenomenon are significant and which should be treated as epiphenomenal."[3] The most important history to the leaders involved in advising and making wartime policy decisions can be grouped into several categories. Recent history, really dramatic history, history with which they were personally involved, and history from a formative period of their development are the types of history on which they most rely.[4] This is the history from which they draw "analogies . . . [to] think about situations and formulate solutions to problems."[5] That "historical sensibility" can provide insights into the efficacy, risks, long-term consequences, and regret that might be associated with each option available during presidents' wartime sunk cost traps.[6] Knowing how previous leaders' choices turned out helps presidents make judgments about the causal factors that led to particular outcomes. Using historical analogies, therefore, can help presidents decide what action to take in the current crisis. In this way, history can be a useful teacher and adviser. Yet "some historical analogies are more powerful, influential, and seductive than others."[7]

Combining a couple of the important categories, policymakers often default to the most recent and traumatic analogy that seems apropos until another traumatic lesson replaces it.[8] Lessons tend to be less impactful the farther in the rearview mirror they become.[9] Nonetheless, some lessons can remain influential for a long time, often until new lessons replace or overshadow them. The lessons of the Vietnam War, for example, have lasted a long time because the conflict was such a significant event for the country's collective memory and psyche. During the war and after it, Americans wondered whether their leaders could be trusted, if the nation's foreign interventions were noble and just, and if future wars were winnable. Yet when historical lessons become dogma, they may lose some usefulness, even becoming dangerous.[10] As a respected scholar and former policy practitioner has put it, "Some reigning lessons become so well known, taught and retaught, that they ossify into one of the small number of master scripts that can mold public policies across whole eras. These aging shibboleths can go on for quite a long time until they are overthrown. . . . When the shibboleths are finally toppled . . . some new collective trauma—a war, a depression—has displaced them, swept them away with compelling needs for fresh social constructions."[11]

Vietnam was so traumatic that it held our historical memory hostage for more than twenty-five years until another searing experience took its place. This dynamic reveals an important truth. "There is a greater likelihood that failure will lead to a more penetrating and nuanced look at the potential contributing factors, whereas there would seem to be a greater danger that success will lead to an unexamined instinct to 'run the same play again' without reflecting on whether the conditions that made the play successful the first time around will prevail in the subsequent case."[12]

So policymakers find historical lessons useful and use them regularly,[13] but according to various assessments, they do not always use them well.[14] During the 1960s and the major escalations of the Vietnam War, for example, Yuen Foong Khong claims that policymakers poorly utilized the lessons of Munich and Korea. In *Analogies at War: Korea, Munich, Dien Bien Phu, and the Vietnam Decisions of 1965*, he argues that decision-makers were "unable or unwilling to put their analogical inferences to tests" before acting on them.[15] This prevented the "closer look at the local realities at work in Vietnam" that was necessary to determine whether the lessons of Munich and Korea—that appeasement does not work and containment of aggressive great powers through proxy wars does—accurately captured the problem and solution.[16]

Instead, Khong claims that the lessons of Munich and Korea were misinterpreted and misapplied. The result was that American decision-makers did not properly understand the threat. By applying these two lessons, they saw the threat as originating from great powers (Russia and China), instead of emanating mainly from North Vietnam, which heightened America's stakes beyond what they actually were. Another result of using the Korean analogy of a limited proxy war was that policymakers underestimated how much commitment would be necessary to accomplish their aim. Fighting against extremely dedicated, nationally oriented political leadership and military forces that had already defeated the French and were willing to outlast the United States was a different type of war that would require more effort than most policymakers initially realized.[17] But America's decision-makers, according to Khong, held to their interpretation and application of Munich's and Korea's lessons during the key 1965 escalation decisions without sufficiently questioning their applicability to Vietnam.

Misunderstanding history affects presidents and their advisers' ability to use past lessons well. It can "cloud and obscure" their path forward, causing them to fight the last war, just as generals are often accused of doing.[18] A lack of historical knowledge can cause presidents to rely on one analogy that may not be the best fit for the current situation—or the way forward.[19] If historical lessons are "narrowly selected" and not deliberately scrutinized, presidents' decision-making processes unnecessarily limit and skew consideration of the current problem, stakes, potential futures, and options.[20] This hinders diplomatic ingenuity, the ability to expose poor assumptions, and the leveraging of historical patterns to suit US interests.[21] Indeed, "thinking-by-analogy can be just as dangerous as historical amnesia: because A looks like B, there's a strong temptation to abandon the immense difficulty of understanding B on its own terms, and instead to let the outcome of A do the thinking for you."[22] The result, therefore, can be an ill-informed and potentially ineffective or counterproductive policy choice. If properly utilized, though, analogies can be helpful in making sense of the situation and determining the broad contours of possible alternative futures.[23]

Given these dynamics of how leaders learn from history, we expect a major shock like the Vietnam disaster to (a) cast a long shadow (i.e., last a long time), and (b) cast a dark shadow (i.e., to be overused even when it may not be appropriate). Based on the literature, we also expect that it takes another such shock to dislodge that shadow. It took Vietnam to dislodge Munich as the dominant theory on which decision-makers based their policy and to which they referred to gain public support. Later, it took 9/11 to dislodge Vietnam as the dominant historical lesson.

HISTORICAL "LEARNING" AND FEAR OF PARTICULAR OUTCOMES

An explanation of presidential decision-making during sunk cost traps should allow for presidents' use of both retrospective and prospective analyses. As President Lyndon Johnson indicated, he "and other American presidents liked to consult the past, as well as anticipate the future in the widest possible ways."[24] As already discussed, presidents use *retrospective* analysis to learn from the past. They employ *prospective* analyses to weigh trade-offs between potential options. Sunk cost and behavioral economics research has tested the impact of retrospective perspectives on reactions to sunk cost traps. These include focusing on responsibility for the decision[25] and sunk costs themselves.[26] Other research has examined future-oriented considerations. The influence of project completion,[27] being "too close to quit,"[28] and anticipating regret[29] are forward-looking factors proven to influence decision-makers contemplating escalation. Still other scholarship has integrated the two approaches.

Experiments by Kin Fai Ellick Wong and Jessica Y. Y. Kwong in 2007 confirm that both approaches, rearward and forward-looking, are significant determinants. Retrospectively, decision-makers responsible for the initial investment decision are more likely to escalate commitment. Prospectively, people are regret-averse and attempt to avoid outcomes they expect to regret. Wong and Kwong found that when presented with two options, fear of one alternative steers individuals toward the other. Those who expect to regret the consequences of withdrawal are more likely to escalate commitment. Those who expect to most regret the possible disadvantages of project persistence or escalation are apt to de-escalate.[30] This represents a potential reverse sunk cost effect in which decision-makers de-escalate—rather than escalate—commitment to a project that appears to be failing. Further, Wong and Kwong found that fear influences the chosen outcome even when controlling for personal responsibility for the initial project decision that resulted in a "sunk cost trap."[31]

Despite the emotional (i.e., fear) component, cognitive factors also play a role. Gillian Ku explored the role of learning from previous escalation-related regret on decisions in future sunk cost traps. He found that escalation-related regret from past decisions reduced *future* escalation of commitment by approximately 60 percent. Ku also tested the impact of anticipated regret through the suggestion of counterfactuals at the time of decision. Like Zeelenberg and Dijk and Wong and Kwong, Ku found that *anticipated regret*—like *past* learning—reduced decisions for escalation as leaders considered the possibility that an alternative choice may yield a better outcome.[32] Further, despite the emotion induced by fear and regret, Ku points out that the mechanism that changed participants' behavior was a combination of emotion *and* cognitive processing. "Although regret is a powerful emotion, its emergence and ability to bring about change are based in counterfactual *thinking*."[33] Applying this to a catastrophic incident facilitates a broader understanding of the dynamics at play.

THE EMOTIONAL AND PSYCHOLOGICAL IMPACT OF 9/11 ON PRESIDENTIAL WARTIME DECISION-MAKING

> [Through 9/11,] the United States had escaped from the confines of the Vietnam syndrome.
>
> —Andrew Priest

September 11 superseded Vietnam as the key reference point for presidents facing hard-to-win military conflicts when other traumas could not because it was a significant, surprising, and uniquely American tragedy. Other shocks between the end of the Vietnam War and 9/11 *reinforced* Vietnam lessons—like Lebanon and Somalia—rather than introducing a new period in which a new lesson was predominant. The Beirut bombings at the US embassy and the marine barracks in 1983 were disastrous but are a case in point. They did not have the emotional or psychological impact of 9/11 because they were overseas. Furthermore, the barracks was a military target, and the military accepts risk as part of its mission. So, too, do State Department employees, especially when serving overseas in a conflict-ridden country like Lebanon. The Black Hawk Down tragedy in Somalia in 1993 again impacted military members in a faraway land. Other tragedies, like those in Rwanda and the Balkans, involved mass killings and were horrendous, but they were not *American* calamities. These events did not occur on American soil, and the majority of lives lost were not American.

September 11 was different because it was the single greatest attack on US soil, surpassing even the attack on Pearl Harbor that dragged America into

World War II. September 11 was also significant because the enemy consisted of nonstate actors—not another great or even second-rate state power. Despite this, the enemy inflicted mass casualties on Americans at home, even without their own state-of-the-art technology.

September 11 was different because it meant that two of America's greatest assets (the Atlantic and Pacific Oceans) were no longer enough to keep those in the continental United States safe.[34] The enemy could attack Americans from afar and from within at the same time. The 9/11 hijackers were largely from the Middle East, but they legally spent months in America and the West preparing for the attacks. Despite a previous attempt to bring down the World Trade Center in 1993, the US had not been successfully attacked by terrorists from around the world on such a scale before.

The 9/11 attackers destroyed symbols of US economic strength, attacked the symbol of American military strength, and attempted to destroy one of the premier symbols of the nation's political strength. Political leaders were, therefore, responsible for acting in ways they were not held responsible for following other post-Vietnam catastrophes.

For these reasons, 9/11 became a galvanizing event that immediately formed a bipartisan consensus for major change. It led to the Department of Homeland Security's creation and the reorganization of national security organizations under it. The government instituted greater airport security. Intelligence, interagency, and defense elements cooperated to a greater extent, creating interagency fusion cells in war zones and Joint Terrorism Task Forces at home.

At its core, 9/11 was a lesson in "how to think about risks, about what weight America's leaders should now attach to certain kinds of risks."[35] While there is no magic casualty threshold that triggers change, 9/11 crossed an emotional, psychological, and political Rubicon, defining a new era in American national security and ushering in new lessons. The tragedy taught presidents that they must prosecute counterterrorism as a war *rather than* as a crime—or face another enormous attack on the homeland.

PRESIDENTS' WARTIME SUNK COST DILEMMAS IN VIETNAM'S SHADOW

Similar to business leaders deciding whether to escalate commitment to a failing financial investment or building project, these dilemmas involve reevaluations of failing (or stalled) conflict endeavors. In both categories, these decisions involve trade-offs among various options, each of which carries the potential for regret if it turns out badly. In both types of traps, leaders face a stark choice between a certain loss, already incurred, and a "risky" option that could result in a larger loss, no loss, or a gain.

Presidents can use political/diplomatic and military measures as two of their main levers to de-escalate, continue the status quo, escalate, or employ a hybrid approach. A combination approach may escalate in one area/phase and de-escalate in another. Presidents' choices reflect the historically based fear that most drives their national security decision-making.[36] If those aims cannot be satisfied by accepting the loss that comes from a sunk cost trap, they will escalate. As Zeelenberg and Dijk point out, though, if presented with "a choice between an uncertain option (which may not satisfy the aim) and a safe option (which satisfies the aim) [experiment] participants [or presidents] having incurred sunk cost may prefer the safe option (showing risk aversion)" and thus de-escalate.[37]

Drawing on this research, I offer two assessments that explain presidential reactions to sunk cost traps in Vietnam's shadow.

Assessment 1 (Avoid a Quagmire): In the sunk cost traps/opportunity between the Vietnam War and 9/11, Vietnam lessons influenced presidents' de-escalation decisions, having taught them that success in a lengthy war via incremental escalation was doubtful and likely to be regrettable.

Assessment 2 (Never Again on My Watch): In sunk cost traps after 9/11, new lessons influenced presidents' escalation decisions, having taught them that proactive counterinsurgency campaigns abroad were necessary to prevent another major attack on American soil.

Assessment 1 follows from Trend 1 above, just as Assessment 2 follows from Trend 2. The first explanatory variable is the impact of traumatically learned historical lessons drawn from previous conflicts or significant events (i.e., the Vietnam War and 9/11). The second, activated by the first, includes presidents' relative fear of the "risky" (escalate) and "safe" (de-escalate) options. The expectation is that presidents gravitate toward the option they least fear and thus least expect to regret. Although domestic and international politics may play a role, they only do so through the most relevant historical lessons. For instance, if a president is concerned about popular support, it is because of the Vietnam War's lesson that public opinion fades as casualties rise.[38]

Assessments 1 and 2 indicate historical lessons' evolving impact on presidents' sunk cost trap decisions. Between the Vietnam War and 9/11, Assessment 1 speculates that presidents, influenced significantly by Vietnam's lessons, believed the "risky" (escalate) option would be worse than opting for the "safer" (de-escalate) alternative. The 9/11 terrorist attacks started a new era in US national security and changed presidents' sunk cost trap prescriptions. As posited in Assessment 2, presidents subsequently focused on different lessons, drawn from 9/11 and the subsequent Iraq conflict. Although aware of Vietnam lessons, they believed victory was possible with additional resources and that the threat warranted escalating commitment. They anticipated that the "safe" (de-escalate) option would be worse than the "risky" (escalate) course. The argument is not that other lessons did not also have some impact in each period but that the more recent defining military conflict or attack shaped presidents' *basic* de-escalation or escalation strategy.

ANALYTICAL APPROACH

I compare presidential decision-making across my five case studies. I orient each on presidential reactions to particular sunk cost traps of important military operations rather than on the conflicts' initiation or termination. For consistency and to ensure objectivity, I use the same set of questions to uncover presidents' rationale in each case.[39] I use four questions to examine each post-Vietnam policy pivot when leaders faced important sunk cost choices.

1. Why was this a sunk cost trap that required a major policy pivot?
2. What were the president's options, and what strategy did he implement?
3. What role did historical lessons and fear play in decision-making?
4. Did internal administration rationale differ from the public justifications?

I start each chapter with a case summary and by stating the president's aims. I then lay out the sunk costs faced and the president's recognition that he was at a major policy juncture (first question). Next, I show the feasible options the president and his team considered and the strategy choice he made (second question). I then detail the historical lessons the president drew on and the type of fear he had based on the dominant historical lesson on which he acted (third question). In this section, I assess how well the presidential rationale aligns with my expectations. In doing so, I demonstrate the extent to which any lessons and related fears were on the president's mind at critical junctures. I also show whether the decision implemented was consistent with the applicable assessment and lesson, the two factors necessary for effective process tracing and a persuasive argument.[40] Last, I compare the way in which private rationale differed, if at all, from the public justifications for the decision. Public justifications can be spun in ways that may not truly reflect the factors most important to the internal deliberations that actually shaped presidents' decision-making. Thus, I look for consistency, or lack thereof, between private decision rationale and public justifications (fourth question). The greater the consistency between the president and his advisers' rhetoric, in private and public, before and after the decision, the greater assurance one can have of a president's rationale. When inconsistencies exist, I make supported judgments regarding presidents' true rationales and why they cast public justifications in a different light.

PRESIDENTIAL HYBRID STRATEGIES

In sunk cost traps, the lesson-induced fear framework suggests that presidents will choose the least bad option. They will escalate or de-escalate based on what they expect they will least regret later. That categorization is useful for understanding the overall trends in the shadow of the Vietnam War. However, presidents' strategies are not always simply a de-escalation or an escalation. Presidents can also continue the status quo or implement a hybrid approach that combines elements of de-escalation and escalation. The cases detail the relevant military options (this book's emphasis) and acknowledge diplomatic and political possibilities.

In fact, in some sunk cost traps, hybrid strategies are how presidents deal with sunk costs in Vietnam's shadow. Multiple lessons cause presidents to fear both de-escalation and escalation. They utilize a combination of escalation and de-escalation over time or across political/diplomatic and military tools to address the conflicting pressures. Conceptually, in the near term, the escalation component allows presidents to deal with their potential proximity to policy attainment or the pressures to deliver on previous commitments.[41] It also demonstrates presidential resolve, consonant with the literature's focus on the justification of previous decisions.[42]

In the long term, the de-escalation component allows presidents to cut losses (sunk cost traps) or bring the troops home while things are still going well (sunk cost opportunities). This enables prioritization of other endeavors that are consistent with the rest of their domestic and foreign policy agendas. It also addresses war opponents' concerns. A simultaneous, rhetorical ramp-up of US accomplishments facilitates such a withdrawal while still claiming victory.[43]

This combination approach recognizes that these are particularly fraught decisions. When faced with such difficult decisions, presidents often try especially hard to have it both ways. Presidents add a bit of de-escalation to a decision that is basically an escalation. The Afghanistan surge combined with a time limit is an example. Presidents also do the opposite. The initial escalation to support a safe and orderly transition to the United Nations as American forces departed Somalia is an example. Even in the cleanest choice, like the departure from Lebanon or the Iraq surge, presidents still invoke rhetoric to show they are sensitive to the downsides. When withdrawing marines from Lebanon, Ronald Reagan framed the policy pivot as a "redeployment" and a series of "decisive new steps" rather than a "withdrawal" because that might signal a failure to achieve US goals.[44] When escalating in Iraq, Bush indicated it was a bridge until America could return to the strategy of transitioning security responsibilities to Iraqi forces.[45]

CONCLUSION

Historical lessons cause presidents to fear certain options due to perceived potential pitfalls. This dynamic makes another basic strategy—either de-escalation or escalation—more fitting in response to sunk cost traps in Vietnam's shadow. The shifting salience of these lessons has contributed to two general trends of presidential strategies across four of the most significant post–Vietnam War sunk cost traps and one sunk cost opportunity. Vietnam lessons were most prominent during major policy pivot decisions pre-9/11. Vietnam lessons included that sunk costs were sunk (and should therefore not be included in decisions about the future). Avoid incremental escalation. Use decisive force and ensure a clean exit. These lessons caused presidents to fear escalation and its potential downsides, creating strong de-escalatory pressures in future conflicts.

After 9/11 and the failed stabilization effort in Iraq suggested that new lessons had become more applicable, escalation replaced de-escalation as presidents' approach to sunk cost traps. This was because the new lessons emphasized the ability to achieve their aims (policy objectives) only through escalation that involved robust ground forces and a counterinsurgency strategy. Moreover, after September 11, 2001, presidents feared another 9/11-like attack on their watch. They came to believe that a war of counterinsurgency, facilitated by a surge of forces and civilians, provided the greatest likelihood of preventing another such attack. Presidents' fear of de-escalation's potential consequences made escalation relatively more appealing, even though it came with its own challenges. When presidents feared both options, they usually adopted a hybrid approach, attempting to charter a middle ground.

The next five chapters use the four questions mentioned earlier to compare hard-to-win, midcourse policy pivots in Lebanon, Somalia, Iraq, Afghanistan, and the Persian Gulf. The conclusion chapter compares these cases to assess commonalities, differences, emerging lessons, and policy prescriptions for future presidential sunk cost dilemmas.

3

Reagan in Lebanon

Vietnam Ghosts and Fear of the Future

INTRODUCTION

Fear of another Vietnam fueled bureaucratic, domestic, and international politics following the October 1983 marine Beirut barracks bombing and subsequent investigations. A divided cabinet and a more assertive Congress combined with the bleak Lebanese political and security outlook to increase the costs of continuing the status quo or escalation. Their confluence demonstrated that prospects for success, arguably always low, had rapidly diminished and change was necessary. Moreover, there was no immediate fix apparent to President Ronald Reagan or his advisers. So the costs rose at a time when Reagan and his advisers were already experiencing a decreased appetite for continuing the operation.[1] This made the marines' eventual redeployment offshore—in reality, a withdrawal—the favored course.

This case confirms Assessment 1 (Avoid a Quagmire; see chap. 2): that Vietnam War–based lessons led President Reagan to de-escalate on February 7, 1984. Reagan had grown to expect a worse outcome if he escalated or continued the status quo than if he withdrew. He indirectly based his decision on lessons from the American military experience in Vietnam that success in a lengthy war via incremental escalation was doubtful and likely to be regrettable. Reagan's autobiography indicates that rising costs and Vietnam lessons caused him to fear continuing the US portion of the Multinational Force (MNF).[2] This obviously was *after* his decision. His advisers, though, demonstrated fear of escalation *beforehand* by not providing any surge options, potentially also reflecting Reagan's desires and fears during the crisis decision-making.[3]

CASE SUMMARY (LEBANON)

President Reagan's military involvement in Lebanon began a few months after Israel's 1982 invasion of Lebanon to clear out Palestine Liberation Organization (PLO) terrorists.[4] Concerned that continued conflict would lead to a greater Soviet presence in the Middle East, Reagan deployed marines with French, British, and Italian troops in what became MNF I on August 1, 1982. Their purpose was to defuse tensions and evacuate the PLO fighters from Beirut. After securing the withdrawal of fifteen thousand fighters from Beirut by September 1, Reagan announced his Middle East peace policy the same day.[5] It was an ambitious policy that called for a new home for the Palestinian people and staked out general US stances on a path toward peace.[6] MNF I withdrew soon thereafter, on September 10.

Stability did not last long. Syrian agents assassinated Christian president-elect Bashir Gemayel on September 14. Bashir's premature death led to his brother Amine's election a week later. Taking advantage of the situation, Israel occupied West Beirut, stating a need to restore order.[7] On September 18, the Israeli Defense Force (IDF) facilitated the Gemayel-linked Phalangist militia's entrance of the Sabra and Shatila refugee camps and tacitly allowed their killing of any remaining PLO "terrorists" who had not evacuated.[8] The result was a massacre of between 800[9] and 3,500 civilians, including women and children, reportedly an act of revenge on Muslim Palestinians for assassinating Gemayel.[10]

Following the ensuing international outcry, Reagan sent marines back to address US credibility and regional security concerns in light of the Cold War[11] and to protect Palestinians that the administration had promised, but thus far failed, to safeguard.[12] His local objectives were the withdrawal of all foreign armies (Syrian, IDF, and Palestinian) and the strengthening of the Lebanese government so it could control its own territory.[13] The marines' mission was envisioned primarily as a presence mission to keep the peace and prevent further atrocities.[14] Consistent with National Security Decision Directive (NSDD) 64, the mission also involved training the Lebanese Armed Forces (LAF). MNF II forces were to be neutral peacekeepers, so their rules of engagement (ROE) were initially restrictive, focused on self-defense rather than offensive measures. The marines' precise goals, the intervention duration—generally thought to be sixty days—and the exit criteria were not well defined.[15]

Reagan's broader goals were to facilitate greater Arab-Israeli peace accords and further regional interests at the Soviets' expense.[16] He saw an opportunity to build on the Camp David Accords and the recent departure of Israel's last troops from the Sinai Peninsula in April 1982. Reagan and Secretary of State George Shultz also wanted an end to the Lebanese civil war and stability through a "comprehensive peace" between Israelis and Palestinians that would be "a long-term settlement of the region's problems."[17]

A divided cabinet hindered these grand ambitions from MNF II's beginning.[18] Charles Hill, Shultz's executive secretary, was privy to one-on-one meetings between the two cabinet principals and described it this way. Shultz and Secretary of Defense Caspar Weinberger "didn't see things in the same way at all. Weinberger's view never changed; the United States should not get involved at all."[19] Weinberger claimed that accounts such as this of reported policy differences between him and Shultz were "largely mythological."[20] Hill's description, however, matches National Security Adviser Robert McFarlane's report of the rift and the challenges Reagan faced in moving his officials forward in unison.[21]

Two important developments in 1983 further complicated the intervention. First, the Islamic Jihad exploded a truck bomb at the US Embassy in Beirut on April 18, killing sixty-three, including seventeen Americans and the top Central Intelligence Agency Middle East expert, in an attempt to rid Lebanon of foreign occupiers.[22] Moreover, when America responded with the May 17 Agreement, calling for Syrian and Israeli forces' simultaneous withdrawal, part of US stabilization through diplomacy, Syrian president Hafez Al-Assad denounced it.[23]

Second, in September 1983, Israeli forces unilaterally withdrew from the Chouf mountains. This removed their security forces from a strategic area that overlooked the Beirut International Airport, which had been protecting US Marines. The withdrawal also undercut the simultaneous withdrawal called for by the May 17 Agreement. The result was a power vacuum filled by Druze militiamen.[24] After increased Druze attacks near the marines' base, the United States changed tactics. Reagan ordered the USS *New Jersey* to move offshore and fire on Druze positions in the Chouf mountains. This move marked the beginning of stabilization through increased military action.

Reagan's new policy of "aggressive self-defense" and naval gunfire to support the LAF caused Syrian and Druze reciprocation and led to the marines' loss of neutrality.[25] After these developments, Congress invoked the 1973 War Powers Act even though it authorized an eighteen-month extension, aided significantly by Democratic Speaker Tip O'Neill's support.[26] This would have allowed Reagan to keep the marines in Beirut until the spring of 1985.[27] Another tragedy intervened, however, ultimately curtailing marine involvement.

On October 23, 1983, a truck broke through the marines' security perimeter and exploded a huge bomb inside their barracks, killing 241. Although this was only one of three casualty events during this period, the Beirut barracks bombing made up 241 of the 260 US deaths (92 percent) in the conflict. Afterward, Weinberger appointed retired admiral Robert Long to head an investigation. As Long examined the tragedy, the administration explored options for (future) deterrence by punishment.

Disagreement among cabinet officials over whether, how, and for what purposes to use force was particularly evident during the first attempt at retribution. Lebanese Hezbollah, an Iranian proxy thought to be responsible, was the target. The government had "seven intercepted Iranian messages since September," pointing to Iranian culpability in the attacks.[28] One of these messages, received on September 22, stated that "the Iranian ambassador in Damascus . . . had instructed Abu Haydar Musawi to 'undertake an extraordinary attack against the U.S. Marines.'"[29] The October 23 barracks bombing appeared to be that attack.

By a couple of accounts, Reagan approved the retaliatory air strike against Hezbollah targets at a National Security Planning Group (NSPG) meeting on November 14. It was to be conducted two days later against the bombing culprits housed in buildings known as the Al Shams Hotel and the Sheikh Abdullah Barracks in Bekaa Valley.[30] Yet, according to Major General Colin Powell, Weinberger's senior military assistant, they did not know who was responsible and therefore could not conduct a strike.[31] Historian Hal Brands corroborates this, indicating that Reagan called it off at the last moment due to inconclusive evidence.[32]

Reagan's diary entries from November 14 through 16, however, offer only partial confirmation. On the fourteenth, Reagan stated there was "additional intelligence but still not enough to order a strike." On November 16, Reagan wrote, "We've contacted [the] French about a joint operation in Beirut." And on November 17: "Surprise call from France—they were going ahead without us. . . . They took it out completely."[33]

Instead of crediting a French reprisal, McFarlane placed the blame on Weinberger. McFarlane recalled that Weinberger's rationale for denying the president's direct order to strike, when the national security adviser confronted the defense secretary, was fundamentally because, in Weinberger's words, "I just don't think it was the right thing to do."[34] Weinberger deeply regretted not having been "persuasive enough to persuade the president that the marines were there on an impossible mission" prior to the barracks bombing and believed that continued intervention was counterproductive.[35] Moreover, Weinberger believed that America lacked a clear mission and was not trying to "win" in Lebanon but was instead "engaging in fruitless tactics in pursuit of unreachable goals."[36] This was a common view across the entire defense enterprise.

> Memories of the Vietnam quagmire contaminated the military's attitude toward the Beirut mission. Vietnam permanently scarred the American military psyche through "the sense of abandonment and betrayal, anguish at being depicted as moral monsters, and resentment at being scapegoated for a decade not entirely of their making."The military learned one overarching lesson from conflict in Indochina: no more Vietnams. Since the end of that disastrous debacle in Southeast Asia, the military had vigorously resisted involvement in ambiguous conflicts, such as Lebanon, for which the United States lacked understanding and skills and where its technological superiority offered little leverage. The Pentagon became increasingly reluctant to involve U.S. forces "without clear public support and a clearly defined mission."[37]

Despite Weinberger and the military's views, Reagan did not immediately drop his retaliatory efforts. On December 4, 1983, a navy pilot, Lieutenant Robert Goodman, was shot down during retaliatory bombing for Syrian troops' earlier firing on US aircraft. The Syrians captured and held Goodman for thirty days until Democratic presidential candidate Reverend Jesse Jackson traveled to Damascus and obtained his freedom.[38] For his part, Reagan was more interested in deterring future attacks than in retaliating for past attacks,[39] took no action against Weinberger for the alleged November infraction,[40] and appeared reliant on Jackson to secure Goodman's release.[41] Moreover, the McFarlane and Hill accounts highlight how differences over the use of force, stemming from varying perspectives on the Vietnam War, divided the cabinet, especially Shultz and Weinberger, with McFarlane supporting the former and military leadership the latter.[42]

Public and congressional support, already tenuous, soon decreased after the barracks bombing. Reagan's pollster Richard Wirthlin had been surveying public opinion before the barracks bombing and continued throughout the week. He found a "precipitous overnight decline in Reagan's approval rating" after the bombings. The polls after Grenada, however, made it more difficult to disentangle the two events since "the pre-invasion survey was never made public." Nonetheless, "it served as a private warning of the consequences of further adventures in Lebanon."[43] As figure 3.1 shows, after an initial spike in support for marine presence, by early December, the public view was clearly changing

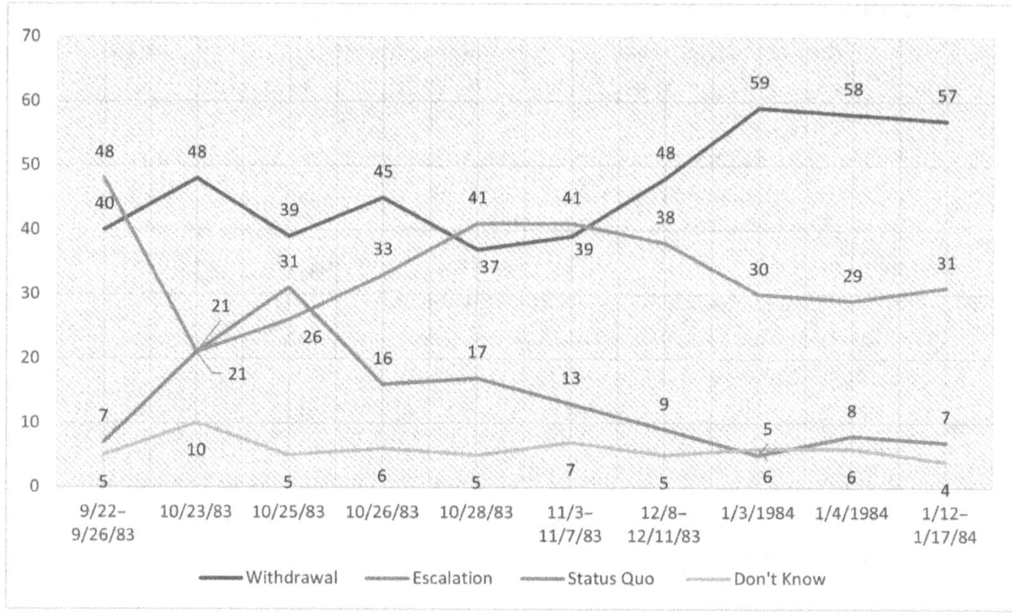

Figure 3.1. Public opinion about marine levels in Lebanon during the early 1980s.

in favor of withdrawal (as shown by an uptick in the red line and a dip in the green line starting October 25–28).[44]

Congressional support had taken a similar turn, souring on the operation following the barracks bombing. Members of Congress grew more concerned about the marine presence in Lebanon, their vulnerability, how they were being utilized, the limited prospects for success, and perceptions that Lebanon was not worth US military involvement. Exasperated with the administration, Representative Sam Hall (D-TX) reflected that "our government leaders have learned nothing from Vietnam. It is axiomatic that when you commit American fighting men . . . you take the necessary military steps to bring it to a quick and decisive conclusion. Our Marines are nothing more than sitting ducks. . . . [They should be allowed to] assume a more aggressive role . . . [or] the administration ought to order them home."[45] Similar concerns and calls for a "prompt withdrawal" from other Congressmen and Senator Joe Biden (D-DE) increased.[46] Congress mentioned the Vietnam War publicly, but the administration did not, leading one to conclude that they were in denial of similarities or that they recognized them and wanted to avoid the label "Reagan's Vietnam." The disagreements between Weinberger and Shultz over whether and how to use force, as well as the Weinberger-Powell Doctrine's emergence ten months after withdrawal, both rooted in Vietnam discourse, suggest it was the latter, not the former.[47]

Reflecting on the president's desire after the barracks bombing, McFarlane stated, "What the President did not want to do, above all, was to pull out of Lebanon immediately, to be seen as running away as a result of the tragedy that had taken place."[48] The country had already lost credibility by suffering a battlefield setback by nonstate actors.[49] An immediate departure risked further signaling to future adversaries that they could "kill and humiliate our people and the United States will immediately retreat."[50] Indeed, after the Black Hawk Down tragedy in 1993, "Al Qaeda and bin Laden . . . told one another, the United States had been humiliated by a Third World country. Just like Vietnam. Just like Lebanon."[51]

Just before Christmas 1983, the Long Commission concluded that military commanders at all levels, along with circumstances beyond their control, contributed to multiple failures and increased vulnerability. Commanders consolidated 350 marines in one barracks that could better protect against indirect fire but offered a "lucrative target." They "prioritized safety over security" by preventing guards at several security posts from chambering rounds until an incident occurred, reducing reaction time.[52] The Long Commission's findings added further impetus for Reagan's team to finalize and publicize their own conclusions.[53]

On February 1, Reagan signed NSDD 123, approving the concept of pulling the marines offshore, but not yet its execution.[54] On February 2, a battle for Beirut began between the LAF and Muslim militias. A deputies-level group had a meeting on February 3 to discuss withdrawal specifics. The topics suggested imminent withdrawal. They included a "timetable for redeployment," "perception management," a search for "any creative political initiatives," and a "presentation for Gemayel" on the new US position.[55]

On February 5, Lebanon's prime minister and cabinet resigned from Syrian pressure. Although purportedly to help Amin Gemayel, the late Bashir's brother, form a more broadly representative government,[56] the government's collapse at that time was a significant blow, the one contingency Reagan had indicated might lead to a US departure.[57] Then the LAF lost effectiveness when one-quarter of its Shia forces resigned or refused to fight fellow Muslims such as the Druze militia.[58] Finally, Muslim militias overran West Beirut on February 6, deepening the civil war.

An "MNF Options" memorandum determined that "the inescapable conclusion is that the current U.S. policy cannot be executed and a change in approach is required. So, the U.S. should be affirmatively looking for an opportunity to withdraw." The NSPG's recommendation on February 7 aligned with this assessment. Reagan finally agreed to withdraw the marines offshore; the last of the contingent left on February 26.[59]

1. WHY WAS THIS A SUNK COST TRAP THAT REQUIRED A MAJOR POLICY PIVOT?

> We are in a quagmire now. This is a trap if I ever saw one.
>
> —Sam Nunn

> There were three loci of that [Lebanon] strategy, and in each one we appeared to be failing.
>
> —Robert McFarlane

By the end of 1983, the military intervention in Lebanon constituted a sunk cost trap. It was a sunk cost trap because it was a failing endeavor, as McFarlane noted in the second topline quotation, and "U.S. credibility had definitely suffered."[60] Furthermore, as Middle East envoy Donald Rumsfeld noted, there were no easy answers to fix it, but Reagan strongly wanted America to remain involved.[61] This left policymakers in a trap in late 1983 and early 1984. They were caught between a floundering effort and Reagan's unchanged aims.

The Lebanon strategy to which McFarlane referred had three facets. The first was the situation on the ground against the Syrians in Lebanon, who, along with Iranian proxies, were opposing both US and Lebanese efforts. The second involved a reconciliation conference among Lebanese factions in Geneva. The third was a struggle for bureaucratic unity among the president's national security team.[62] McFarlane's assessment, beyond accounting for the bombings at the American embassy in April and the marine barracks in October, was that the prospects for success were low.[63] Following the Syrians' downing of a couple of planes that were attempting a punitive strike on December 4, McFarlane reflected that "it was an embarrassing demonstration of American military ineptitude . . . I knew it was time to step back and take a hard, rigorous look at the realities of our very ability to forge viable strategy in the Middle East."[64]

Lebanese prime minister Shafik Dib Wazzan's resignation was one key indicator, beyond the bureaucratic and domestic politics at home, that led American leaders to reach the type of assessments expressed by McFarlane. Another was the resignation of Gemayel's cabinet, and the mass desertions or refusal to fight anti-Gemayel militias by some LAF units. King Hussein of Jordan expressed to Donald Rumsfeld that things in Lebanon had reached "a point of no return."[65] In addition to McFarlane's accounts, memorandums at the time also reflected a realization that the situation was bleak and required a policy change.[66]

The decision to reevaluate America's military commitment and foreign policy approach in Lebanon and the greater Middle East came after eighteen months of investments. This temporal sunk cost measures the time from MNF I's creation in August 1982 until Reagan's sunk cost trap decision on February 7, 1984. This time frame is substantially shorter than the post-9/11 decisions in the Iraq and Afghanistan Wars, which are also among this book's cases. Yet among my pre-9/11 cases, it represents the longest period from the start of US military involvement until a sunk cost decision was made. In the other two cases, the time was approximately seven months in the Gulf War and ten months in Somalia, respectively.

Perhaps more important than the length of the conflict was the effort invested. Secretary of State Shultz and initial Reagan Special Envoy to the Middle East Philip Habib and his deputy, Morris Draper, had traveled continuously among the United States, Lebanon, Israel, and other regional capitals. Their shuttle diplomacy was central to the successful brokering of ceasefires and the May 17 Agreement—though all proved ephemeral.[67] This demonstrated Reagan's commitment to Lebanese stability not for its own sake but in support of regional US interests, as would be true later in the Persian Gulf, Somalia, Iraq, and Afghanistan.[68]

The human toll was an important dimension of the sunk costs as well. As with the temporal component, the numbers did not approach the level of casualties later experienced in the Iraq and Afghanistan Wars. Nevertheless, the casualties were important because they came primarily in two major mass casualty-producing attacks: the bombings of the US Embassy (seventeen deaths) and the marine barracks in Beirut (241 deaths). The enormity of these losses in single events weighed heavily on Reagan and other DC political elite.

Indeed, the perception of the bombings, especially that of the barracks, was powerful. It resulted in the largest single-day loss of life for the US Marine Corps since Iwo Jima in 1945.[69] It reaffirmed that the mission was not going well and cast doubt on whether active learning was occurring. Why had the country's and marine leaders not learned from the April embassy bombing, also conducted by a suicide truck driver, and improved the security measures to prevent such a tragedy? Why had the administration chosen sides, abandoning

TABLE 3.1
Reagan's Lebanon Sunk Costs (1984)

Time	18 months (August 1, 1982–February 7, 1984)
Casualties	260 dead[1]; 4 nonservicemen killed; 137 wounded
Financial Investment	Approximately $500 million total, including $249.6 million for military operations and $251 million in emergency relief aid[2] (est. August 1, 1982–February 13, 1984)
Personal Credibility (Reagan)	Accomplishment of Reagan's peace plan was at risk.[3] He suffered an 18% decline in popular support for the MNF as measured by an increase of support for withdrawal from 40% to 58% across the time period from before the barracks bombing to mid-January 1984, potentially jeopardizing his reelection.[4]
National Prestige	There was a risk of allowing terrorists to change US foreign policy and of increased Soviet influence in Syria and the Middle East.[5]

[1] Ronald Reagan, "Letter to the Speaker of the House and the President Pro Tempore of the Senate on the Termination of United States Participation in the Multinational Force in Lebanon," March 30, 1984; online by Gerhard Peters and John T. Woolley, *The American Presidency Project*, accessed January 25, 2016, http://www.presidency.ucsb.edu/ws/?pid=39709.

[2] Total military deployment costs from October 1, 1983, to February 13, 1984, are listed at $62.4 million in Memo, "Lebanon Report: February 13, 1984—U.S. Foreign Policy Interests Served by U.S. Participation in the MNF," Lebanon–MNF (Multinational Force) 1984 (1)–(3) folder, box 91136, Near East and South Asia Affairs Directorate: Records, Ronald Reagan Library, 5. Since other cost compilations were not available, the $249.6 million figure comes from extrapolating these costs for four and a half months over the eighteen months of MNF I and II. Robert Shepard, "The House Overwhelmingly Approved a 251 Million Emergency Aid," June 2, 1983, http://www.upi.com/Archives/1983/06/02/The-House-overwhelmingly-approved-a-251-million-emergency-aid/3528423374400/.

[3] President Ronald Reagan, "Address to the Nation on United States Policy for Peace in the Middle East," September 1, 1982, https://reaganlibrary.archives.gov/archives/speeches/1982/90182d.htm.

[4] John Mueller, "American Public Opinion and Military Ventures Abroad: Attention, Evaluation, Involvement, Politics, and the Wars of the Bushes," Annual Meeting of the American Political Science Association, Philadelphia, August 2003, 47.

[5] President Ronald Reagan, "Address to the Nation on Events in Lebanon and Grenada," October 27, 1983, https://reaganlibrary.archives.gov/archives/speeches/1983/102783b.htm; Caspar W. Weinberger, *Fighting for Peace: Seven Critical Years in the Pentagon* (New York: Warner Books, 1990), 151–52, 160.

any modicum of neutrality, by firing on Syrian and Druze positions in support of the Lebanese government?

As is usually the case, the financial investment was the least relevant. As reflected in the middle column of table 3.1, Reagan spent an estimated $500 million on the intervention, roughly equivalent to $1.15 billion today.[70] Like the temporal and human sunk costs, the financial sums would not match the amounts spent in latter, larger interventions. Yet for a president whose political rhetoric revolved around smaller government and reducing the national debt, spending even that much on a flailing foreign policy represented a substantial commitment.

Reagan's personal credibility was also on the line, and not only as the commander in chief seeking a successful military outcome in Lebanon. Reagan's relatively new foreign policy aim of Middle East peace was now tied up in how these events unfolded. His September 1, 1982, peace initiative was a way to capitalize on the recent success of MNF I. Reagan saw intervention in Lebanon as a clear investment toward Middle East peace and increased regional influence vis-à-vis the Soviet Union.[71] He sought to break the Cold War stalemate by "exploiting Soviet weaknesses and asserting western strengths."[72] Reagan made this clear in his British Parliament address on June 8, 1982. His hope was that the "march of freedom and democracy . . . will leave Marxism-Leninism on the ash-heap of history."[73] MNF I's success and Lebanon's need for US involvement provided an opportunity to assert Western influence. Failure to achieve his goals, however, could diminish Reagan's political standing. Moreover, having labeled the Soviet Union as the "evil empire"[74] and advocated against standing by while "the Middle East [was] incorporated into the Soviet bloc,"[75] his aims were not easily retractable.

Reagan recognized the worsening situation in his September 10–11 diary entries. "The situation is worsening. We may be facing a choice. . . . If it [naval gunfire] doesn't work then we'll have to decide between pulling out or going to Congress and making a case for greater involvement."[76] Reagan conceded a few days earlier that, "the civil war is running wild and could result in collapse of the Gemayel government and [then] the stuff would hit the fan."[77] Later he expressed that a Lebanese government collapse would risk further US participation.[78]

Reagan's political advisers' fear of bad outcomes in Lebanon led them to favor pulling the marines offshore. Their fear was based on a combination of Vietnam lessons and domestic political challenges.[79] As Reagan neared a reelection campaign season, they wanted him free of foreign entanglements that might prevent the American people from again answering the question "Are you better off now than you were four years ago?" in Reagan's favor, this time in the affirmative.[80] If average citizens saw Lebanon as a quagmire, the issue could become a focus of election-year politics—to Reagan's detriment.[81] It is unclear whether political realities impacted Reagan's personal thinking,[82] but his memoirs show the Vietnam War's impact.[83]

Finally, some members of the administration—other than Secretary Shultz—believed they were in a sunk cost trap because national prestige was at stake.[84] A quick withdrawal after the barracks bombings could send the message that the United States was unwilling to pursue its aims when bloodied.[85] An administration memo in early February 1984 stated that national prestige is the "main U.S. strategic interest now . . . Lebanon itself is of little intrinsic strategic value."[86] Reagan himself asked, "If we were to leave Lebanon now, what message would that send to those who foment instability and terrorism?"[87] The message would be that terrorism was successful, could prompt immediate American disengagement, and that waiting out the United States works.[88] Interestingly, this question-and-answer foreshadowed President William (Bill) Clinton's concern following the 1993 Black Hawk Down tragedy in Somalia.[89]

SUNK COST SALIENCE

> "When America sends its forces to perform a legitimate mission, asked for by the legitimate Government involved, and it does so and then the minute some trouble occurs we turn tail and beat it, I think that sends a gigantic message around the world."
>
> Lyndon Johnson in 1965? No, George Shultz on Sept. 21, 1983.
>
> —Anthony Lewis

The perception of a flailing Lebanon policy "was clear [to policymakers by Christmas 1983;] we were at a moment of truth"[90] that required major change. The sunk costs and the linkage of Lebanon's stability with vital goals delayed Reagan's recognition of the need for change.[91] A couple of developments made that clear. First was the marine barracks bombing. Second, "national reconciliation [among various Lebanese factions] was set back by the serious deterioration in the security situation in Beirut in early February."[92] This called into question the accomplishment of US goals. So Reagan and his team explored other alternatives.[93]

2. WHAT WERE THE PRESIDENT'S OPTIONS AND WHAT STRATEGY DID HE IMPLEMENT?

As the "MNF Options" memorandum indicated, this set of circumstances left President Reagan and his advisers with a narrowing set of options they were considering. This winnowing of apparently feasible options had been in the works for a few months. Admiral William N. Small, commander of US Naval Forces Europe, presciently summarized the American position and options, even before the Lebanese government's and LAF's collapse. On a November 3, 1983, visit to Lebanon, he wrote, "The American Multinational Force contingent forfeited its neutrality on the occasion of the bombardment of Suq al-Gharb [in the Chouf mountains, and], having been publicly declared the enemy, then had [only] two alternatives: accept their status as co-belligerents and consider them[selves] as combat troops or retire to the amphibs [amphibious ships]."[94] It was impossible to simultaneously be a neutral broker and support a particular side. A month after that assessment, Reagan himself indicated conditions for a marine withdrawal.

On December 14, 1983, Reagan told reporters that the marines would only be withdrawn if there was a complete withdrawal by all foreign forces from Lebanon (i.e., mission accomplishment), or if there "was a complete collapse" of the Lebanese government and "there was no possibility of restoring order."[95] Regarding the former condition, State Department cables during January 1984 indicated that America's MNF partners were contemplating withdrawal whether the United States remained or not.[96] The latter condition occurred on February 5, 1984, as Prime Minister Wazzan and key cabinet members resigned. Combined with the LAF woes and Muslim militias overrunning parts of Beirut the next day, the capital descended into civil war and Reagan's second condition was met.[97]

Despite his December remarks, Reagan conceptually had a choice among three main alternatives, with variants thereof. The first course was to withdraw completely and stop all MNF activity, maintaining only diplomatic ties (vertical military de-escalation). The second option was to make the status quo more tenable by a "legislative strategy" that tried to convince Congress of Lebanon's importance to America and clarify the mission.[98] The administration could have undertaken this by using diplomacy and intelligence to persuade international and domestic audiences that Syria and Iran were the real culprits and that resoluteness was what was necessary to achieve US ends. The status quo approach could simply involve a change in talking points (no movements along the political, military, vertical, or horizontal dimensions). The third alternative was to support Gemayel's government and the LAF with increased forces (horizontal military escalation) or more robust ways of using those forces (vertical military escalation). Retaliatory military action against those responsible for the bombings would have been an example of this type of escalation. Another variant could have entailed the pursuit of new partners for the MNF (horizontal diplomatic and military escalation).

In reality, the options Reagan's advisers prepared demonstrated less diversity. They developed several nuanced options that varied primarily based on the amount of withdrawal they directed. In what foreshadowed the narrowly conceived options presented to President Barack Obama in 2009 for an adjustment to Afghanistan war policy, all the options mentioned focused on the number of marines that would remain.[99] This was likely because it was the most salient political factor. Nevertheless, the options did not include the full range of conceptual alternatives, likely reflecting that the administration did not see other courses as viable.

All the proffered options focused on maintaining either the status quo or drawdown variants.[100] Option 1 (Status Quo) left the current contingent of marines at the airport. Though not specifically addressed, the implication was that Reagan's aims, the strategy, and the level of diplomatic dialogue would also remain unchanged. The intention was to monitor the domestic political situation closely and unify the executive branch behind this approach. Though no end date was provided, this course presumably hoped to complete the mission at least by March 1985. That was the point at which the eighteen-month extension Congress approved in September 1983 expired. The rationale proffered for this strategy was all negative in nature. It included the adverse impact that withdrawal of any sort was likely to have on Lebanon, MNF partners, the region, and US credibility.

Option 2 (Partial De-escalation) involved reducing the marine presence by about half, to approximately eight hundred to one thousand personnel. Those departing would go to ships offshore, constituting a surge capability, and could come ashore to conduct patrols. The rest would remain at the Beirut International Airport.[101] This option would continue LAF training as well as retain offshore naval/air power and counter-battery equipment that would help if Reagan wanted to add a security umbrella, possible with any option. This umbrella would protect the remaining MNF units and Beirut by demanding that Syria remove its artillery from within shelling range of the capital and threatening punitive air/naval responses to any artillery fired at the US or friendly elements. Option 2 had an open-ended time commitment where further policy adjustments would be conditions based. One perceived advantage of this option included its ability to enhance America's staying power by partial adherence to domestic critics who wanted the marines out of Lebanon. The downside was that assuring Lebanon of enduring US commitment would be difficult, and domestic opposition could continue.

Option 3 (Large De-escalation and Security Umbrella) involved the removal of most of the marines, coupled with the definite implementation of the security response plan. Most of the marines would be withdrawn to ships offshore. The marines that were left (one hundred to three hundred) would hunker down at the most secure portion of the Beirut International Airport.[102] The LAF training, air/naval presence, and counter-battery equipment would remain, while a security umbrella and a small antiterrorism and embassy protection special operations force would be added.[103]

Diplomatic measures were also an important part of Option 3.[104] Israelis would be expected to continue air attacks against the PLO and to declare a redline against any forward movement by Syrian forces following the departures of the MNF and Israeli Defense Forces. The United Nations Interim Force in Lebanon (UNIFIL), a separate peacekeeping operation that predated the MNF, would be invited to protect the refugee camps, and MNF partners would be encouraged to keep their contingents. This reflected the administration's welcoming of a recent UN proposal to substitute UN peacekeeping forces for the MNF. They thought the UN idea came at just the right time, allowing the United States to use that substitution as a pretext for withdrawal, even though they believed the move would not produce a political solution in the next nine months.[105] Option 3's trade-offs were perceived as much the same as those faced under Option 2. The near-complete withdrawal was a move that could swiftly deflate congressional opposition, while the security mechanism was central to an uphill attempt to convince the Lebanese government that the plan could provide the support they needed. The other key element was to follow through if Syria tested US resolve by shelling remaining US forces, the MNF, or the LAF around Beirut.

Option 4 (Complete Withdrawal) would involve pulling all the marines onto ships offshore.[106] It would acknowledge that the prospects for Lebanese reconciliation and a national unity government were "nonexistent" and that "indefinite de facto partition of Lebanon is inevitable."[107] Beyond the troop exit, it could involve most of the same elements as Options 2 and 3 and the possibility of a UNIFIL role. Yet complete withdrawal would require less ambitious goals, rely on Israeli power, afford the marines greater safety, and retain the ability to quickly reinsert marines if the parties reached a peace deal.[108] Option 4, however, was perceived as the most likely to trigger Israeli withdrawal and subsequent MNF pullouts by other nations. It also presented the greatest challenge to the administration's bilateral relationship with Lebanon. Yet all the options the administration put forward suggested withdrawing while still pursuing Reagan's aims and trying to assure Lebanon of US commitment.

Figure 3.2 depicts these options along political/diplomatic and military escalation/de-escalation spectra. It also enables a comparison of the options across these factors—conceptually and for this case. Conceptually, presidents can manipulate options in the number of additional troops deployed or

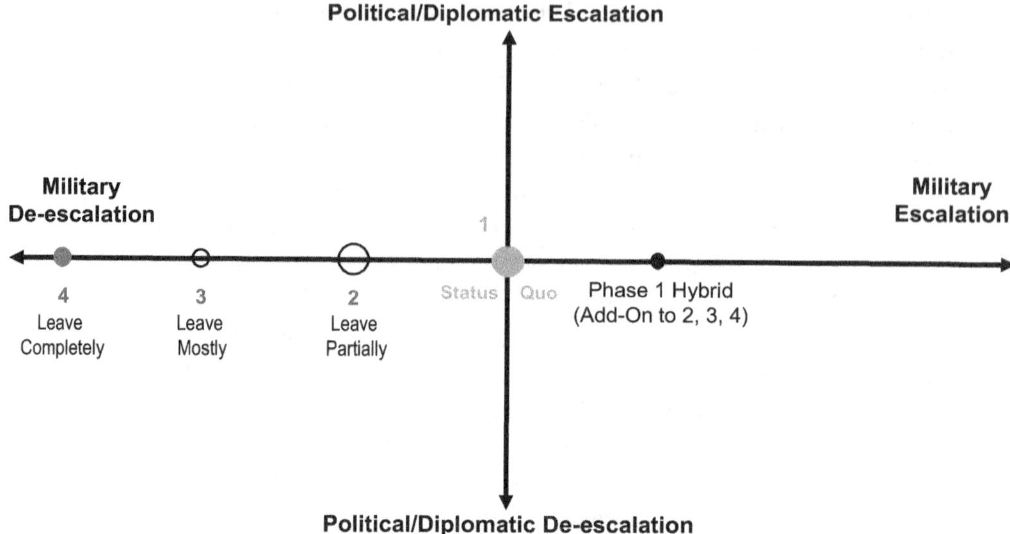

Figure 3.2. Potential presidential policy options in Lebanon in 1983–1984.

withdrawn. They can change the type of mission those forces conduct. They can adjust the intensity of diplomacy undertaken and the breadth of its focus bilaterally, regionally, or globally. They can modify the amount of political capital expended on domestic politics to secure popular and congressional support. They can determine the pace at which those changes will be implemented and how long they will last—within certain feasible logistic parameters.

None of the options considered explicitly involved military escalation or diplomatic de-escalation. In fact, the options were very uncreative and limited. They only differed in the amount of military de-escalation and whether to add a temporary military escalation. The only potential change in diplomatic partners was the possible substitution of a UN peacekeeping element for the MNF. These dynamics point to an administration that slowly and reluctantly perceived its options as narrowing.

THE STRATEGY IMPLEMENTED

> Decisions are easy when no options are left.
>
> —P. V. Narasimha Rao

Reagan made the de-escalation decision during a brief phone call with Vice President H. W. Bush while on a trip out West.[109] His decision on February 7 when Shultz was traveling[110] may have been due to the recent disintegration of Lebanese institutions. The timing of Reagan's decision may instead have been opportunistic. Since Reagan had a divided cabinet and found it hard to refuse either his secretary of defense or secretary of state, he may have waited until Shultz was not present to make the decision.[111] On February 7, Shultz was conveniently in the middle of a nine-day trip around Central and South America and the Caribbean when the key developments in Lebanon transpired. This was the same time during which the decisive balance among Reagan's advisers swung in favor of removing the marines.[112]

McFarlane's perspective had shifted; he and Vice President Bush sided strongly with Weinberger and the Joint Chiefs of Staff against a continued marine presence onshore. Lawrence Eagleburger was the only dissenter, on behalf of the traveling Shultz, when Bush asked the NSPG about the withdrawal proposal on February 7.[113] After the meeting, Bush reported the results to Reagan during a brief phone conversation. Bush reached Reagan after the president's speech to a Nevada Republican Party fundraising luncheon. Bush recommended a redeployment of all marines but continued support of the Lebanese government with air and naval forces.[114] "The Vice President emphasized that all of Reagan's advisers except Shultz favored the decision." Speaking from a Las Vegas airport hangar, "Reagan agreed, ending the U.S. commitment [of marines] in a phone conversation even briefer than the one in which he had originally authorized Habib to commit the United States to participation in the MNF."[115]

Deputy National Security Adviser John Poindexter oversaw the release of President Reagan's written statement to reporters traveling with the president later that day. It indicated that Reagan had directed "decisive new steps" in changing the Lebanon strategy and had instructed Secretary Weinberger to present a redeployment plan to pull the marines at the Beirut International Airport (BIA) back to their ships but that LAF training would continue when the circumstances stabilized. In addition, as Bush had recommended, the American military would conduct air/naval strikes against any threats to the MNF or Beirut.[116]

As you can see from this description and figure 3.2, the strategy Reagan chose was complete withdrawal (Option 4), with the add-on hybrid. The marines' departure to ships offshore was a de-escalation. The publicly expressed intention to respond to Syrian artillery against Beirut (not just against the MNF) would have been an escalation if enforced. So, too, would have been the privately articulated potential for an infusion of a small special operations team for antiterrorism and additional embassy protection.[117] The combination made for a hybrid solution on paper. In practice, the withdrawal dominated the other dimensions since the LAF training ended a month after the marines pulled offshore, and there was no real testing or enforcement of US redlines regarding artillery strikes. By February 26, all the marines had left; by March 30, the trainers had departed.

3. WHAT ROLE DID HISTORICAL LESSONS AND FEAR PLAY IN LEBANON DECISION-MAKING?

> Vietnam was a shadow over Lebanon.
>
> —Lou Cannon

> The lesson of Vietnam was continually being cited to reject any use of military force unless in exceptional circumstances and with near total public support in advance.
>
> —George P. Shultz

These quotations illustrate the Vietnam War's impact on decision-making during the US peacekeeping operation in Lebanon during the fall of 1983 and early 1984. The first reflects the cloud that Vietnam cast over officials' views as to the wisdom of US involvement in and execution of the MNF mission. Then senator Dan Quayle expressed a similar belief when he remarked that "Vietnam has made us paranoid, it has terrorized us, it has blinded us to our own interests."[118] He saw traumatic lessons from Vietnam adversely affecting leaders' ability to make sound decisions about foreign policy and military force—decisions based on *present* interests rather than on paranoia about *past* conflicts or sunk costs. Instead, leaders were paralyzed between fears of losing national prestige that hindered an exit from Lebanon and fears of casualties that prevented consensus about pursuing the status quo or escalation. The second topline quotation reflects Secretary of State George Shultz's observation that the lesson of Vietnam was behind every attempt to thwart the use of military power in Lebanon. After the Beirut barracks bombing in October 1983, the goal to excise Vietnam ghosts by confidently exercising power[119] gave way to references to Vietnam as a harbinger of a looming Lebanon quagmire.[120] Vietnam's influence, which then pushed toward the withdrawal of the marines—played out in three arenas: the administration, Congress, and declining popular support.

Vietnam's impact during Reagan's policy reevaluation on Lebanon widened the preexisting fissure in his cabinet.[121] It influenced Secretary of Defense Caspar Weinberger in favor of exit. Powell later indicated that the secretary "never wanted to ever preside over anything like a Vietnam involvement by U.S. forces."[122] Weinberger continually tried to persuade Reagan that the marines were on an impossible mission and needed to be withdrawn.[123] Weinberger worried that Lebanon had some of the same characteristics that marked the Vietnam War effort. As for the military writ large, Vietnam-era wounds of perceived political micro- and mismanagement, and of not producing a decisive victory, were still deep. "Only a decade after the end of Vietnam, the uniformed services had strong reservations about being dragged into another open-ended military commitment with no clear end-state."[124] The connection to national interests was arguable, policy objectives were vague, and the administration was falling prey to incrementalism. Yet Reagan lacked the will to invest at the level necessary to accomplish his aims. There was an ends-means mismatch; the number of resources allocated did not match Reagan's robust objectives.[125] For his part, Shultz wanted to continue what he considered an important mission in Lebanon, but he recognized that Vietnam lessons were leading toward an exit.[126] He criticized Weinberger for "the Vietnam Syndrome in spades, carried to an absurd level, and a complete abdication of the duties of leadership."[127]

The shadow of Vietnam was also central to congressional debates.[128] Members of Congress had been speculating for a year that the current conflict would lead to a Vietnam-like entanglement.[129]Senator Ernest F. Hollings (D-SC) said the nation "must avoid 'getting bogged down there' as it did in Vietnam."[130] Representative James Florio (D-NJ) argued against an eighteen-month extension because "the priority of the Congress must be to ensure that our Nation is not again pulled into a quagmire like Vietnam."[131] Representative Sam Gibbons (D-FL) declared, "I have only three words to say: Lebanon, Reagan's Vietnam."[132] Representative Samuel Stratton (D-NY) questioned Reagan's decision-making. "I don't like to see Marines wasted. If you're smart, you know when to cut your losses. That's what we didn't understand in Vietnam."[133] The opposition was bipartisan. Representative Michael Bilirakis (R-FL) said Lebanon was "haunted by the specter of our Vietnam experience . . . critics . . . express not just the fear but the conviction that our present actions will lead us down the same path. . . . It is a fear that is very real for all of us."[134]

A third front where Reagan faced Vietnam-linked pressure was the public opinion arena.[135] In early October 1983, prior to the barracks bombing, public concern was at 35 percent that "Lebanon could turn into a situation like Vietnam . . . that the U.S. would be more and more deeply involved as time goes on."[136] By December, 57 percent agreed that the country was "risking American lives in Lebanon without any clear mission" and that "we are going to get bogged down there, just as we did in Vietnam."[137] Thus, comparing Reagan's Lebanon withdrawal with previous presidents' Vietnam policies, one scholar assessed that

> the fact of defeat in Vietnam encouraged the Reagan administration to cut its losses in Lebanon far earlier than did Lyndon Johnson and Richard Nixon in Vietnam. Reagan believed that America had a powerful stake in creating a stable Lebanon, but he seemed to recognize, in the wake of the Beirut disaster, that continued U.S. military intervention was not the solution to what was essentially an intractable local political problem. This had also been the case in Vietnam, but the outcome of that war proved that a prolonged lost war is a far worse foreign policy outcome than an early decision to back out of a bad intervention. Wars of choice involve not only choosing to intervene but also choosing to halt a mistaken intervention in progress. Reagan did in Lebanon what Johnson could not bring himself to do in Vietnam.[138]

Reagan later wrote of his decision that "no one wanted to commit our troops to a full-scale war in the Middle East . . . [and] we couldn't remain in Lebanon and be in the war on a halfway basis, leaving our men vulnerable to terrorists with one hand tied behind their backs." Reagan's language and reasoning here indicate his rationale and demonstrate another Vietnam War lesson—that of using decisive force when in a military operation or, if it becomes unsustainable or unwinnable, to leave.[139] Reagan opted for the latter course to avoid an even worse situation that might undeniably become his own "Vietnam."[140]

4. DID INTERNAL ADMINISTRATION RATIONALE DIFFER FROM THE PUBLIC JUSTIFICATIONS?

> Defeat isn't bitter if you don't swallow it.
>
> —Chinese proverb

> Reagan framed the policy pivot as a "redeployment" and as a series of "decisive new steps,"[141] but "to even neutral observers it seemed as if Hezbollah's use of terrorism had achieved at least one of the organization's political goals."[142]

The administration's public justifications were consistent in some ways and differed from private rationale in others. They were consistent regarding the enduring desire to support Lebanon and regarding congressional influence on the policy change. They differed in who originated the change, beliefs about the Lebanese government's viability, and the nature of the change. Together, the differences highlighted the administration's spin on a bad situation.

One consistency between the private deliberations and public explanations of the new approach involved an initial desire to continue support to Lebanon. Privately, in an internal administration memo dated February 13, 1984, just six days after the announcement that Reagan was pulling the marines out, the administration explained the move. "The intention is to redeploy our military resources in a way that can best help the Lebanese, without signaling a lessening in our resolve. The United States will remain fully engaged."[143] Although illogical, publicly, it was the same line. The new strategy was "to help the Lebanese confront the terrorist threat that poses such a danger to Lebanon."[144] This language seemed to demonstrate that Washington did not intend to abandon Lebanon and thought it possible to sell the redeployment in a way that others might understand America's commitment to be ongoing.

Another area of relative congruence was the recognition of congressional influence. The "MNF Options" memorandum explicitly discussed the need to frame a new Lebanon policy assertively, both domestically with Congress and internationally with Gemayel, as well as with MNF and regional partners. It wanted to link the strategy change to an increase in "American staying power"—the positive outcome gained by appeasing Congress by removing the marines from BIA. In fact, the political bargain that the administration had sought with Congress was an "expanded ROE in exchange for total MAU [Marine Amphibious Unit] withdrawal."[145] The public reference to this compromise involved a more tacit recognition of Congress's role but did make it into the February 7 statement. It implied that the new steps were cognizant of domestic political realities since they were "consistent with the compromise joint resolution worked out last October with the Congress."[146]

One key discrepancy between the private deliberations and public justifications concerned the impetus for a strategy change. The move was ostensibly at the request of President Gemayel,[147] though the Reagan administration pushed him to make the request to increase its legitimacy.[148] A request from President Gemayel for such a "reorientation" would enhance Reagan's ability to characterize the changed war policy as something other than a cut-and-run. NSDD 123 admitted this. "The objective is to encourage President Gemayel to request the type of reorientation described above [US MNF] departure to ships, continued LAF training, and stronger ROE for naval and air responses to threats against Beirut] from the U.S. and other MNF contributors."[149] Having secured this "request," it became part of the public justification in Reagan's February 7 written explanation of the changed strategy.[150]

Portions of the question-and-answer session following the policy change announcement reveal a second discrepancy. As Poindexter answered questions, he spoke of American support for the Lebanese government and stated that the Reagan administration still saw it "as a viable entity."[151]

In reality, US officials no longer saw the Lebanese government as "a viable entity." Instead, it had been seen as "impotent" for more than a month.[152] Specifically, "it was now evident to McFarlane [Poindexter's direct boss] that Amin Gemayel was incapable of making the concessions needed to form a united government of Lebanon, and the national security adviser thought it irresponsible to risk more American casualties in this cause."[153] Moreover, US officials realized that the developments in Lebanon were so bad that they would need to wait until the situation stabilized to resume LAF training.[154]

A third difference was over the characterization of the strategy change, as indicated in Poindexter's statement. Publicly, it was a "redeployment"[155]; privately, it was acknowledged to be a "withdrawal."[156] A fourth difference regarded what the sunk cost trap decision meant for US foreign policy. Publicly, it was a move that would "strengthen our ability to do the job we set out to do and to sustain our efforts over the long term."[157] Privately, it was "one of the worst defeats of the Reagan administration."[158] These discrepancies showed that things were going badly in Lebanon and the administration knew it but did not want to acknowledge it openly. It also meant that Reagan was not likely to redeploy forces back into Lebanon. His threat to re-escalate when withdrawing Marines was likely a fig leaf for departure regardless of how future events transpired in Lebanon.[159] As the Chinese proverb at the top of this section indicates, the Reagan administration hoped defeat would not be bitter if they did not swallow it (i.e., accept it as a defeat).

CONCLUSION

> While these [Weinberger Doctrine] tests are drawn from lessons we have learned from the past, they also can—and should—be applied to the future.
>
> —Caspar Weinberger

In September 1983, a month before the barracks bombing, Anthony Lewis of the *New York Times* asked, "Might we be heading for another Vietnam in

Lebanon? Involvement on such a scale seems unlikely. But there is every reason to fear self-inflicted wounds of a lesser but still significant kind, military and political. For the American military role in Lebanon is growing in that same incremental way, accompanied by deceit and ignorance."[160] Evaluated in light of President Reagan's withdrawal decision four months later, Lewis's assessment proved mixed. He was correct that the Lebanon intervention resulted in what Secretary Weinberger regarded as self-inflicted wounds.[161] Lewis was incorrect about continued incremental escalation. Instead, Reagan cut losses and brought the marines home sooner than his predecessors had done during the Vietnam War.

Therefore, this case is consistent with expectations. It meets both of Alexander George's requirements to prove historical influence through process tracing. The chapter shows that in addition to the decision being consistent with Assessment 1 (a de-escalation), the relevant lesson was "on the minds of the central decision-makers and that it was used at important junctures in the policy process."[162] This was true for Secretaries Shultz and Weinberger (as well as key senators and members of Congress),[163] if not conclusively for the president at the time. Historical accounts differ on whether Reagan was thinking about Vietnam lessons when he decided to withdraw, or if that only came afterward.[164] Yet the Vietnam lesson-driven policy rift within the administration, along with Congress's impact on the administration's thinking, memorandum writing, and option development demonstrated Vietnam's centrality to decision-making.[165] Moreover, Secretary Shultz, the one most adamant about the mission's importance and the least inclined to see historical analogies pointing toward an exit, said "the lesson of Vietnam" was behind every attempt to thwart the use of military power in Lebanon.[166]

Like Shultz, Weinberger and the entire military reflected on the use of military power following the operation. As a result of the Vietnam and Lebanon hangover, Weinberger (with help from Powell) developed six lessons from common themes encountered in Lebanon and Vietnam, but that he feared had not truly been "learned." These lessons constituted tests he believed presidents should apply to determine whether circumstances warranted US military action. The United States' vital national interests must be at stake. America should apply sufficient resources to ensure it would win, "have clearly defined political and military objectives," match appropriate resources to the ends sought, have popular and congressional support, and use force as a last resort.[167] Weinberger's prime motivation, and the purpose behind the tests, was to keep America from "being drawn inexorably into an endless morass, where it is not vital to our national interest to fight."[168] Weinberger hoped his tests would influence future presidential decisions to use or adjust the use of force. He wanted to save presidents the trouble of unnecessarily finding themselves in sunk cost traps but to provide some means by which to extradite themselves should it happen.[169]

Although the timing is inconclusive, Reagan's later reflections on these lessons are compatible with Vietnam-induced, contemporaneous fear of the status quo or escalation.[170] Saddened by MNF II's results, Reagan called it "the source of my greatest regret and my greatest sorrow as president."[171] Reagan wrote that the Lebanese experience led to "a set of principles to guide America in the application of military force abroad, and I would recommend it to future presidents."[172] This illustrated Reagan's recognition that he had escaped a sunk cost trap and that his defense secretary's tests might help future presidents avoid them altogether.

Within ten years of Reagan's decision, a much different president—from a different political party—would make a similar decision for similar reasons. Chapter 4 examines President Clinton's decision-making during military operations in Somalia.

4

Black Hawk Down

Vietnam (and Lebanon) Ghosts Remain

INTRODUCTION

> Exactly like Vietnam, Somalia became a symbol of everything that could go wrong in a foreign military operation; it seemed, indeed to revalidate the Vietnam syndrome for a new generation.
>
> —Arnold R. Isaacs

Lessons from the Vietnam War and Lebanon intervention *directly* influenced President William (Bill) Clinton's decision to leave Somalia after the 1993 Black Hawk Down tragedy (named for the downing of two Black Hawk helicopters). These lessons were amplified by their impact on Congress and changed Clinton's risk calculus.[1] They were a filter through which he deciphered the risks of feasible options. Vietnam lessons had shaped Clinton's thinking during his formative years as a college student and an intern for Senator J. William Fulbright.[2] When he encountered his own sunk cost dilemma over an unfruitful military intervention in a country with limited relevance to US national security interests, Clinton had already learned from that experience. He preferred informed reassessment, admitting failure, and de-escalation over reflexive incremental escalation.[3]

Lessons from US involvement in these conflicts led Clinton to anticipate greater regret with the status quo or escalation than with cutting losses and withdrawing forces. In addition to Clinton's predisposition against sunk cost inclusion for sunk cost trap decisions,[4] influential members of Congress raised a Vietnam-era lesson against incremental escalations at the critical juncture when Clinton was determining whether and how to change course.[5] At the same time, Lebanon provided a relatively recent example that reinforced

Vietnam's lessons by demonstrating that a president could withdraw from an overseas intervention and still be reelected.[6]

By early October, the first year of Clinton's presidency was not going well on the foreign policy front.[7] The Somalia intervention was part of his assertive multilateralism and enlargement foreign policy, shaped by Clinton being the first entirely post–Cold War president.[8] Events started out well but quickly took a turn for the worse in June. A faction acting under the direction of Somali warlord Mohamed Farrah Aideed ambushed a Pakistani unit acting under a United Nations (UN) mandate in early June.[9] US and UN forces had been unable to apprehend Aideed. A US helicopter was shot down at the end of September. The Balkans were erupting in violence and needed a diplomatic breakthrough and peace enforcement mission.

Things were not going well on the home front either. Unemployment remained high, and Clinton had been unable to gain traction on his domestic agenda.[10] The push for universal health care, arguably Clinton's number one policy agenda, had not made progress. His administration was attempting to stop the hemorrhaging of foreign policy and refocus on domestic policy.[11] Clinton wanted to shift US efforts in Somalia from military to diplomatic-centric[12] to foster reconciliation among Somali clans and put a greater onus on UN leadership.[13] Yet the president and his team had not yet worked out the practical elements of this shift. Furthermore, they had not communicated them to the military,[14] despite the military's involvement in all the administration's meetings about military matters.[15]

Finally, civil-military relations were at a low point. Clinton's status as a reported draft dodger did not sit well with uniformed personnel and, in a way, haunted him during the early months of his presidency as his personal Vietnam ghosts.[16] His "Don't Ask, Don't Tell" policy further alienated a military that was more conservative than the general population[17] and that was not ready for what it saw as a social experiment that endangered morale and readiness.[18] Employment in humanitarian and peacekeeping efforts rather than being reserved for conventional wars exacerbated these other factors. For these reasons, some thought the military had never wanted to be in Somalia in the first place and was pushing for an exit.[19]

Given all of these dynamics, the existing literature suggests that Clinton's decision-making was either a result of his nonculpability for the initial intervention decision or a by-product of domestic politics. According to the first theory, leaders responsible for the initial intervention decision have a stronger incentive than nonculpable leaders to escalate in a sunk cost trap because domestic audiences will only blame the culpable for a loss.[20] The second alternative suggests that congressional opposition and public opinion, influenced partially by casualties and a lack of success, explained Clinton's decision to withdraw.[21] The other element of the domestic politics argument is that Clinton already felt that Congress had been inhibiting his domestic agenda, then Congress erupted again immediately after the Black Hawk Down incident.[22] Clinton realized he did not want to spend the political capital on Somalia when he had bigger requests to make of Congress. The nonculpability explanation lacks strength because Clinton had owned and expanded the mission over a period four times the length of his predecessor. The domestic politics theory ultimately fails to identify the underlying rationale for prevailing sentiments to withdraw—past lessons and fear of the future. My framework, however, explains the reasons for presidential sunk cost decision-making in a way consistent with their choices.

CASE SUMMARY (SOMALIA)

> The policy was, in fact, changing dramatically, and no one was aware of it.
>
> —David Halberstam

During the sunk cost trap that accompanied the Black Hawk Down tragedy, Clinton had to decide how to adjust war policy. The United States had lost eighteen soldiers at the hands of Somali warlords and their militias, who had captured one helicopter pilot and dragged a dead American through the streets of Mogadishu. Shocked that a group of nonstate actors did this to the highly trained American army, Clinton reevaluated the US mission in Somalia.[23]

Clinton's aspiration to establish a foreign policy marked by assertive multilateralism and enlargement influenced his view of the United Nations Operation in Somalia (UNOSOM) II effort as well as those that had preceded it. Some argued that there was a logical link between Somalia and the Balkans. Both were seen as candidates for humanitarian assistance missions. According to this interpretation, President George H. W. Bush intervened in Somalia *instead* of Bosnia at the end of his term in office.[24] Clinton, on the other hand, saw Somalia as a test bed for his assertive multilateralism. He thought he could eventually intervene in Bosnia *after* a successful humanitarian mission in Somalia.[25]

Clinton's foreign policy perspective also contributed to increasing aims in Somalia. When Clinton took office, the mission of the Unified Task Force (UNITAF) was narrowly scripted to deliver humanitarian assistance and ensure its safe distribution to the Somali people. The George H. W. Bush administration purposefully limited the operation's scope to narrow the mission and reduce the time necessary to complete its mandate.[26] The Bush administration designed UNITAF, led by and composed primarily of American military forces, to concentrate on the areas hit hardest by the crisis, not on the entire country.[27] Another limiting mechanism put in place by the Bush team involved not taking sides among competing warlords (neutrality) and rendering aid without bias (impartiality).[28] US Special Envoy Robert Oakley, a former ambassador to Somalia, and Lieutenant General Robert Johnston, UNITAF's commander, were adept at these approaches and avoided robust nation-building activities.[29]

The Bush decision for UNITAF not to engage in institution-building and economic reconstruction aligned with the lesson Oakley learned from his involvement as a foreign service officer in the Vietnam War. Oakley understood that lasting change could only occur if the host country took ownership of the process.[30] Accordingly, UNITAF encouraged Somalis to provide their own local security, police reconstitution, and reinstitution of a judicial code.[31]

Initial UNITAF efforts met with rapid success. UNITAF accomplished its mandate during Clinton's initial months in office and facilitated national reconciliation conferences in January and March 1993 with fourteen clan-based factions led by rival warlords, leading to the sporadic observation of an agreed-upon ceasefire.[32] UNITAF restored order, secured the road networks, and provided security for aid delivery to meet humanitarian needs, stemming the famine and saving lives without attempting broader nation-building activities.[33] Clinton inherited the Oakley- and Johnston-led team from Bush and kept them in place for a few months until UNOSOM II replaced UNITAF on May 4.

In line with his broader foreign policy agenda, Clinton had cooperated with the UN as it added nation building as an aim through the United Nations Security Council Resolution (UNSCR) 814 in March. This broadened the UN mandate in Somalia and represented a significant increase in US and UN aims. UNOSOM II was now to stabilize broader swaths of Somalia, build a Somali police force, and support reconciliation among various clans—in addition to delivering humanitarian assistance.[34]

In line with Oakley's predictions, and contrasting with UNITAF's success, operations started going poorly. Somalis, apparently under Aideed's control, killed twenty-four Pakistanis and wounded fifty, including three Americans, when a UN force inspected five of Aideed's weapons sites on June 5, including at one of his radio stations.[35] UNSCR 837 passed on June 6, approving "all necessary measures" against those responsible and adding raids on warlords as another goal.[36]

Clinton's assertive multilateralism and inattention to the operation created a permissive environment for mission expansion and a policy-strategy mismatch.[37] At the same time the aims were growing, Clinton applied dwindling resources to accomplish those ends. The tension among these conflicting pressures—to do more with less—was increasingly evident as the summer passed. National Security Adviser Anthony Lake later reflected that the Clinton administration "attempted too much" in Somalia.[38] Military leaders in Somalia made repeated requests for heavy assets and Special Operations Forces to address the ends-means gap[39] that were usually denied.[40] Civilian and military leaders in DC deliberately did not offer more resources as they were conflicted about the intent—accomplishing stated aims or biding time until the UN could assume the mantle.[41] To critics, Somalia was developing into a Vietnam-like quagmire[42] with the potential to absorb increasingly more resources without offering better prospects for success.[43] In reality, the operation's evolution was not mission creep but "a deliberate experiment in 'assertive multilateralism'" gone wrong.[44]

As a result, Clinton's aims had become less ambitious and more distinct from those of the UN by summer's end, but civil and military officials still lacked clarity about Somali policy and how best to implement it.[45] Despite casualties over the summer and an inability to capture Aideed, the administration voted in favor of UNSCR 865 on September 22.[46] This affirmed the nation-building mission just eleven days before Black Hawk Down but also coincided with the administration's private signal to the contrary that same day.[47] Secretary of State Warren Christopher had "met with [UN Secretary-General] Boutros-Ghali and handed him a memo that explained the American belief that there had to be a new emphasis on finding a political settlement. The search for Aidid had to stop."[48] The president quietly began seeking a way out of Somalia.[49] Accordingly, Lake foreshadowed an imminent departure. "We have reduced our military presence by 80 percent and transferred lead responsibility for peacekeeping and reconstruction to the UN. The withdrawal of our remaining combat troops is only a matter of time, but it must not come in a way that undermines all the gains made."[50] The clarity of Lake's statement, however, coming only a month after deploying Task Force (TF) Ranger, was not universally shared.

Instead of making it explicit that the administration was heading for the exits in Somalia, the relevant policy addresses sent mixed, if not status quo, signals. On August 27, Defense Secretary Les Aspin said that Clinton's deployment of TF Ranger led to a "focus [that] is really much too narrow . . . if there is to be a solution to Somalia's problems, it must be much more than a military solution.... Our overall criteria for success should include progress in the three focal elements: economics, political, and the security elements of the Somali problem."[51] This would include security operations in South Mogadishu, disarmament of Somali militias, and nation-building activities.[52] Aspin opened the aperture from a security focus to one that would involve more priority placed on the political realm. Yet his security plan would tackle some of the most challenging dimensions of the problem not yet tried or successfully accomplished by either UNITAF or UNOSOM II, and it ran contrary to UNITAF's narrower approach—not security measures likely to be completed in a short time frame. On September 28 at the UN, contrary to Lake's clear call for a pending exit, Clinton praised "a stunning humanitarian rescue" and reaffirmed the need to "complete our mission and to ensure that anarchy and starvation do not return just as quickly as they were abolished."[53] Accordingly, "the president and Lake did not seem able to give the administration a clear voice."[54] Thus, taken together and separated by only six days, these addresses signaled status quo continuation more than a major departure.

As a result, military and civilian leaders were unclear on Clinton's Somalia policy right up until the Battle of Mogadishu.[55] General Colin Powell had been a staunch advocate of limiting the Somalia operation[56] and so should have been keen to identify any presidential directives in line with his inclinations. In his final two weeks of military service, however, Powell twice urged national leadership to pull out of Somalia because he did not see a national security interest in continued intervention there and because he saw no clear intention on behalf of the administration to do so.[57] The first occurred at a meeting of the National Security Council (NSC) in late September[58]; the second was during his retirement breakfast with the president on October 1.[59]

Contrary to the understanding at lower levels of the NSC staff during the same period,[60] and Clinton's statements after the tragedy that he had been on the way out of Somalia,[61] General Powell sensed administration ambivalence, if not resistance to a withdrawal from the Somalia mission.[62] Counterterrorism Security Group Director Richard Clarke affirmed this, saying he and the administration "did not deemphasize the military effort."[63] Then-Brigadier General Anthony Zinni, Director of Operations for UNITAF, did not perceive any tangible efforts to get out of Somalia before Black Hawk Down or a timeline for exit.[64] UN Special Envoy Jonathan Howe indicated multiple times that he "did not sense that the [Clinton] administration was on its way out during the months prior to Black Hawk Down."[65] This had been the consistent theme for so long that Powell finally determined he must support the commanders in the field if the administration was not going to withdraw.[66] This is why he recommended that Aspin approve the deployment of TF Ranger at the end of August. A month later, when he retired, he still saw no movement toward an exit from Somalia.[67]

Civilians serving within the administration were also confused and stymied in their ability to implement the president's intent. An interagency team led by Ambassador David Shinn, the State Department's coordinator for Somalia, concluded after a trip to Somalia in July 19 through 27 that "political and humanitarian activities were not—and must now become—closely integrated with military efforts."[68] US Ambassador to Somalia, Robert Gosende, sent a cable on September 18 outlining a political way forward that was designed to address this shortcoming. Doing so signaled that he was unaware of clear guidance and was offering recommendations to Secretary Christopher and the president. His cable suggested establishing a commission with representation from Aideed's Habar Gidir clan and reaching a plan with them for a ceasefire, heavy weapons cantonment, and demobilization. Gosende believed that Aideed would reject the plan, which would alienate many of his fellow clansmen and motivate them to provide information leading to Aideed and his lieutenants' arrest.[69] Instead of being rejected because of the impending exit, Gosende's cable went unanswered. This left him, like some on the Joint Staff, to conclude that the policy of hunting Aideed remained in place.[70]

For some, the discrepancy was a matter of where individuals sat. Civilians in DC thought that emphasizing diplomatic efforts implicitly downgraded emphasis on military tasks.[71] Military members on the ground saw raids against Aideed as complementary—even necessary. Military pressure might force Aideed to cooperate with reenergized political measures. Raids would do that, result in his capture or killing, or lead to house arrest or exile.[72]

Mission expansion stemming from the new UNSCRs and these types of deliberative calculations is not mission creep. It has its own logic, which mission creep does not. For those inattentive to the mission's evolution, it did appear to be mission creep. In reality, it was an issue of perception and leadership. For those awakened to a new and enlarged mission by the tragic events unfolding in Somalia, the change seemed to have occurred unintentionally. In fact, it had been the result of deliberate, repetitive decisions by US and UN officials who had not first counted (or understood) the potential cost. It also reflected the absence of strong leadership and communication from the White House and the Pentagon.

Yet the approach against Aideed had not improved the situation over the four months (June through September) during which UNOSOM II had tried it. Things had actually gotten worse. It was an approach bound to encounter casualties and would most likely make the situation worse before it got better.[73] This strategy might have proved workable had it been pursued with complete support from the president, as well as appropriate coordination between the military and civilian elements in Somalia and between the United States and the UN. It would also have required congressional and public support, which would have necessitated the exercise of significant political capital from President Clinton. TF Ranger either did not anticipate the political consequences of a raid gone wrong or believed that continuing the raids was necessary to political objectives.[74]

Recognizing and mitigating political risk was not TF Ranger's job, however. It is impossible to eliminate all risk in armed conflicts, and TF Ranger had been given a mission to get Aideed. It was the decision-makers' responsibility, not theirs, to determine the policy parameters within which TF Ranger was to conduct its mission. TF Ranger had what they believed to be good intelligence and their best chance to date to capture Aideed.[75] They had orders to do just that, with no clear boundaries as to "no-go" locations or times of the day.[76]

Clinton later professed he thought he had ordered a ramp-down of military activity.[77] Apparently, he thought that the directive was communicated directly through military channels or the various policy addresses[78] and through Aspin's repeated declination of requests for additional equipment.[79] However, the directive was neither clearly decided on nor implemented effectively. Some senior Pentagon officers saw the administration changing trajectory, but it was not translated into practical implications for field commanders.[80] Military units received no orders to leave Somalia, to change TF Ranger's approach—whose sole job was to go after Aideed and his lieutenants—or to decrease military efforts in support of increased diplomatic engagement.[81] Even if he did not understand the raid's risks, Clinton had approved it "in general," if not in the "particulars."[82]

Further, when the president questioned the military's execution of the operation against Aideed, Clinton forgot his responsibility.[83] He overlooked the fact that he, as commander in chief, could have centralized approval of certain missions. That would have required his approval, or that of his Secretary of Defense, before TF Ranger launched certain operations—in a certain area of Mogadishu or during daylight. That would have caused a delay in TF Ranger's ability to respond to emergent intelligence, but it would have increased control. Moreover, Clinton had defended the raids against the warlord following the loss of four American soldiers on August 8 and eight more in September.[84] Finally,

Clinton's approval tied him to the operation despite any desire—whether in place beforehand or contrived afterward—to pursue diplomatic efforts to the exclusion of military actions.

1. WHY WAS THIS A SUNK COST TRAP THAT REQUIRED A MAJOR POLICY PIVOT?

President Clinton faced a sunk cost trap in Somalia because the costs expended were not producing a positive return on investment; it was a failing foreign policy endeavor. The United States had experienced few recent successes and some noteworthy setbacks under UNOSOM II. Although much less temporal, human, and financial costs had been invested in Somalia at the point of decision than would later be the case in Iraq and Afghanistan, the effort was not inconsequential. It was the United States' first post–Cold War peacekeeping operation and Clinton's first major overseas military operation. Moreover, it had lasted longer than originally envisioned by the Bush administration. UNITAF undertook a noble cause and was initially successful in reducing the famine's effects. An expanded UN mandate (from UNSCR 814) accompanied by decreased resources and flawed strategies, however, caused a downward trajectory after the transition to UNOSOM II. The operation did not capture Aideed, lost soldiers, appeared untenable, precipitously lost domestic support, and was failing to achieve Clinton's nation-building aims: interclan reconciliation, security, disarmament, police support, and judicial reform.[85]

SUNK COSTS QUANTIFIED

The American investment in Somalia at the time of President Clinton's policy pivot had experienced sunk costs in multiple dimensions: temporal, human, financial, and in terms of personal credibility and national prestige. Table 4.1 summarizes the sunk costs, by category, at the time of Clinton's sunk cost trap decision. Ten months had passed from the initial deployment under President George H. W. Bush to Clinton's sunk cost trap (December 1992 to October 1993). The human death toll included 29 dead, with another 146 wounded during this same period.[86] Financially, the United States spent $1.2 billion from December 1992 to September 1993 on combined expenditures, including military expenses, humanitarian assistance, and payments to support UN efforts.[87]

Clinton's personal credibility was also at stake, as shown by using opinion polls about his handling of the situation as a proxy measure. Clinton had lost a great deal of political capital since spring. Polling shows that the public's

TABLE 4.1
Clinton's Somalia Sunk Costs (1993)

Time	10 months (December 9, 1992–October 7, 1993)
Casualties	29 dead; 146 wounded[1]
Financial Investment	Between \$885 million[2] and \$1.2 billion[3] (December 1992–September 1993)
Personal Credibility (Proxy Measure)	Support for the president's handling of the operation dropped 51% between early April and October 1993, from 84% to 33%.[4] Poor polling data and alleged inattentiveness to Somalia meant Clinton's personal credibility was at stake with his October 7 sunk cost trap decision.[5]
National Prestige	Prestige lost by suffering a battlefield setback from nonstate actors.[6] "The potential message [that an immediate departure would signal to adversaries]: Kill and humiliate our people and the United States will immediately retreat."[7] Indeed, "Al Qaeda and bin Laden . . . told one another, the United States had been humiliated by a Third World country. Just like Vietnam. Just like Lebanon."[8]

[1] Carolyn Logan, "US Public Opinion and the Intervention in Somalia: Lessons for the Future of Military-Humanitarian Interventions," *Fletcher Forum of World Affairs* 20, no. 2 (1996): 156, 166–67.
[2] *Peace Operations: Cost of DOD Operations in Somalia*, Chapter Report, March 4, 1994, GAO/NSIAD-94-88.
[3] John G. Sommer, "Hope Restored? Humanitarian Aid in Somalia 1990–1994," RPG Refugee Policy Group, Center for Policy Analysis and Research on Refugee Issues, 1994, C-4–C-5.
[4] Logan, "US Public Opinion and the Intervention in Somalia," 156, 166–67; Bruce W. Jentleson and Rebecca L. Britton, "Still Pretty Prudent Post-Cold War American Public Opinion on the Use of Military Force," *Journal of Conflict Resolution* 42, no. 4 (1998): 395–417.
[5] David Halberstam, *War in a Time of Peace: Bush, Clinton, and the Generals*, vol. 34 (New York: Simon & Schuster, 2001), 254, 256, 258–60.
[6] Hal Brands, *From Berlin to Baghdad: America's Search for Purpose in the Post-Cold War World* (Lexington: University of Kentucky Press, 2008), 270.
[7] Anthony Lake, *6 Nightmares: Real Threats in a Dangerous World and How America Can Meet Them* (2000), 129.
[8] Richard A. Clarke, *Against All Enemies: Inside America's War on Terror* (New York: Free Press, 2004), 88.

approval of his handling of the operation had dropped some 50 percent since early April. Support for the president's handling of the Somalia intervention had ranged between 77 and 84 percent from assuming office through early April. By October, those numbers hovered around 33 percent.[88] As a proxy measure for the change in Clinton's credibility on Somalia, this change in polling numbers shows that—in just six months—he had suffered a reduction in more than half of his political capital for managing the intervention.

Less political capital translated to less operating freedom. It did not help that there was a persistent perception that Clinton's foreign policies were ineffectual and that he was inattentive to Somalia.[89] Even Secretary Aspin felt that way, "complaining to his close friend [Democratic representative] Lee Hamilton that getting instructions from the White House about the policy in Somalia and other issues was hard."[90] In addition, Clinton's leadership of the military was compromised due to a bungled effort to lift the ban on homosexual service and because of his reputation as a draft dodger.[91]

Clinton's overall job approval, like his polling on Somalia specifically, had declined significantly from January to June. However, over the ensuing few months, and headed into his sunk cost trap, the president had recovered most of the lost ground. Interestingly, he bottomed out on June 5–6, the same time Aideed-inspired fighters ambushed the Pakistanis. Clinton's numbers then were at 37 percent approval and 49 percent disapproval rates.[92] This was a 21 percent drop in support from when he took office.[93] It would be the lowest point of his entire eight years as president. By the time of the Battle of Mogadishu, Clinton had rebounded to between 50 and 56 percent approval overall—a substantial improvement.[94] This recovery meant Clinton's hand was not completely forced, but his domestic support base was tenuous because of his rocky trajectory thus far[95]; senior military leaders' distrust[96]; and his domestic agenda, for which he needed congressional support.[97]

The damage affected not just the president but also the nation. American military forces had been stymied for several months in their efforts to capture a warlord in a developing country. Elite US units had just lost eighteen soldiers and had two helicopters shot down at the hands of nonstate actors. In addition, the stakes changed after October 3. Deterrence of future adversaries would be more difficult *if* they perceived that America would always abandon its foreign policy aims and head home after losing some soldiers.[98] This became apparent a few years later when Osama bin Laden and al-Qaeda used Somalia as an example of American fecklessness in its declaration of war against the United States. Bin Laden assessed that America had left Somalia "defeated," "in humiliation," and having revealed "weakness and powerlessness" because Clinton's promises of revenge "were merely preparation for withdrawal."[99]

To an extent, that was true. Clinton believed that multiple components make up national prestige. Despite the United States' capability as a superpower, he said, "We are also not gonna flatten Mogadishu. . . . Everybody in the world knows we could do that. We don't have to prove that to anybody."[100] Clinton's appraisal followed Hans Morgenthau's line of reasoning that credibility derives from a combination of resolve *and* judgment.[101] Nonetheless, Clinton and his team focused on appearing strong despite leaving. "It was all about how to get out, or more accurately, how to cut and run without looking like we were cutting and running."[102]

Clinton's address to the nation and his letter to Congress announcing his policy change reinforced the importance of credibility as perceived by others. On October 7, Clinton told Americans, "I am proposing this plan because . . . if we were to leave today, . . . our own credibility with friends and allies would be severely damaged. Our leadership in world affairs would be undermined at the very time when people are looking to America to help promote peace and freedom in the Post-Cold War world. And all around the world, aggressors, thugs, and terrorists will conclude that the best way to get us to change our policies is to kill our people."[103]

On October 13, Clinton wrote to Congress, "Having been brutally attacked, were American forces to leave [Somalia] now we would send a message to terrorists and other potential adversaries around the world that they can change our policies by killing our people. It would be open season on Americans."[104] That showed Clinton's belief that any loss of prestige would result not so much from the battlefield losses but from adversaries' perceptions of weakness, which risked becoming a self-fulfilling prophecy.[105]

SUNK COSTS SALIENCE

Human sunk costs were more relevant than other sunk costs in shaping President Clinton's decision-making.[106] The commander in chief was "casualty phobic," and because of his personal Vietnam shadows, he "doubted his own moral authority to order people to their deaths."[107] While communicating his policy change decision to Richard Clarke, Clinton said, "No more U.S. troops get killed, none. Do what you have to do, whatever you have to do."[108] Thus, the casualties experienced so far influenced the implementation of Clinton's new policy.[109] John Mueller's casualties hypothesis predicts this outcome, but it goes against what some researchers on the sunk cost effect would anticipate.[110] Instead of leading Clinton to double down on the investment already paid in blood, the casualties were an expenditure he did not want to repeat. In this way, the casualties contributed to his desire to cut losses, extracting himself and the country from the Somalia endeavor.

Previous temporal and financial investments were low-level factors but were not primary considerations.[111] The ten months already sunk into efforts to improve Somalia's humanitarian crisis and to set it on a sustainable path had led to low-level war weariness since there was little recent progress to show for it.[112] In fact, even in the weeks before the events of Black Hawk Down, the administration recognized that things were getting worse, not better, and wanted to change direction.[113] In Clinton's words, he wanted to "get the U.N. to finally show up and take over."[114] Financially, the $1.2 billion already spent was not a concern for the president or his administration.[115] It was for Congress, though, and had come up during congressional testimony.[116] Moreover, Senator Robert Byrd's proposed amendment to the National Defense Authorization Act threatened to defund all Somalia operations after November 15.[117]

Clinton's Somalia decision became a major policy pivot point because of intense executive and legislative branch reactions to the Battle of Mogadishu. The incident "haunted" Clinton.[118] US Ambassador to the UN Madeleine Albright reflected on it as a "nightmare."[119] Lake characterized it as "a failure" that led to "terrible humiliation" because the United States was again "unable or unwilling to bring American power to bear in effective ways."[120] Congress was in an uproar.[121] Support among Americans had reached its lowest point since the operation began.[122] The tragedy's psychological impact on Clinton and his key advisers, coupled with his professed intent to focus on political solutions,[123] ensured the tragedy prompted an immediate policy overhaul.[124]

2. WHAT WERE THE PRESIDENT'S OPTIONS AND WHAT STRATEGY DID HE IMPLEMENT?

Clinton believed he faced a less-than-satisfying array of choices. "The president felt trapped between two bad options: accepting failure by abandoning an ill-conceived operation, or avenging today's losses by going in with 'decisive force' to defeat the Somali warlords."[125] The status quo was untenable, so Clinton looked to make an immediate change.[126] "Continuing the old policy, now fully orphaned, was not discussed" during a six-hour meeting with his closest advisers.[127] The question was whether to escalate, de-escalate, or try a combination approach.[128]

Clinton's national security team presented him with four options when they met on Tuesday, October 5, following his return from California.[129] Figure 4.1 illustrates these options on a quadrant graph depicting military escalation and de-escalation on a sliding scale on the x-axis. On the y-axis, political/diplomatic escalation is at the top and political/diplomatic de-escalation is at the bottom.

Clinton's team included National Security Adviser Dr. Anthony Lake, Secretaries Les Aspin and Warren Christopher, and political advisers David

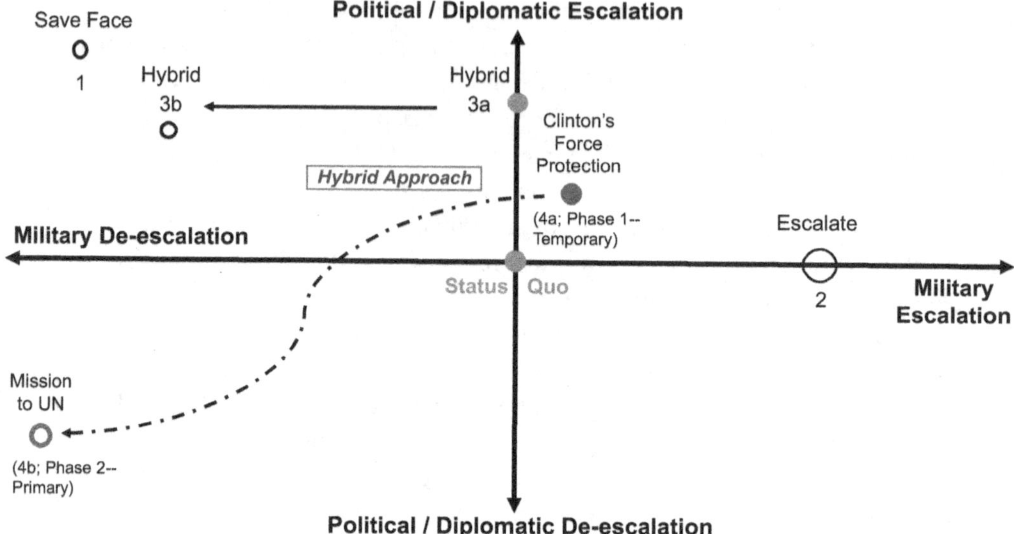

Figure 4.1. Potential presidential policy options in Somalia in 1993.

Gergen and George Stephanopoulos. Clinton could have ordered an immediate withdrawal,[130] continued to press Aideed militarily, or sought a diplomatic settlement with a phased US withdrawal.[131] Option 1 in figure 4.1 involved military de-escalation and diplomatic escalation. The purpose of this option, as discussed by the principals, would be to "drop the military approach and try to find a face-saving way to get out."[132]

Option 2 was a military escalation, which would have increased the military presence and attempted to pacify South Mogadishu, per Secretary Aspin's recent focus on the continued violence there.[133] It is labeled as the "Escalate Option" in figure 4.1.[134] Senators Sam Nunn (D-GA) and David Pryor (D-AR) told Clinton that if he wanted to escalate the American commitment in Somalia, he should ask for all the troops he would need at once instead of in gradual increments. This, they implied, would prevent the "ghosts" of gradual escalation lingering from Vietnam.[135] Option 3 involved a political and diplomatic escalation, followed by a time-phased or conditions-based military de-escalation. It would limit military operations and focus on diplomatic efforts to reach a political settlement.

Option 4 developed by Clinton and his advisers involved a hybrid approach that would increase the number of troops (vertical escalation) and keep the pressure on Aideed (a status quo activity), and yet focus on negotiating a political settlement with him.[136]

No one advocated simply continuing the mission with the same strategy and the same number of forces (the status quo).[137] Nor did anyone argue for withdrawing immediately. That was the general sentiment in Congress[138] and arguably among some of the American people initially—though a strand of popular opinion also favored retaliatory strikes against Aideed.[139] Clinton's desire to protect US forces' withdrawal, facilitate the transition to the UN, and guard against bad signals that a cut-and-run approach might send to terrorists made the hybrid option more attractive than the other courses discussed.[140]

Clinton's inclination aligned with the domestic political situation—based on both congressional opposition and popular support trends. Multiple polls showed declining support for the operation, and for the president's handling of it, based on the type of mission being pursued.[141] As the mission became more robust, fewer resources were levied against it, prospects for success for the new missions diminished, and approval ratings dropped precipitously. After having lost three US soldiers on August 8 and another three on September 22, support was already at 40 percent. It was down from a high of 80 percent as late as early spring. Although suffering a slight dip after Black Hawk Down, support remained relatively constant despite fallout from the battle. Moreover, 77 percent said that an attack on US troops, like the one on October 3, warranted a stronger response,[142] and 71 percent wanted to continue hunting Aideed.[143] So, while some assert that Somalia reinforced the "powerful myth" of a casualty-phobic public, a closer reading of polling data shows the importance of mission type providing "more evidence of a defeat phobic public than a casualty phobic public."[144]

THE IMPLEMENTED STRATEGY

Clinton announced his new policy on October 7, 1993. It no longer involved an active attempt to capture Aideed. The decision was a return to UNITAF's policy in that regard—an approach of engaging rather than targeting Aideed. This man had American blood on his hands, his actions had facilitated the desecration of American bodies, and he still held Chief Warrant Officer Michael Durant. Instead of conducting operations to kill or capture Aideed, however, the administration directed them to ferry Aideed to diplomatic engagements that sought political and social reconciliation among Somali tribes.[145]

Clinton's sunk cost trap decision sent 1,700 additional soldiers and 104 more armored vehicles under US command. He also deployed two amphibious-ready

TABLE 4.2
Escalation Typology

	Vertical	Horizontal
Political	Increased number of aims	Seeking/gaining more allies; increased diplomatic activity
Military	Using more lethal weapons or more troops	Attacking other countries/sanctuaries

groups with 3,600 marines, stationed offshore with the aircraft carrier USS *Abraham Lincoln*. Clinton also ordered four AC-130 aircraft to the area.[146] Those deployments situated 5,300 additional military members in and off the Somali coast, bringing the total troop levels in the area to approximately 10,700, plus the 6,000 sailors onboard the USS *Abraham Lincoln*.[147] The decision increased the political track. President Clinton sent Robert Oakley back to Somalia, based on his relationship and credibility with the warlords.[148] Clinton gave Oakley a mandate to get Chief Warrant Officer Durant back safely and to facilitate diplomatic efforts.[149] Clinton also centralized decision-making in the NSC and with the creation of five task forces, all headed by an assistant secretary or a three-star general, which oversaw the intervention's functional requirements and its transition to the UN from Washington.[150]

The decision is best understood as a low-grade hybrid strategy. It did not entail what a true hybrid would have or what popular opinion would have preferred to see: an escalation to kill or capture Aideed, followed by a withdrawal.[151] What it did involve was a horizontal escalation diplomatically (top-right quadrant in table 4.2) and a vertical escalation militarily in the short term (bottom-left quadrant in table 4.2). The midterm approach entailed military de-escalation along the vertical dimension (inverse of the bottom-left quadrant) as the nation redeployed its troops by March 31, 1994. Politically, the United States also ramped down its engagement as it tackled other issues at home and abroad after the troop withdrawal. Clinton's political aim for Somalia after October 7, when he announced the new policy first to congressional leaders and then to the American people, was focused on the short to mid term.[152] Clinton wanted to extricate the United States and replace the American void with UN leadership and force contributions from other UN member states.

Following that transition, Clinton did not pursue significant goals in Somalia, but he did send troops back to assist UN forces in withdrawing from December 1994 to March 1995. So, America was not permanently disengaged after the withdrawal of its troops. Political de-escalation decreased the number (and intensity) of aims sought (inverse of the top-left quadrant), though, and Somalia received even less attention after the military's departure.

The option 4 dots in figure 4.1 are a characterization of the strategy President Clinton implemented. It initially involved some escalation militarily in force size but also political and diplomatic escalation. The initial option 4 dot is not farther to the right because it was coupled with an immediate equivalent of a ceasefire. Additionally, the intent and actual activity of the escalation was for force protection, not more missions to get Aideed, disarm Somali factions, or train local police. Although Clinton did not intend to continue raids against Aideed in difficult Mogadishu neighborhoods, he did plan "to prevent a return to anarchy."[153] The task became unnecessary, however, after Oakley convinced Aideed to implement a unilateral ceasefire and return Durant.

3. WHAT ROLE DID HISTORICAL LESSONS AND FEAR PLAY IN SOMALIA DECISION-MAKING?

> After an election campaign shadowed by the Vietnam ghosts in his own past, Bill Clinton took office only to find Vietnam still hovering as it had for twenty years. . . . In case anyone still thought the Vietnam syndrome had been vanquished, the events surrounding the bungled U.S. intervention in Somali brought it back, with a vengeance, less than a year into the Clinton presidency.
>
> —Arnold R. Isaacs

> Vietnam overshadowed everything else.
>
> —William (Bill) Clinton

Fear of a Vietnam-like Somalia quagmire drove President Clinton's decision to withdraw forces after the Black Hawk Down tragedy.[154] The Vietnam experience provided relevant, influential lessons. On a personal level, Clinton's reputation as a draft dodger during the Vietnam War put his relationship with the military at a disadvantage, affecting his leadership. "Vietnam was a ghost Clinton couldn't shake. He was aware that his credentials as Commander in Chief were in question . . . men in uniform in the Pentagon looked down on him."[155]

Moreover, Clinton did not want to repeat President Lyndon Johnson's mistakes of incremental escalations. Clinton recognized this lesson, and the related unwillingness to cut losses, while working for Senator J. William Fulbright as an intern during the war.[156] Clinton remarked that letting sunk costs be sunk was the appropriate response to a wartime sunk cost trap presenting a major presidential dilemma. Clinton wrote that

> when you find yourself in a hole, the first rule is to quit digging; if you're blind to the possibility of error or determined not to admit it, you just look for a bigger shovel. The more difficulties we had in Vietnam, the more protests at home, the more troops we sent in. We topped out at more than 540,000 in 1969, before reality finally forced us to change course. I watched all this unfold with amazement and fascination. I read everything I could, including the material stamped "confidential" and "secret" that I had to deliver from time to time, which showed clearly that our country was being misled about our progress, or lack of it, in the war. And I saw the body count mount, one at a time.[157]

In Clinton's estimation, American presidents had mistakenly taken the "big shovel" approach during the Vietnam War, digging in deeper despite the lack of a vital national interest. In his policy dilemma, Clinton was determined to admit the "possibility of error" and to "quit digging."[158]

In addition to Vietnam's shadow, Lebanon also provided Clinton with a useful political reference point. Reagan's reaction to his Lebanon policy dilemma proved that a president could show restraint, eschew ambitious foreign policy objectives, register a military "loss," and still survive politically. Reagan had wanted military participation in Lebanon to pave the way for a broader Middle East peace initiative.[159] Instead, Reagan withdrew the marines after the Beirut bombing and the Lebanese government's collapse, yet he still won reelection later that year. His response set a precedent that Clinton could follow in Somalia. During the critical Tuesday, October 5, meeting, "Clinton asked Gergen how it was that Ronald Reagan had been able to remain unscathed after the tragedy in Beirut in October 1983, when 219 Americans were killed in a suicide bombing of the Marine barracks. Gergen replied, 'Because two days later we were in Grenada, and everyone knew that Ronald Reagan would bomb the hell out of somewhere.'"[160]

What Clinton took away from Lebanon reinforced the lessons he had drawn from Vietnam—but with a twist. Similar to the situation in Vietnam, Clinton must have seen the Lebanon case as another example that when a president conducting a military operation finds himself in a hole, the first thing to do is stop digging.[161] A president should be willing to admit mistakes, recognize the limits of American power, and make tough choices about priorities. A president should also make corresponding policy adjustments before the only option left is to leave with a complete loss. Finally, a president must move forward with purpose on other policy efforts that capture the nation's attention, turning headlines and perceptions back in a positive direction.[162]

The twist, similar to President Richard Nixon's desire to pursue peace with honor by leaving Vietnam, was that Clinton wanted to display strength on the way out. This came from his perception of Reagan's intervention in Grenada immediately after the Beirut bombing.[163] Clinton doubled the military presence on and off the Somali shore, therefore, to facilitate a safe and orderly transition to the UN.[164] Nonetheless, Reagan's and Clinton's withdrawals from Lebanon and Somalia, respectively, generally reinforced Vietnam's shadow.

4. DID INTERNAL ADMINISTRATION RATIONALE DIFFER FROM THE PUBLIC JUSTIFICATIONS?

The president's private deliberations present a mixed consistency with the public justifications. Clinton did not openly acknowledge the role of historical lessons as a rationale for the course he selected, but he did use fear as a public justification. Clinton claimed he was pursuing a responsible exit that would do everything possible to give the Somali people a chance for peace. In making that case, Clinton argued that an immediate departure would be regrettable because it would result in more starvation and the loss of progress made thus far, and it would not be consistent with US values. It was an argument that combined sunk costs and expected regret as justification for staying a bit longer. Further, the sunk cost element of his justification was not based on human sunk costs, as the literature would expect.[165] Instead, it was based on past accomplishments and attempted to prevent two administrations' successes from unraveling.[166]

Clinton elaborated with several specific justifications to explain the temporary escalation and six-month withdrawal timeline, some of which diverged from his private rationale. Publicly, Clinton said that the increased forces were a way to carry out the remaining missions he had given the military, including keeping "pressure on those who cut off relief supplies and attacked our people."[167] The six months until withdrawal, at least double what Congress wanted,[168] was to allow time to transition efforts to the UN and for other member states to deploy more forces of their own to backfill US units.[169] The troop escalation and phased drawdown were also designed to communicate American resolve in the wake of the tragedy. The administration did not want future adversaries, of whom al-Qaeda was to become one, to perceive the new policy as a "cut-and-run" approach.[170] If they did, "terrorists will conclude that the best way to get us to change our policies is to kill our people,"[171] and they would declare "open season on Americans" all around the world.[172] This later happened in places like Saudi Arabia, Tanzania, Kenya, Yemen, New York City, Washington, DC, Pennsylvania, Afghanistan, Iraq, Texas, Libya, and Western Europe, among other places.

Behind closed doors, Clinton made it clear that he wanted to give the military every resource it needed to transition safely and effectively to the UN and return home without further loss of life.[173] In these respects, he was concerned with implementing a responsible strategy during his internal deliberations—not just in his public justifications. The steps he took to centralize control of the operation, ensure proper planning, avoid foreseeable problems, and facilitate a smooth withdrawal were consistent with that desire.[174]

There were ways in which the public justifications diverged from the private deliberations, though. Privately and different from the public indications,[175] the president and his national security team realized that the hybrid solution was a veiled cut-and-run.[176] The six-month period did provide some time to mobilize more international forces and transition leadership of the Somalia effort to the UN. However, it was also a logistic limit set by the military—one that Clinton was not going to challenge.[177] Moreover, the publicly expressed hope to send a strong signal to future adversaries[178] overlooked the reality that the withdrawal was announced at the same time as the policy change, just four days after the Battle of Mogadishu. The proximity connected the withdrawal to the casualties. Additionally, US forces did not put any pressure on Aideed for the remainder of the mission.[179] The only pressure amounted to sending Oakley to deliver a message that the United States wanted Durant returned immediately, would not negotiate for him,[180] and might back off if Aideed ceased attacks against American forces.[181] In fact, elements of TF Ranger that had hunted Aideed actually escorted him within a matter of weeks to peace negotiations with other Somali tribal factions.[182] Clinton also centralized control of operations at the NSC staff to ensure that the military did not take any actions the warlord could perceive as hostile—perhaps a responsible move, but contrary to the publicly stated mission.[183] Finally, Clinton's stated intent regarding terrorist perceptions was not met. Al-Qaeda interpreted American actions as weakness and later used them as rhetorical ammunition in its plot against its far enemy.[184]

CONCLUSION

> Somalia was in all ways a fiasco . . . Dick Holbrooke eventually came up with a name for the syndrome that followed the debacle—Vietmalia, combining *Vietnam* and *Somalia.*
>
> —David Halberstam

> The [Weinberger-]Powell Doctrine lived on—Somalia was ammo for it.[185]
>
> —David Halberstam

\UN and US officials made a series of deliberate decisions to expand operations from humanitarian assistance to include nation building and manhunting during the spring and summer of 1993 without a full understanding of the potential implications and inherent risk.[186] These decisions contributed to the casualties experienced during Black Hawk Down and increased the sunk costs associated with Clinton's sunk cost trap. Even before that tragedy, though, Clinton wanted out of Somalia,[187] sensing the beginnings of his own Vietnam-like quagmire.[188] This sense motivated his administration's move to extricate itself from Somalia,[189] but its policy change before October 3 was feeble and misunderstood by key military elements.[190] The Battle of Mogadishu added tangibly to a sense that the status quo or escalation of commitment would lead to entrapment.

Although not the primary driver behind Clinton's decision-making, the sunk costs already incurred leading up to and during Black Hawk Down were still important. They reminded Clinton and other key actors of salient historical lessons, which triggered Clinton's fear of the potential pitfalls of continuing the status quo or pursuing escalation.[191] Those lessons, particularly the collective memory about the Vietnam War, impacted the domestic political context. The Lebanon and Persian Gulf War experiences reinforced those lessons in different ways. The exit from Lebanon and its subsequent political outcome for Reagan demonstrated to Clinton that a president could withdraw from an unsuccessful military operation, quickly rebound, and still win reelection.[192] The Persian Gulf War predisposed the public and Congress against suffering many casualties in Somalia given the seemingly less important mission there than in the Gulf, and the low number of casualties experienced in the Gulf.[193] Thus, the impact of these lessons on Clinton's decision-making was both direct and indirect. They influenced him through his experiences and perspectives[194] as well as through congressional and public pressure derived from them.[195] Identifying this as the fundamental driver confirms my explanation's validity in this, the first post–Cold War sunk cost trap.

The Somalia chapter of American foreign policy reinforced the Weinberger-Powell Doctrine as well as Vietnam-era lessons. A young David Petraeus observed in his Princeton dissertation, "[T]he debate over how and when to commit American troops abroad has become a debate over how to avoid, at all costs, another Vietnam."[196] The Weinberger-Powell Doctrine had this aim. It codified a series of questions developed to guide presidential decisions about if, when, and where to use force. After experiencing quagmires in Vietnam and Lebanon, Caspar Weinberger, President Reagan's secretary of defense, and Weinberger's senior military assistant, then Major General Powell, wanted America to avoid future sunk cost traps. As Weinberger said it, "These tests can help us to avoid being drawn inexorably into an endless morass, where it is not vital to our national interest to fight."[197] The Clinton administration recognized a need to update these lessons' application to the new missions of the post–Cold War world. Administration members codified their own lessons learned from Somalia in *Presidential Decision Directive 25 (PDD-25): Reforming Multilateral Peace Operations*. It emphasized careful intervention selection, clear objectives, US forces serving under American commanders, and avoiding casualties.[198] The genesis for this was the Vietnam War and Lebanon peacekeeping operation.

Somalia added to the impetus and foreshadowed the character of future wars in Afghanistan and Iraq. There, the "greater part of the warrior's role involve[d] not killing but muting the antagonism caused by the warrior's own unwelcome presence."[199] *PDD-25* was a pre-9/11 recognition that embarking on a military intervention warranted great caution as well as deliberate policy, planning, and execution. For, "if American forces find it difficult to adjust to the peculiar demands of such wars, then those responsible for formulating basic national security policy should consider the possibility that the wars themselves just might be futile."[200] The next two presidential decisions fall under Assessment 2 ("Never Again on My Watch") rather than Assessment 1 ("Avoid a Quagmire"), as discussed in chapter 2. The terrorist attacks of 9/11 served as the dividing line between them. Before 9/11, the "Avoid a Quagmire" lesson was dominant. After 9/11, lesson dominance shifted to maintaining and expanding a robust war footing abroad to prevent another spectacular attack on the homeland during each president's "watch."

THE IMPACT OF 9/11 AND WHY IT WAS DIFFERENT FROM OTHER TRAGEDIES

9/11 dislodged Vietnam as the key lesson for presidents facing hard-to-win military conflicts when other traumas could not because it was a uniquely

American tragedy. Other shocks between the end of the Vietnam War and 9/11 reinforced Vietnam lessons—like Lebanon and Somalia—or did not happen to "us," like calamities in Rwanda, the Balkans, and elsewhere. The events of 9/11 were different because they happened to us, at home, and in a surprising and spectacular way. September 11 was the single greatest attack on US soil. Despite being a nonstate actor, the enemy on 9/11 showed that they could reach out and kill us where we lived and worked. The 9/11 tragedy also had a live-on-television impact. Not only was technology more pervasive than in the past but, unlike the Beirut barracks bombing or Black Hawk Down, the attacks unfolded dramatically in real time before a large and captivated audience. These dynamics led to a massive psychological impact. For all these reasons, political leaders were responsible for acting after 9/11 in ways they were not held accountable for following other post-Vietnam tragedies.

The next two examples illustrate how 9/11-generated lessons changed presidents' greatest fears and subsequently the way they made midcourse corrections to military operations abroad. They now escalated and employed counterinsurgency strategies after prolonged stalemates instead of de-escalating. Their risk calculus was different, as were the outcomes they most wanted to avoid. They took on the political risk associated with a possible failure of an overseas operation (i.e., the possibility of another Vietnam) to avoid another stunningly "successful" terrorist attack on the homeland during their watch (i.e., another 9/11).

The Iraq and Afghanistan surge decisions provide additional context to explore the veracity of my claims about commanders in chiefs' sunk cost trap decision-making. They are two of the most salient sunk cost traps in recent history: decisions to implement the 2007 Iraq and December 2009 Afghanistan surges. The chapters examine both presidential application of lessons learned and how the sunk costs already incurred influenced their decisions.

5

The Iraq Surge

Governmental Lesson Learning and Adaptation

INTRODUCTION

The 2003–2011 Iraq War is well known for the insurgency against the US occupation and Iraqi government fueled by al-Qaeda in Iraq (AQI) and other elements. Another, different type of bureaucratic insurgency, better understood as a bottom-up and outside-in push to change American war policy is less well known, but is an important part of the first post-9/11 presidential sunk cost trap. This chapter tells the story of how President George W. Bush and his national security team came to believe that their policy was flawed and headed toward strategic failure. Ultimately, it explains why Bush made a major course correction.

Historical lessons acted as a filter through which Bush made strategic calculations about the stakes involved, due to the new security reality after 9/11 and three years of failure in Iraq. Given these new stakes and the lessons learned from them, Bush most feared failure. His advisers indicated that a surge was the only option that carried with it the possibility of success. Correspondingly, and consistent with my expectations, Bush feared status quo efforts or de-escalation, realizing that would require going against a strong domestic political headwind. Nonetheless, recent lessons from 9/11 and the early Iraq War years, some of which were relearned from the Vietnam War, taught him such a response and counterinsurgency strategy was necessary[1]—as did a new interpretation of the Vietnam War's key strategic lesson. Bush's belief that Vietnam showed the necessity of winning wars differed from its Avoid a Quagmire lesson that influenced previous and subsequent commanders in chief in their sunk cost traps. Given these influences, Bush surged with a new commander and a counterinsurgency strategy.

CASE SUMMARY (IRAQ)

Since the rapid, successful invasion, ouster of Iraqi president Saddam Hussein, and Bush's "mission accomplished" declaration on May 1, 2003, events in Iraq had not gone well. This included the military occupation and development of a new government. Paul Bremer, head of the Coalition Provisional Authority and initially charged with establishing stability after major combat operations, issued two disastrous edicts.[2] The first was de-baathification. Designed to show Iraqis that Hussein would not return, this policy prevented the old regime leadership from serving in a new government.[3] The result, however, was the loss of important bureaucratic and administrative leaders necessary to run the government—most of whom were Baathist in name only to secure employment under Hussein.[4] The second order disbanded the Iraqi Army, creating the potential for four hundred thousand armed and unemployed insurgents.[5] Over the ensuing years, the war progressed with events that both sides could claim as successes, while violence rose considerably. The Iraqi government experienced punctuated successes involving constitution development and national elections but was struggling to protect the Iraqi people. Elements of the disbanded military, the former regime, terrorists, and foreign fighters began what became a violent and volatile cocktail of violence aimed at the new government, the US military, and across sectarian divides.

Bush's aims had evolved from regime change to building a democracy and counterterrorism. Regime change was the initial goal due to the belief that Iraq had weapons of mass destruction and terrorist linkages.[6] Democracy promotion was part of Bush's Freedom Agenda, perceived as an obligation to the Iraqi people and seen as the only way to bring Iraq's Shia and Sunni together.[7] By 2006, the added rationale was to confront terrorists there "so we do not have to face them here at home."[8] Further, Secretary of State Condoleezza Rice had adopted Lieutenant Generals David Petraeus and Ray Odierno's terminology of "clear, hold, and build." This Vietnam-era strategy became the bumper sticker advertising the overarching components of what US strategy should entail.[9]

National Security Council (NSC) staffers Peter Feaver and Meghan O'Sullivan orchestrated a meeting with administration outsiders at Camp David on June 12–13 designed to trigger a full policy review.[10] Michael Vickers, Fred Kagan, Eliot Cohen, and Fred Kaplan presented differing views about what should be done in Iraq. Vickers favored a light footprint that emphasized special forces and working with Iraqis. Kagan favored escalation through a surge. Cohen agreed but said the main thing was what was done with the additional troops. Kaplan was less critical of the current strategy but said there was a need for counterinsurgency practices.[11] However, the timing was not conducive to a comprehensive policy review. Bush left Camp David early to visit the Iraqi prime minister in Baghdad.[12] The administration's reaction against the Revolt of the (Retired) Generals in April and in support of Secretary Donald Rumsfeld delayed any change atop the Defense Department for six months.[13] The seating of the Iraqi government on May 20 signaled that Iraq was making political progress and should be given some time to turn things around. The killing of AQI's leader, Abu Musab al-Zarqawi, on June 7, demonstrated US military success, casting doubt on how much change was necessary. Bush's desire to depoliticize any review during the midterm election campaign also contributed, as did entrenched assumptions of key leaders, both civilian and military, that had to be overcome.[14]

Nonetheless, an informal and highly secretive policy review did begin in mid-2006. The group conducting it began to see the fundamental issue as determining the character of the war. Was the situation in Iraq a counterinsurgency or a civil war?[15] Each drew on different historical analogies and presented different policy prescriptions. An insurgency suggested a counterinsurgency such as General Creighton Abrams employed at the end of the Vietnam War to quell the violence, protect the people, and provide time for the Iraqi government to take hold. If the root of the problem was a robust civil war, assuming the role of neutral peacemakers, such as America initially did in Lebanon in 1982, might be apropos.

After the midterms, a formal, publicly acknowledged review ran from November 10 to 26.[16] The group did not reevaluate American objectives, which were assumed to be constant.[17] They did question US influence on Iraqi leaders and addressed "the relationship between security and political reconciliation . . . [and] between U.S. force levels and security."[18] On the last day, a key meeting in the solarium on the roof of the White House illustrated there was still no emerging consensus among principals. Rice and Rumsfeld both opposed the surge the NSC staff supported. Both secretaries believed security was Iraq's responsibility.[19] Rice thought that America could not end the Iraqi feud and so should focus on counterterrorism.[20] Rumsfeld favored the current approach of transitioning security to Iraq. Too much US involvement for too long would create an unhealthy dependency like he had seen as Reagan's Lebanon envoy.[21]

Other analogies were also relevant to Rumsfeld and the vice president. "'If Rumsfeld saw a Kosovo on steroids, Cheney's image was that last helicopter lifting off the roof of the Saigon embassy,' J. D. Crouch said."[22] The different analogies suggested divergent stakes, solutions, and likely outcomes. The Vietnam reference suggested higher stakes for the United States. It heightened the importance of winning and suggested escalation was necessary to avoid a really bad outcome, as was the case with the domino theory during the Vietnam War. The Kosovo analogy—while not at all apt—had the opposite effect, suggesting that the situation could eventually stabilize without an infusion of more resources. The solarium discussion did not result in a consensus, but it had been important for Bush to see opposing views firsthand.[23]

The Iraq Study Group, a congressionally commissioned, bipartisan committee led by former Secretary of State James Baker and former Congressman Lee Hamilton (D-IN), published its report on December 6, 2016. The report recommended a new diplomatic-centric strategy, a train-and-advise mission, and requiring Iraqis to meet security, reconciliation, and governance benchmarks to obtain more aid.[24] It was an exit strategy. Bush's team, however, relied on relatively minor comments that supported a temporary surge if commanders endorsed it.[25]

Another meeting on December 11 with academics Eliot Cohen and Stephen Biddle, as well as retired Generals Wayne Downing and Jack Keane further shaped Bush's decision-making. Keane pointed out a mismatch between the president's goals of victory in Iraq and the current strategy.[26] Keane "reinforced the president's thinking: add more troops, get them off the big bases and into local communities, change the priority to protecting the Iraqi people and focus on Baghdad."[27] Keane warned that casualties would initially go up but would decrease in the long term because the war would end more quickly and on US terms. All attendees emphasized that history showed the occasional need for presidents to overrule generals during wars.[28] Keane said having the right leaders and accountability to the president—unlike the last three years—were "absolutely essential" for success, or "we will have squandered . . . lives by escalating the war."[29]

Likewise, Bush's new chief of staff, Josh Bolten, realized that the president he saw during Iraq meetings was different from the one he saw during all non-Iraq sessions. The former was deferential to those in uniform because of his great respect for their hard work, tough conditions, and their willingness to make the ultimate sacrifice. The latter was a leader who pushed the agenda, asked tough questions, and held his subordinate leaders accountable to deliver success on his policy aims. Bolten and National Security Adviser Stephen Hadley sought a better process that would help Bush evolve into being a strong leader of his generals in a way that could reshape war policy.

The most tangible initial test of Bolten and Hadley's emphasis was when Bush met with the Joint Chiefs of Staff (JCS) on December 13 in the Pentagon's "Tank"—their briefing room.[30] Army chief of staff, General Peter Schoomaker, said that an escalation's required deployment timelines might break the force. Bush replied that another Vietnam-like loss was more likely to do that. The JCS begrudgingly agreed, an important, historically based moment.[31] Bush announced the surge, counterinsurgency strategy, and new commander, General David Petraeus, on January 10, 2007.

1. WHY WAS THIS A SUNK COST TRAP THAT REQUIRED A MAJOR POLICY PIVOT?

> The costs of the Iraq War were staggering, and were "not perceived to be generating a level of benefits that can be convincingly described as proportionate to the costs."
>
> —Christopher Dandeker

> The human, financial, and strategic costs of the war far outweigh its benefits.
>
> —Matthew Duss and Lawrence Korb

Bush was in a sunk cost trap because the war was not going well and America lacked a strategy for success, and yet Bush wanted to maintain his aims.[32] The Al-Askari ("Golden Dome") Mosque bombing in Samarra in February 2006 marked a significant milestone. The deliberate targeting and destruction of one of Shia Islam's most holy sites by Sunni extremists fueled even more heightened sectarian violence. "Iraq was devolving into civil war. . . . The number of attacks was soaring, civilian casualties were skyrocketing, the Iraqi government couldn't keep the country from unraveling, and our own forces didn't have the right strategy."[33] Between December 2005 when the elections were held and mid-May 2006, the Iraqis were unable to form a government, further inhibiting effective responses to the downward spiral.

According to many experts, Iraq was quickly descending into civil war. On August 3, Senator Carl Levin of the Senate Armed Forces Committee asked General John Abizaid, commander of US Central Command, whether Iraq was sliding toward civil war. Abizaid responded, "I believe that the sectarian violence is probably as bad as I have seen it, in Baghdad in particular, and that if not stopped it is possible that Iraq could move towards civil war."[34] In October, when more than 3,700 Iraqis were killed, the highest monthly death toll since the beginning of the war, prompted UN Secretary-General Kofi Annan to say that Iraq was close to a civil war.[35] Others assessed Iraq as having already crossed that threshold. In November, a classified report categorized the conditions in Iraq as a "civil war."[36] At the Council of Colonels meeting on November 27, 2006, there was "one thing that [everyone] could agree on. Iraq was in a civil war, and we were on the road to defeat."[37]

The associated costs are captured in table 5.1. The United States had been fighting for nearly four years, already longer than its involvement in World War II. The nation had lost nearly three thousand of its troops, with almost 23,000 wounded.[38] The number of attacks had skyrocketed from 250 to more than 3,500 per month by May 2006, and the numbers increased during the fall.[39] Iraqi civilian deaths, which would grow another threefold before US troops departed, were approaching 45,000.[40] Weekly expenses had grown to nearly $2 billion. Cumulative financial costs from the war's start to Bush's war policy change announcement were around $335 billion, just for direct military operations.[41] This does not include expenses for homeland security, other War on Terrorism missions, future Iraq operations, additional veteran medical costs, or other macroeconomic and social costs, the total of which has been estimated to exceed $4 trillion.[42]

The loss of international credibility at home and abroad were other costs, though less quantifiable ones. America's credibility was at stake, and Bush's personal reputation was on the line.[43] Like military participation in Vietnam, there were few other nations with significant troop contributions. This was partially because of how the administration had conducted the lead-up to the war, disagreements about the justification for war, and the decision not to get a second UN Security Council resolution. Events like the Abu Ghraib prison scandal did not help once the war began. Domestically, Bush's overall approval rating was at 37 percent, down from 89 percent after 9/11 and 70 percent after the Iraq invasion.[44] Using public opinion as a proxy, Bush had lost half of his political capital since the start of the war. Public opinion had generally been on the wane since early war successes. However, the administration noticed a palpable difference sometime between 2005 and 2006. "Speeches had lost their ability [to influence public opinion]. They no longer had any purchase. Only events were going to influence them [to change their perspective on the war]."[45]

By the fall of 2006, the war had lost a large amount of congressional support as well. On November 17, 2005, John Murtha (D-PA), a decorated Vietnam War

TABLE 5.1

George W. Bush's Iraq Sunk Costs (2007)

Time	47 months (March 20, 2003–January 10, 2007)
Violent Incidents and Casualties	Attacks increased from approx. 250 to 3,500/month.[1] (May 2003–May 2006) 2,998 military members had died since the war began.[2] 22,834 wounded military members.[3] 43,772–64,523 Iraqi civilian deaths.[4] (March 19, 2003–December 31, 2006)
Financial Investment	$335.75 billion in estimated war funding, based on budget requests[5] (FY2003–1st Qtr., Y2007)
Personal Credibility (Bush)	Bush's presidential legacy at risk. Bush's overall approval rating was at 37%, down from 89% after 9/11 and 70% after the Iraq invasion. Using public opinion as a proxy, Bush had lost half of his political capital since the start of the war.[6]
National Prestige	International credibility at risk if US allowed terrorist hotbed. Middle East stability at risk. Heightened sectarian conflict. Iran gained increased leverage in Iraq. Democracy promotion stifled.[7] Advanced IED components and training targeting US military in Iraq increasingly linked to Iran.[8]

[1] Bob Woodward, *State of Denial* (New York: Simon & Schuster, 2006), 472.

[2] Joseph Stiglitz and Linda Bilmes, *The Three Trillion Dollar War: The True Cost of the Iraq Conflict* (London: Allen Lane, 2008), 251.

[3] Ibid.; "Operation Iraqi Freedom," iCasualties: Iraq Coalition Casualties Count, accessed April 15, 2016, http://icasualties.org/Iraq/Index.aspx.

[4] "Iraq Body Count database," accessed April 15, 2016, https://www.iraqbodycount.org/database/.

[5] Richard D. Hooker Jr. and Joseph J. Collins, *Lessons Encountered: Learning from the Long War* (Fort McNair, DC: National Defense University Press, 2015), 432; Amy Belasco, *Cost of Iraq, Afghanistan, and Other Global War on Terror Operations since 9/11* (Darby, PA: Diane, 2009).

[6] Bush Job Approval, *American Presidency Project*, Gallup Poll data, compiled by Gerhard Peters, accessed July 7, 2016, http://www.presidency.ucsb.edu/data/popularity.php?pres=43&sort=pop&direct=DESC&Submit=DISPLAY.

[7] Matthew Duss and Peter Juul, "The Iraq War Ledger (2013 Update): A Look at the War's Human, Financial, and Strategic Costs," March 19, 2013, Center for American Progress, https://www.americanprogress.org/issues/security/report/2013/03/19/57173/the-iraq-war-ledger-2013-update/.

[8] Woodward, *State of Denial*, 449.

veteran, called for withdrawing all 153,000 troops from Iraq within six months. That timeline would have been the fastest possible, even if all transport assets were available and no other strategic precautions were taken to stabilize Iraq.[46] Harry Reid, Senate minority leader, said, "We need leadership from the White House, not more whitewashing of the very serious issues confronting us in Iraq."[47] Ranking member of the Senate Foreign Relations Committee, Senator Joseph (Joe) Biden, later called for decentralizing power in Iraq.[48] Republican leadership, also disenchanted, urged members of Congress up for reelection to distance themselves from Bush and the war to avoid defeat.[49] Mitch McConnell, the Republican whip in the Senate, pleaded with Bush to bring some troops home because not doing so would cost Republicans seats in the midterms.[50]

SUNK COST SALIENCE

> To invoke a word from the unmentionable Vietnam era, Iraq was looking more and more like a *quagmire.*
>
> —Fred Kaplan

The war's sunk costs had salience at a micro and macro level. At the micro level were the impact felt by families who had lost loved ones and the effect those human losses had on the president. Cindy Sheehan, in a meeting with a couple of Bush aides, used the sunk cost argument against the president's strategy of perseverance in Iraq. "'Don't let the president say that he needs to send more troops to get killed in order to honor the sacrifice of my son,' she told them."[51] Other parents felt differently, consistent with sunk costs' relevance. One of the same advisers who had met with Sheehan reflected, "'The most prominent emotion was. . . . Don't let my son have died in vain.' One slain soldier's mom told Bush, 'He did his job. . . . Do yours.'"[52]

Undersecretary of Defense for Intelligence Stephen Cambone characterized a continued effort as an important way of "keeping faith in the people who have fought this war, and making certain that what was gained, wasn't lost."[53] Peter Baker, the *New York Times* White House correspondent, concluded that "for Bush, withdrawing troops before Iraq was secure would mean admitting their sons and daughters had indeed died in vain, and that was something he just could not let happen."[54] Philip Zelikow, Rice's State Department counselor, shared Baker's sentiment. "The President said, 'We knocked this thing down, and we have . . . to discharge our responsibilities.'"[55] James Jeffrey, at the time a State Department adviser for Secretary Rice on Iraq and a future ambassador there agreed. "I cannot emphasize enough the need [for Bush] to have a result that justifies the sacrifices of our troops."[56]

At a macro level, although the situation was unraveling, many foreign policy experts, generals, and administration officials realized the strategic value of a stable Iraq. Secretary Rice "knew that the U.S. couldn't afford to lose; U.S. credibility and power would have diminished more severely than at any time since the Vietnam War." Given the importance of the Middle East, "the damage would have been deeper and more lasting."[57] Analysis done for the Pentagon's Office of Net Assessment concluded similarly that "the costs of failure are likely to be high, . . . much higher than was incurred following the U.S. withdrawal from Haiti, Somalia, Lebanon, or even Vietnam."[58] In fact, comparing Iraq to the circumstances in Vietnam some thirty-five years before led to the conclusion that the current situation "was even worse considering that the level of violence existed after two years spent training, equipping and funding 263,000 Iraqi soldiers and police. The cost had been $10 billion, and American teams had been embedded with most of the Iraqi units for over a year. At an equivalent time in 1971, after several years of Vietnamization, the trend lines of insurgent violence had been down, not up."[59]

Before Bush could ask for options for a war policy change (the second question addressed in each of the cases), however, he had to realize he was facing a sunk cost trap. It took a long time, but Bush increasingly came to that realization between late 2005 and fall 2006.[60] During that period, he and his administration were no longer able to ignore the grim reality that had been evident for some time to Congress, the press, and the American people.[61] For Bush, his aims and his legacy were in jeopardy. He had one chance left to improve the situation and to save dwindling political capital that would be necessary for other initiatives.[62]

Belief that the country had done the right thing had dropped 30 percent, from approximately 70 to 40 percent from the invasion to the surge announcement. Over the same period, popular support for Bush's handling of the war had dropped even further, from roughly 70 to 30 percent. This was a personal credibility indicator, alongside human losses, violence levels, and financial costs, that Bush was in a serious sunk cost trap and needed new policy options.[63]

2. WHAT WERE THE PRESIDENT'S OPTIONS AND WHAT STRATEGY DID HE IMPLEMENT?

Sunk cost considerations had delayed policy change during several years of increasingly worsening sectarian violence. The thought had been: "We have invested so much in Iraq, we must not lose it. [And] we have invested so much in defending the Casey-Abizaid strategy, we should be careful about sabotaging it by critiquing it publicly."[64] Once key players accepted the direness of the situation, however, that perspective began to change. Eventually the JCS, NSC staff, interagency, and the current team in Iraq considered a wide variety of options. One the military examined was to send more forces (Go Big). The second was a lighter footprint focused on advising Iraqi Security Forces (ISF) for up to a decade (Go Long). The third was to withdraw completely (Go Home).[65]

O'Sullivan's informal review team drafted a memo detailing potential risks and benefits associated with four options.[66] They included an option (Adjust at the Margins) that diverged from the status quo only in hastening the transition of security responsibilities to Iraqis even faster than had been intended. It assumed that a major escalation risked Iraqi support for the Nouri al-Maliki government by increasing the US military presence. Another alternative (Target Our Efforts) entailed focusing US efforts against al-Qaeda, letting Iraqis handle the sectarian violence since only the former posed a direct threat to America and the latter was an internal threat. It threatened to leave US soldiers in a moral quandary as they saw the Iraqi bloodbath unfold and were unable to intervene. It might also abandon Iraq before it could secure itself.

A third possible strategy (Double Down) infused additional troops and civilians, changed to a population-centric counterinsurgency strategy, extended deployments, expanded the armed forces, and prioritized the fight for Baghdad. The risks were multifaceted. American political support would be difficult to maintain. Maliki was unproven. There had been no Iraqi request for additional forces. More forces and a counterinsurgency strategy that pushed US troops off the large bases and into a role of securing the Iraqi population would result in more casualties until violence abated and could increase Iraqi dependency. This approach could break the US military if not accompanied by raising end strength levels. Violence could return once America left, rendering the extra effort for naught.

The final option the O'Sullivan memo listed "would focus more resources exclusively on Maliki and his government" if he proved capable of being a national versus sectarian leader (Bet on Maliki or the 80 Percent Option). It focused efforts on exploiting political success among the 80 percent of Iraqis that composed the Shia and Kurd populations.[67] This alternative differed from the double-down strategy because it sent additional resources straight to Maliki's government instead of investing them across the board. This would put Iraqis in the lead whether they were ready or not. It risked stoking the insurgency by leaving the Sunnis out of the equation.

The current chain of command under General George Casey, the commander in Iraq, backed by Secretary Rumsfeld, also offered several options. Their four options included "acceleration of the transition to Iraqi control; reinforcement; status quo; and . . . a fixed withdrawal schedule."[68] All but the reinforcement (i.e., escalation) option involved the current approach or slight variants of it. A December 8 memo from Rumsfeld to Bush and Vice President Cheney continued to back the train-and-transfer policy. In it, the outgoing defense secretary argued that "no increase in the level of U.S. forces can substitute for successful diplomacy . . . in getting the Iraqi Government to act."[69]

After conducting their own reviews, various positions solidified. The Joint Staff favored the status quo. The NSC staff recommended a surge. The State Department argued that it was too late for a surge.[70] Rice was later won over, however. Her concern had been that the change would involve more than simply adding troops, which would increase American deaths in vain. Because the new strategy would involve an approach that Rice believed might prove successful, she supported it.[71] Casey was still against anything more than a one- or two-brigade surge. The Iraq Study Group recommended increasing diplomatic engagement to "build stability in Iraq and the region" and an increase in advisers embedded in the Iraqi Army.[72] Figure 5.1 portrays the main options seriously considered. The chart captures differences among alternatives across an escalation/de-escalation spectrum, both militarily and diplomatically. The closer the options are to the graph's middle, the more they resemble status quo efforts.

This chart shows that between the Bush administration, the military, and the Iraq Study Group, a wide range of options were explored. It also enables a better comparison of the options across diplomatic and military factors—conceptually and for this case. Conceptually, presidents can manipulate options in the number of additional troops deployed or withdrawn. They can change the type of mission those forces conduct. They can adjust the intensity of diplomacy undertaken and the breadth of its focus bilaterally, regionally, or globally. They can modify the amount of political capital expended on domestic politics to secure popular and congressional support. They can determine the pace at which those changes will be implemented and how long they will last—within certain feasible logistic parameters.

The strategy Bush implemented (Option 6) involved the greatest amount of military escalation but less overt regional diplomacy than recommended by the Iraq Study Group report, for instance. The Go Home option involved a complete military de-escalation. The other options fell in the middle. They

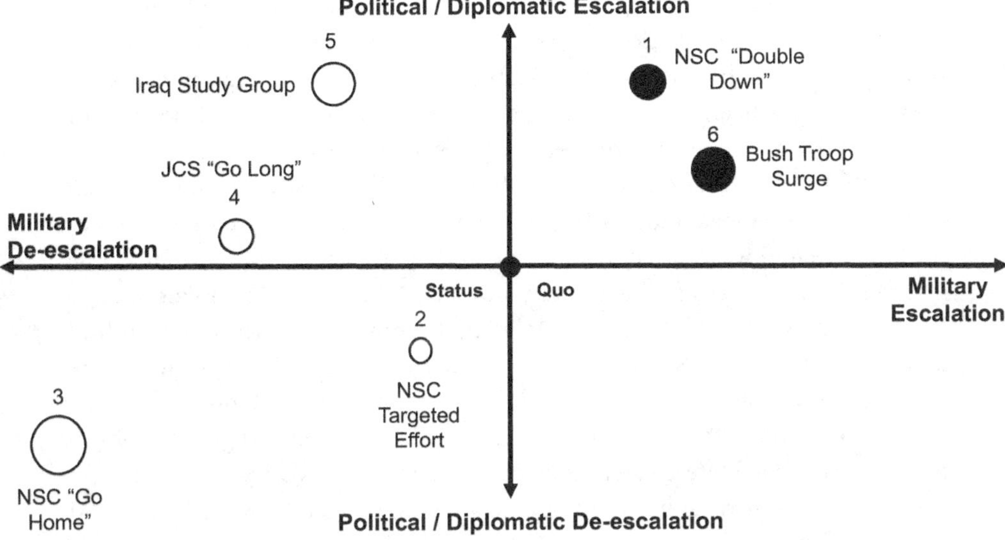

Figure 5.1. Potential presidential policy options in Iraq in 2006–2007.

were the most diverse set of options of this book's cases, both in terms of what they would involve politically/diplomatically and what would be required militarily. Under the options in the top-right quadrant of the graph, diplomacy with Maliki would increase and involve a civilian surge. That would be most notable in a doubling of the number of Provincial Reconstruction Teams that provided economic development assistance to local Iraqis. Yet the surge did not involve the level of engagement with Iran and Syria, among others, that the Baker-Hamilton report had envisioned.

To change war policy, the administration had to see security rather than Iraqi political reconciliation or reducing the US signature as priority one. Originally, the thought was that Iraqi political development and security force growth would decrease the number of attacks. Yet an established Iraqi government under a ratified constitution, with its own security forces, did not reduce violence.[73] After an NSC staff visit to Iraq in October 2006, civilian policymakers' logic flipped.[74] Security was more fundamental than political progress. The latter could not occur without the former.[75] US forces were necessary, and "the Iraqi people's desire for security trumped their aversion to occupation."[76] Bush realized escalation might lead to "throwing more lives away in a losing cause," but the gamble was worthwhile if victory were possible.[77]

After deciding on a surge, the question for Bush became twofold: whether Maliki would act in a national versus sectarian fashion, and how large of a surge to conduct. These were the subjects of discussion among the principals at the president's ranch in Crawford, Texas, at the end of December. Coordinator for Iraq and senior adviser to the secretary of state David Satterfield had written that Maliki's "actions and failures to act increasingly reflected a Shia sectarian identity."[78] US Ambassador to Iraq Zalmay Khalilzad attempted to convince Bush that Maliki was a serious politician and leader. Unlike the former Prime Minister Ibrahim al-Jaafari, Khalilzad thought Maliki wanted to do more to go after the insurgents and terrorists. Maliki had summoned Casey and Khalilzad and criticized America's approach; he wanted the United States to use more force. Moreover, since Maliki believed the United States acted too slowly to be effective against the threats, he wanted more forces trained and greater control over the ISF to facilitate greater security.[79] Some US officials argued that Maliki wanted more control so he could pursue a sectarian agenda. But when Maliki was cajoled into public announcements that the law would be applied evenly across sectarian lines and that he would allow US troops freedom to maneuver and target Shia extremists, the Bush administration's view was that he could become a national leader and reliable partner.[80] Given this assumption, the risk of the surge seemed mitigated. Bush decided to help Maliki with additional resources and regular mentoring via video-telephone conference meetings.[81]

As for the size of the surge, the debate had shifted from if to how much and what the sequencing of the additional forces should be. How many brigades should be included, and should there be a separate decision for each additional brigade after the first two? An idea had floated around the interagency in mid to late December to send two brigades initially, with additional brigades sent only if needed. This was a compromise typical of interagency solutions and similar to the Vietnam War's incremental escalations.[82] Not wanting to repeat that war's infamous presidential decision-making, Bush decided that he would only make the decision for escalation once and would send all five brigades simultaneously.[83]

3. WHAT ROLE DID HISTORICAL LESSONS AND FEAR PLAY IN IRAQ DECISION-MAKING?

> I recognize that history cannot predict the future with absolute certainty. . . . But history does remind us that there are lessons applicable to our time.

> And we can learn something from history. . . . The worst mistake would be to think that if we pulled out, the terrorists would leave us alone.
>
> —George W. Bush

> The "willingness to tolerate risk [of inaction] had gone down after 9/11."
>
> —Eliot Cohen

"The events of 9/11 altered the "calculus of risk."[84] One manifestation of this was to change default reactions of commanders in chief to sunk cost traps from de-escalations to escalations. The first escalation occurred in Iraq five and a half years after 9/11 when Bush surged troops and changed strategy to avoid disastrous regional outcomes and another spectacular terrorist attack at home. In line with the Never Again on My Watch assessment, the 9/11 attacks displaced Vietnam's shadow and lessons from their dominant place shaping policy shifts during major post-Vietnam conflicts. "The 9/11 attacks were the most consequential global event since the dissolution of the Soviet Union. . . . [They shifted Bush's thinking and] catalyzed major change . . . almost immediately."[85] No longer could America afford to prosecute terrorist threats with a defensive and criminal-based approach. The United States had to hunt terrorists proactively—abroad and on a war footing—before they scored another major terrorist attack against the homeland.[86] America would also go on the offensive and take out state-based threats thought to be harboring terrorists, Bush's doctrine of preventive war.

The president laid out his new doctrine's central tenets during a West Point graduation speech on June 1, 2002. "The war on terror will not be won on the defensive. We must take the battle to the enemy, disrupt his plans, and confront the worst threats before they emerge. In the world we have entered, the only path to safety is the path of action. . . . If we wait for threats to fully materialize, we will have waited too long."[87]

Complete or partial withdrawal not only went against 9/11's lesson, but it also scared Bush because it would have let Iraqis' sectarian bloodletting turn into a full-blown genocide and have dire implications for America. While explaining his decision, Bush said he "concluded that to step back now would force a collapse of the Iraqi Government, tear the country apart, and result in mass killings on an unimaginable scale. Such a scenario would result in our troops being forced to stay in Iraq even longer and confront an enemy that is even more lethal. If we increase our support at this crucial moment and help the Iraqis break the current cycle of violence, we can hasten the day our troops begin coming home." Bush indicated that "failure in Iraq would be a disaster" whose "consequences . . . are clear" for radical Islamic extremists, Iran, the region, and the United States. "On September the 11th, 2001, we saw what a refuge for extremists on the other side of the world could bring to the streets of our own cities. For the safety of our people, America must succeed in Iraq."[88]

Bush repeatedly reiterated the reasons for his fear, tying them to the lessons he had learned from 9/11 and the first three years of the Iraq War. "To step back from the fight in Baghdad would have disastrous consequences. . . . The Iraqi Government could collapse; chaos would spread; there would be a vacuum; into the vacuum would flow more extremists, more radicals, people who have stated intent to hurt our people." Bush explained, "What's different about this conflict than some of the others is that if we fail there, the enemy will follow us here. . . . And that's one of the main reasons why I made the decision I made."[89] It was also why he did not cut losses and withdraw, as Reagan had done in Lebanon and Clinton had done in Somalia.

In a news conference on May 24, 2007, the president expounded on implications to US interests and why he feared de-escalation (i.e., premature withdrawal, in his view). "Failure in Iraq will cause generations to suffer . . . Al Qaida will say, yes, once again, we've driven the great, soft America out of the region. It will cause them to be able to recruit more. It will give them safe haven. They will be a direct threat to the United States."[90] In his memoirs, Bush wrote about the nonescalation options. "I worried [that with them] we might not succeed. If Iraq split along sectarian lines, our mission would be doomed. . . . I didn't think it was practical to withdraw from the cities and let the violence burn out. . . . I worried Iraq could be broken so badly that it would be impossible to put back together."[91]

During this postdecision period and even during the surge's darkest days, Bush returned to the necessity of proactive overseas action to explain his logic. At an American Legislative Exchange Council speech on July 26, 2007, Bush said, "September the 11th changed my way of thinking. . . . I believe it [the threat] requires . . . relentless pressure on an enemy that wants to do us harm again. I would rather defeat them over there than face them here."[92] That Bush highlighted this theme in many 2007 speeches demonstrated that the 2002 West Point speech still accurately reflected his conflict decision reasoning for the Iraq surge. In a September 2007 speech just after Ambassador to Iraq Ryan Crocker and General Dave Petraeus testified before Congress for the first time on the surge's progress, Bush contrasted what he believed his new policy would achieve versus the ghastly ramifications of an early withdrawal.

> The success of a free Iraq is critical to the security of the United States. A free Iraq will deny Al Qaida a safe haven . . . counter the destructive ambitions of Iran . . . marginalize extremists, . . . be our partner in the fight against terror, and that will make us safer here at home. If we were to be driven out of Iraq, extremists of all strains would be emboldened. Al Qaida could gain new recruits and new sanctuaries. Iran would benefit from the chaos and would be encouraged in its efforts to gain nuclear weapons and dominate the region. Extremists could control a key part of the global energy supply. We would leave our children to face a far more dangerous world. And as we saw on September the 11th, 2001, those dangers can reach our cities and kill our people.[93]

Bush's fear of de-escalation or withdrawal saturates this impassioned speech and adds more evidence to the Never Again on My Watch assessment.

Bush's administration shared his fear of de-escalation. Cheney was determined not to continue the policy of counterterrorism responses pursued in the 1980s and 1990s. It was a new era after 9/11, and those policies had failed the country. They had convinced terrorists that you could change US policy if you killed enough Americans, and they invited more attacks.[94] A former marine who had served in Vietnam, Ambassador James Jeffrey, wanted to avoid "a defeated American military like in Vietnam" at all costs "so that we could withdraw with honor at least."[95] That was what military leaders most feared during the decision-making. Initially, the JCS most feared breaking the force, and that escalation would cause public opinion to plummet further, as in the Vietnam War. After Bush agreed to grow the US Army and the Marine Corps, and assured them he could handle the politics, their fear shifted to the consequences of a Vietnam-like strategic failure.[96]

In his *Decision Points* memoir years later, President Bush again defended his consistent thinking, still rooted in 9/11.

> Before 9/11, Saddam was a problem America might have been able to manage. Through the lens of the post-9/11 world, my view changed. I had just witnessed the damage inflicted by nineteen fanatics armed with box cutters. I could only imagine the destruction possible if an enemy dictator passed WMD to terrorists. With threats flowing into the Oval Office daily—many of them about chemical, biological, or nuclear weapons—that seemed like a frighteningly real possibility. The stakes were too high to trust the dictator's word against the weight of

> evidence and the consensus of the world. *The lesson of 9/11 was that if we waited for a danger to fully materialize, we would have waited too long.* I reached a decision: We should confront the threat from Iraq, one way or another.[97]

Despite the importance of 9/11, and given the Iraq experience and sunk costs to date, there were other lessons shaping the strategic lens through which Bush made his policy change decision.

IRAQ WAR LESSONS

> If we had learned one lesson from . . . Iraq, it was that we had to give the people a sense of security before anything else could work.
>
> —Robert Gates

After a persistent and increasingly violent, complex cocktail of sectarian conflict and an insurgency that convinced the administration of the strategic failure of its current policy, policymakers were primed for additional lesson learning. They drew an important lesson from the Iraq War that they layered on top of the 9/11 lesson. The early Iraq years showed them that counterinsurgency was necessary to make lasting security gains and promote democracy.[98] Some lessons had their genesis from the bottom-up.[99] For instance, the informal NSC review began with an analytic effort to determine what had been learned from the Iraq and Vietnam Wars.[100]

The bottom-up developments followed two general tracks on the military side: failure- and success-induced learning. Failure during the early Iraq War years prompted some leaders to reevaluate the strategy. One of these was Lieutenant General Ray Odierno. Having adopted a conventional, heavy-handed approach as a division commander that failed to produce the desired results, he searched for a better way. While working for Secretary Rice as her liaison to the Joint Staff, Odierno realized that US forces were turning over security responsibility to the ISF too early; American units needed to "clear *and* hold."[101] This lesson also became important to the White House. "Very important were the lessons internal to the Iraq war, in particular how quickly gains during the 'clear' phase were lost because we were unable to 'hold' and then how much harder it proved to 'clear' the next time. This convinced him [Bush] that the costs of 'trial and error' and 'taking our hands off the bicycle' was too costly."[102] Thus, these Iraq War lessons, rediscovered from Vietnam, persuaded Bush that he feared the possible implications of de-escalation more than those of escalation, because he did not want to lose hard-won gains.[103]

Other military leaders were influenced primarily by success rather than failure. They wanted to take to scale the success they had experienced at lower levels. Petraeus was influenced by his doctoral research on the Vietnam War's military lessons as well as by his success in Mosul early in the Iraq War.[104] He had an opportunity to influence the broader military effort in Iraq during his next two assignments, and he specifically set out to do so. While serving as the commander of the element responsible for training the ISF, Petraeus included counterinsurgency principles in the training regime.[105] Then, as the leader of the Combined Arms Command, he led the writing of the counterinsurgency manual, which he helped ensure the military would apply in the contemporary fights.[106]

The new manual drew extensively on the lessons learned in previous conflicts. These experiences included those of French Army intelligence officer and author David Galula while fighting insurgencies in Indochina and Algeria, the American military experience in the Vietnam War, and the Iraq War's early years from 2003 to 2006.[107] In her *Introduction to FM 3–24 Counterinsurgency*, Sarah Sewall wrote of the institutional dogma that the new doctrine was pushing against and its attempt to turn the military into a learning organization. "This counterinsurgency manual challenges much of what is holy about the American way of war. . . . Those who fail to see the manual as radical probably don't understand it, or at least understand what it's up against. . . . The side that learns faster and adapts more rapidly—the better learning organization—usually wins."[108] Daniel Serwer, executive director for the Iraq Study Group, assessed that the new war policy "implementation was directly related to the counterinsurgency manual."[109]

America's strategic failure, contrasted with a few tactical successes during the 2003–06 period—including Petraeus's own—had served as his impetus for writing the new manual. Beginning in late 2005 when Petraeus assumed command at Fort Leavenworth, he sought broad, sweeping changes to the way the army trained for and fought in Iraq. This was months before the informal review began and a year before the formal review was announced.[110]

These changes eroded an entrenched, anticounterinsurgency military culture, in place since the Vietnam War, and prepared the military to embrace counterinsurgency.[111] During the 2005–06 period when Petraeus was implementing these changes, his publications came to O'Sullivan's and Cheney's attention.[112] They had come to believe, like Fred Kagan and then lieutenant general Stan McChrystal, that counterinsurgency was necessary. They thought it not a winning strategy to simply use "special forces with decapitation raids."[113]

The early recognition of this lesson led the administration to seize on the "clear, hold, build" catchphrase in late 2005 to describe its strategy. Yet that refrain was disconnected from the reality of what the Pentagon was actually doing in Iraq at that time.[114] "The mantra of clear, hold, and build was an elaborate bumper sticker for the White House and, in the final analysis, an egregious bit of deceptive advertising, since the hope-inspiring military effort it highlighted—Tal Afar—was the exception rather than the rule" throughout 2006.[115] What the administration's attachment to "clear, hold, and build" at that point showed, however, was that they were in search of a better strategy and thought that counterinsurgency might be it and that contrasting lessons of success and failure from the last couple years were shaping decision-making.

Another officer who wanted the military to embrace counterinsurgency and apply it throughout Iraq was Colonel H. R. McMaster. He had successfully utilized a counterinsurgency approach during 2004–05 in Tal Afar, Iraq, as a brigade commander. McMaster had also passed off the successful game plan to his replacement, Colonel Sean MacFarland, who also experienced success with the same approach in Tal Afar, and later in Ramadi. The latter coincided with and spurred the Al-Anbar Awakening in the fall of 2006, at the same time officials in DC were seriously relooking at war policy.[116] These successes added to those experienced by Petraeus and McMaster to provide light in an otherwise dark security situation.[117]

Additionally, McMaster's published doctoral thesis about the Vietnam War had argued that generals' failure to properly advise civilian policymakers constituted a "dereliction of duty"—also the title of his subsequent book. This failure on the part of senior military leaders contributed, McMaster argued, to the first war America lost.[118] When on the JCS' Council of Colonels, this Vietnam-era lesson contributed to McMaster's frank assessment of the situation and his belief that America needed to act like the superpower it was and win the war.[119] Through McMaster's role on the Council of Colonels and Petraeus's role in developing and implementing the new doctrine across the force, each exerted a bottom-up influence, along with their requisite organizations, in the eventual decision for the new policy.[120] In both cases, the influence was informed by a study of Vietnam's lessons and seen through the filter of recent Iraq War experiences.[121] In both cases, what drove them was a desire to transform the army into a learning organization by exporting these lessons.

VIETNAM WAR LESSONS

> The President felt his greatest obligation was not to create another Vietnam.
>
> —Condoleezza Rice

> Petraeus . . . applied the lessons of Vietnam to the Iraq campaign.
>
> —Doug Lute

One of the reasons that early lessons from the Iraq War were influential was because of their connection with lessons learned and forgotten from the Vietnam War, which had so deeply impacted the military. A major operational lesson of the Vietnam War was that the "population is the prize."[122] This cross-war connection spurred Keane to action. He was energized by seeing Rumsfeld respond to Senator Clinton during testimony on August 3, 2006, before the Senate Armed Services Committee. Rumsfeld replied to Clinton's critique that he was presiding over a "failed policy" with "happy talk and rosy scenarios." "I do not know that there is any guidebook that tells you how to do it [to meet the security requirements in Iraq without unduly feeding the insurgency against the US occupation by having too many forces there]. There is no rule book, there is no history for this."[123] But Keane insisted there were counterinsurgency lessons from Malaya, the Vietnam War, and elsewhere.[124] Yet those lessons were no longer in most of the army's institutional memory, as Keane told Chairman Peter Pace in the fall of 2006. "The U.S. Army is ill-prepared to deal with this. . . . We're trained to fight big conventional war. . . . We purged ourselves of the lexicon of everything that dealt with how to fight counterinsurgency because of the result of the outcome of the Vietnam War."[125]

Moreover, leaders during the Iraq War had recognized parallels with the Vietnam War and repressed the connections because of the negative connotations. Casey was severely limited by what he could do because of Rumsfeld's hardwired resistance to treating the threat as an insurgency.[126] In a *New Yorker* article, George Packer explained this state of denial as the lingering influence of Vietnam's shadow. "'They [senior leaders] didn't even want to say the "i" word [insurgency],' one officer in Iraq told me. 'It was the spectre of Vietnam. They did not want to say the "insurgency" word, because the next word you say is "quagmire." The next thing you say is "the only war America has lost." And the next thing you conclude is that certain people's vision of [the] war is wrong.'"[127] This story captured the sentiment of how Vietnam's impact still affected military operations more than thirty years later. Bush eventually turned this aversion to reality on its head by using a Vietnam analogy to emphasize the need to win in Iraq.

Bush acknowledged the parallels with the Vietnam War era in an August 22, 2007, speech to the annual convention of the American Veterans of Foreign Wars. "Then, as now, people argued that the real problem was America's presence and that if we would just withdraw, the killing would end."[128] Bush saw it differently. One of his Vietnam War lessons was based on National Security Adviser Henry Kissinger's famous 1969 memorandum to President Richard Nixon. In it, Kissinger said that troop withdrawals would become like "salted peanuts" to the American public: the more they had, the more they would want.[129] This was an important consideration to the Bush White House as well, leading to a different diagnosis of the problem.[130] The issue was not the US presence. "In fact, asserted the president, the problem in Vietnam was that U.S. forces had not fought long enough. He contended that giving up before the fight was won had damaged American credibility in the eyes of its Cold War adversaries."[131] "For Kennedy, the Vietnam War taught the need to understand the limits of American power; for Bush it taught the need to use that power boldly."[132]

Bush's comparison of the Vietnam and Iraq Wars with the JCS on December 13, 2006, showed he was thinking similarly when deciding.[133] Bush believed that failure to act on 9/11's lesson would result in "a repeat of Vietnam—a humiliating loss for the country, a shattering blow to the military, and a dramatic setback for our interests. If anything, the consequences of defeat in Iraq would be even worse than in Vietnam" because of the national security repercussions the September 2007 speech highlighted.[134] More terrorist attacks could occur on American soil if the United States pulled out of Iraq before it was stabilized and could provide for its own security. "We had to stop that from happening."[135]

Keane later explained Bush's thinking about how the Vietnam War provided a lesson about winning that was relevant to the Iraq endeavor. Keane did so by drawing on Lewis Sorley's *Better War* thesis about the change in war strategy from General William Westmoreland to General Creighton Abrams.[136] After employing an inappropriate attrition strategy under Westmoreland, the military implemented a counterinsurgency strategy in 1968 under Abrams and began achieving more favorable effects. "We had defeated the insurgency by '71 but we lost political support. We had the wrong strategy for three years. The irony of what took place in Iraq"[137] is that the similarities with Vietnam are so strong. From his perch in the State Department, James Jeffrey saw things similarly. In 2006, he thought the United States was still in the Westmoreland phase of "search and destroy" instead of the Abrams phase of protecting the population.[138] Despite the few success stories where tactical-level military leaders used counterinsurgency successfully, the military had not yet fully embraced it.

Similarly, comparing the strategies used in Vietnam before and after 1968 was relevant in determining what should be done in Iraq for at least one important Bush adviser. Karl Rove was thinking about Vietnam strategies in considering what needed to be done in Iraq. "In a way, the [2006] American strategy was replicating General William Westmoreland's 'search and destroy' strategy of the Vietnam War, with a similarly unsatisfactory outcome. We needed an updated version of General Creighton Abrams's 'ink blot' strategy, which called for concentrating forces on key areas, securing them, and spreading out to secure ever larger sections of the country."[139]

The influence of Vietnam War lessons extended beyond picking an overall strategy to how that strategy should be implemented. Considering an incremental escalation of war policy versus a decisive application of force conjured up memories of President Lyndon Johnson's incremental escalations during the Vietnam War. Bush wanted to avoid the incremental approach because it would prolong the Iraq War, as it had the Vietnam War, contributing to a quagmire instead of a decisive outcome. That lesson also resonated with others in the White House. When some advisers recommended an incremental approach to the surge whereby Bush would approve one or two additional brigades at a time, Rove disagreed. "We'd already gone through [incremental troop increases] in the 1960's, and we kept stepping up the number of troops over the period of time, and the American people had some sort of memory of that. Better to say 'Bam!' then to say, 'Little bit, little bit, little bit, little bit.'"[140] Bush agreed. He told those who proposed the idea, "I'm not going to make this decision five times. That looks like incrementalism."[141] Thus, to effect a positive change, Bush believed he needed to heed Vietnam-era lessons about strategy selection and implementation.

The Bush administration would also have been well served to heed a Vietnam lesson about measuring progress. Civilian and military leaders had "learned" from the Vietnam War that the right metrics are important, but before the Iraq War policy review, the administration relied on inappropriate measures to assess progress. Policymakers and generals had come to decry the use of body counts during the Vietnam War as a deceptive measure of success. The United States suffered fifty-eight thousand casualties to North Vietnam's one million. America had won every battlefield engagement, but this was irrelevant, as North Vietnam had won the political victory.[142] Similar dynamics were taking place during the first few years in Iraq. "Even though it raised the ghosts and anguish of Vietnam," policymakers, including Rumsfeld and Bush, utilized comparative body counts to discuss US and Iraqi progress.[143] American officials also relied on Iraqi political milestones and the number of ISF trained as measures of progress, hoping those metrics would eventually result in a reduction in the number of violent attacks.[144] However, that proved elusive until the surge.

The use of the number of ISF trained as a measure of effectiveness toward the achievement of US aims was a mistake; it was only a measure of performance. It was a necessary component of increasing Iraqi capacity and capability to provide for their own security. It was not a real measure of effectiveness in the fight, however. The number and quality of the ISF in the field as well as the frequency and type of operations they were undertaking and against what type of targets, how long they could hold terrain, and whether they pursued a sectarian or nationalist agenda were more true reflections of Iraqi's readiness to assume control over its own security in a way consistent with US goals. Also important were the quality of the judicial system and Maliki's leadership—whether it galvanized national support or increased sectarian divides. Increased levels of trained ISF showed movement toward a performance benchmark but did not necessarily demonstrate effectiveness toward achieving policy aims.

Although informed by Vietnam lessons, this failure of understanding and metrics is a large part of why it took until 2006 before the administration identified the extent of the problem. It contributed to wrong assumptions and clouded judgment about the real nature of the problem, lasting a few months beyond the bombing of the Golden Dome Mosque, when matters could have come into focus. Another factor contributing to the length of time before the war policy change was "the President wrestling with the challenge of violating the 'don't micromanage' lesson."[145] Bush did not want to repeat the perceived mistakes of President Lyndon Johnson picking bombing targets or otherwise micromanaging military tactics from the White House. However, the academics and retired generals at the December 11, 2006, meeting with George W. Bush encouraged him that history, instead of affirming a lack of micromanagement, pointed out that presidents sometimes had to overrule generals during wars.[146] This effectively freed Bush to change course—against the advice of his current field commanders.

The Never Again on My Watch assessment is consistent with why George W. Bush made the surge and counterinsurgency decision.

> Assessment 2 (Never Again on My Watch): In post-9/11 sunk cost traps, new lessons taught that proactive counterinsurgency abroad was

> more effective in protecting America from another major homeland attack than reactive counterterrorism, influencing presidents' escalation decisions to avoid that regret.

As I postulated, historical lessons influenced Bush's decision to escalate. Moreover, some of these lessons were ones that came to the forefront because of 9/11 and after hard-fought battles in the initial years in Iraq. What I did not account for in Assessment 2 is the extent to which Vietnam lessons remained significant, were linked to the "new" lessons, and provided an added rationale for escalation.

The reason Vietnam-era lessons remained relevant was because leaders influenced by that war had positions of influence during the Iraq decision-making. The Vietnam War triggered a traumatic learning experience for key civilian and military leaders shaping policy during Iraq.[147] It explains lesson learning by the likes of Petraeus, Keane, McMaster, and Jeffrey.[148] As Petraeus wrote in his 1987 dissertation, "For the military . . . the debate over how and when to commit American troops abroad has become a debate over how to avoid, at all costs, another Vietnam."[149] Had it not been for the deep impact of the Vietnam War on the military, and their understanding of its impact on the country, Bush's efforts to obtain JCS buy-in for a surge might have turned out differently. George W. Bush may not have had such a persuasive trump card. As it was, Bush could point to a commonly understood Vietnam analogy to convince them of the need to win in Iraq when addressing their concern about breaking the force.

Hence, two matters are clear. First, historical lessons were "very much on the minds of the central decision makers" and were "used at important junctures in the policy process."[150] Second, while Vietnam remained relevant to Bush's decision, as I hypothesized, the most recent lessons mattered most and were "consistent with the option chosen."[151]

4. DID INTERNAL ADMINISTRATION RATIONALE DIFFER FROM THE PUBLIC JUSTIFICATIONS?

Lessons from Vietnam, 9/11, and Iraq were all important factors that George W. Bush considered privately to make his sunk cost trap decision. Lessons from 9/11 and Iraq dominated his public justifications, however. This section explains this discrepancy, while also telling the story of the president's evolution from an inconsistent to a primarily consistent private-public posture. Bush had a reputation before the surge of being unwilling to officially recognize reality. His unfailing optimism and characterizations of the war painted a picture of the war that seemed disconnected from the grim truth. His refusal to publicly acknowledge the true state of the war "was an inept political tactic, because it made it appear that the president was divorced from reality."[152] It also masked his private recognition in 2005–06 of the challenges faced.[153] Yet the reality is that Bush's private rationale and public justifications were consistent.

Before deciding to surge, George W. Bush focused publicly on positive developments. His March 2006 radio address indicated there was "evidence of real progress that is too often lost amid the more dramatic reports of violence."[154] Bush thought "the situation was manageable but exacerbated by a press corps that emphasized failure."[155] After the Revolt of the (Retired) Generals, Bush publicly supported Rumsfeld despite private concerns that he needed to go.[156] In late 2006, Bush, Cheney, and Rumsfeld's public comments attacking critics as "intellectually confused . . . abetting terrorists . . . [and] wrong" belied an ongoing administration debate.[157]

It was not until Bush had decided on the surge and was considering the details of its size and implementation that he publicly acknowledged how bad the situation was. On December 20, 2006, Bush utilized Pace's paradigm "We are not winning; we are not losing" as a way to describe the situation.[158] Cheney reinforced this view. There was "a view that we weren't winning. . . . That doesn't mean we were going to be defeated."[159] The Council of Colonels saw this as a distortion of their assessment that "we are not winning, so we are losing."[160]

Chief of Staff Andrew Card realized that incompetence and arrogance had come to define the public perception of Bush.[161] Republican members of Congress implored Hadley to rein in the tone-deaf Bush. "'Don't talk about winning!' . . . 'Stop talking about success!' . . . It sounded arrogant, triumphant and overconfident"[162] at a time when everyone else recognized that bad news far outweighed good news. Since the situation was clearly spiraling downward, this resulted in a perception that "his strategy was to make repeated declarations of optimism and avoid adding to any doubts. . . . The strategy was denial."[163] The president's overemphasis on the positive was out of touch with reality. George W. Bush recognized the disconnect between his messaging and common perception. His other audiences, like Maliki, the Iraqi people, allies, and US troops, led him to use optimism as a morale-boosting technique. His staff did not want to undermine the military or the current strategy until they had a new one in place.[164] Bush explained that his view "'stay the course' means let's get the job done, . . . [not] staying stuck on a strategy or tactics that may not be working." Even so, he began to realize he needed "to do a better job of explaining that we're constantly adjusting."[165]

So Bush's rhetoric began to evolve from being characterized by optimistic rigidity to also including recognition of failure and the need for adjustments.[166] The logic for his previous inconsistency was that while he *privately* had recognized that the situation was going very poorly, Bush did not want to *publicly* undercut the current strategy, commanders, or troops until another strategy was in place.[167] While this was understandable, the NSC's belief (before the midterms) that even acknowledging a public review of the war policy was ongoing would demoralize the military is a canard. The truth is that the military's wartime morale depends more on an assurance that their civilian policymakers and, ultimately, their commander in chief, have crafted a sound, feasible policy that has a chance of success. If it appears that is not the case—and it had long since been clear that was not true in Iraq—soldiers want to know that the president recognizes and is fixing the problem. Yet from a popular support perspective, President George W. Bush and his administration had to be careful during the review not to undercut their own case for congressional resources should they decide to continue the war effort. Therefore, Bush's job during the address to the nation about the new policy was to strike the appropriate delicate balance between admitting past errors while also making the case for continuing the fight with greater resources and a new strategy.[168]

Earlier cases show that when presidents de-escalate commitment during a sunk cost trap, they tend to downplay the ambitious elements of their initial aims and claim success in limited ways warranted by the situation, while still heading for the exit. Presidents Reagan and Clinton followed this pattern in Lebanon and Somalia, respectively. In this case, with Bush deciding to escalate commitment, Stephen Cambone saw a different response as appropriate. "If we're going to make an adjustment, it has to be one that is going to lead to success defined as the original set of aims . . . to get a functioning government in place."[169] Bush's speeches, and those of his administration, made that case, aligning public justifications with private rationale.[170]

One inconsistency between the administration's private deliberations and their public justifications is that a few of the lessons that facilitated Bush's bucking public opinion and the advice of his senior military leaders did not make it into his public justifications. The Vietnam War lessons to win and avoid a broken military reaffirmed to Bush the importance of the stakes at home. The lesson about presidential vindication in the long term confirmed his inclination to ignore domestic politics and to push back against the resistance from the JCS. Lessons from 9/11 and the "within-Iraq success of Petraeus, McMaster, and others" were the primary drivers behind the new war policy itself, would resonate with average Americans, and were therefore "far more influential than Vietnam."[171] Thus, they were what George W. Bush referred to publicly when explaining his decision. They were also what steadied him when faced with greater US and Iraqi casualties and low congressional and declining popular support—not Vietnam lessons.[172]

CONCLUSION

When faced with his sunk cost trap, "Bush . . . invoked historical analogies, narratives, and insights in choosing or justifying policies" and "relied heavily on the presumed lessons of the past in charting routes forward."[173] As in the past, policymakers and legislators referred to Vietnam analogies. The dominant lessons and resultant fear, however, were from 9/11 and Iraq.

September 11's strategic lesson to keep military pressure on terrorists overseas influenced George W. Bush's decision *for* escalation. The operational-level lesson about *how* to escalate was from Iraq—originally from Vietnam—that counterinsurgency worked.[174] The NSC backed the surge because it assessed that cutting losses would not free assets for unencumbered investment elsewhere in the way envisioned by the economic literature. "In the real world of war making, you don't just lose the investment already made, but that loss diminishes your remaining stock of capital."[175] Leaving Iraq as a violent mess would preclude rather than facilitate other aims.[176]

The relevant Vietnam War lessons were not the same ones most prevalent during the sunk cost trap/opportunity evaluations between the Vietnam War and 9/11. Before 9/11, those who opposed continued intervention referenced Vietnam's "let sunk costs be sunk" and Avoid a Quagmire lessons when they thought the United States should withdraw. For Bush, the two most important Vietnam references during the Iraq War decision-making—the interrelated lessons to win and to avoid incrementalism—instead pushed toward escalation.[177] Unlike the de-escalatory pressures generated by previous Vietnam lessons, these reinforced the 9/11 and Iraq War lessons—the latter rediscovered from Vietnam—to surge and conduct counterinsurgency.

During the decision-making, the internal lesson learning (and application) confirmed for Bush there was a feasible path toward achieving his original aims—albeit a difficult one.[178] Having gone "through a lot of very bad outcomes and false starts," George W. Bush learned lessons and pushed the military and agencies to embrace a strategy to which certain leadership was initially opposed.[179] Eventually, the administration and military became learning organizations, but it took a long time due to the entrenched assumptions that military leaders and top civilian policymakers had to overcome.[180] The lengthy period suggests that the Iraq War's shadow should influence future presidents to conduct semiannual war policy reviews to facilitate rapid identification and implementation of major war policy changes.[181] Reviews are not a silver bullet solution; they will not always produce change, nor will change always lead to victory. However, reviews are more likely to produce needed change than conducting wars without them.

Bush thought that cutting losses through de-escalation would have negative implications for the broader fight against terrorism, lead to even greater violence in Iraq and the region,[182] and embolden adversaries—as had withdrawals from Lebanon and Somalia.[183] So Bush decided to surge forces and change to a counterinsurgency strategy. He believed that provided the best possibility of preventing another 9/11. Although the lessons were different from those before 9/11, the decision-making for the Iraq surge—like in Lebanon and Somalia—is a story of past lessons informing the present war effort. Within two years of Bush's decision, a much different president—from a different political party—would make a similar decision for similar reasons.

6

Afghanistan

Lessons from 9/11, the Iraq War, and Vietnam Coalesce

INTRODUCTION

> Obama . . . relied heavily on the presumed lessons of the past in charting routes forward.
>
> —Hal Brands and Jeremi Suri

Lessons from the Vietnam War, 9/11, and the ongoing war in Iraq influenced the fall 2009 decision to surge in Afghanistan. Each played important roles in President Barack Obama's decision to escalate commitment. These historical lessons changed his risk calculus. They were a filter through which he deciphered the risks of action and inaction and judged the trade-offs of possible options—none of which were appealing. The dominant lesson and accompanying fear that most shaped Obama's propensity for escalation were from 9/11.[1] That was the prism through which Obama as senator, then candidate, and later president, came to favor an increased focus on and eventual escalation in Afghanistan.[2] The Iraq War influenced his decision to employ a counterinsurgency strategy. The Vietnam War lesson against both sunk cost inclusion and incremental approaches—because they ensnare a president—contributed to Obama's decision to limit the surge's duration.[3]

CASE SUMMARY (AFGHANISTAN)

This case study involves President Obama's December 1, 2009, decision to escalate and change strategies in the face of a prolonged stalemate in Afghanistan, paired with a simultaneously announced withdrawal timeline. The decision-making began with Obama's rhetoric about Afghanistan on the campaign trail. Obama touted it as the "good war," compared to the Iraq War, which was the "bad war" and one he felt was unnecessary, had derailed the country's foreign policy, and had been a resource drain, diverting much-needed assets away from the original terrorist threat in Afghanistan and Pakistan.[4] Pursuant to his campaign rhetoric, once in office, on February 17, 2009, President Obama approved approximately seventeen thousand additional soldiers and marines to join the war effort—a troop request left over from the Bush administration.[5] Obama also approved a mini escalation of four thousand additional enablers later in the spring.[6]

These earlier escalations—not yet completed—added to Obama's "sticker shock" when presented so soon with *another* military request for more troops.[7] Arguably, they also reduced his options during the latter decision-making. This was less because Obama had already escalated a couple of times as it was the military's greater appetite—relative to the White House—to undertake a fully resourced counterinsurgency campaign. The military's perception was that the earlier escalations in Afghanistan would be insufficient to achieve the desired outcomes. This was fed by counterinsurgency doctrine and recent escalation success in Iraq.[8] This ran contrary to the commander in chief's interpretation of what was necessary. Obama intended to implement a limited counterinsurgency strategy to buy time for Afghan security forces to meet the threat.[9] Military leaders wanted a fully resourced counterinsurgency strategy as a means of bringing stability and peace to Afghanistan. At bottom, the military saw counterinsurgency as a strategy for winning the war.[10]

The particular escalation decision in this case study came in the fall of 2009, after the completion of formal strategy, military, and policy reviews. Obama commissioned Bruce Riedel, a longtime intelligence community professional and an expert on Southwest Asia, to lead the strategy review in the spring. Later, General McChrystal conducted a separate commander's assessment in the summer after Obama installed him as the new commander in Afghanistan. These reviews facilitated the president's goal from the campaign to reevaluate and reenergize a war that had reached a stalemate by 2009—despite the effort over the previous eight years.[11] The United States had been unable to kill or capture Osama bin Laden, the head of al-Qaeda, or his number two, Ayman al-Zawahiri. Perhaps more importantly, the Taliban had reconstituted since being routed in 2001–02 and was putting up a strong fight.

Obama's decision about how to handle Afghanistan intensified with McChrystal's *Commander's Initial Assessment* at the end of the summer. In McChrystal's report, Obama's new commander stated that the prospect for victory was bleak but not lost.[12] Similar to Riedel's policy review, McChrystal viewed a counterinsurgency approach favorably. Additionally, to achieve US policy objectives in Afghanistan and Pakistan, McChrystal's report recommended another surge of troops. The general's escalation request triggered an intense period of strategic reflection and multiple National Security Council (NSC) meetings during the fall.

The subsequent leaking of McChrystal's report to the *Washington Post* increased civil-military tension. The president and some of his advisers felt that the military's now-public request for more troops limited his options. Some thought the military had leaked the report for that purpose, to box the president into their preferred course of action: a significant escalation. The source of the leak was unconfirmed, but it had the very real effect of increasing the friction between the administration and the military.[13] The relationship had already been strained when, in its initial escalation request in the spring, the military did not include the four thousand combat enablers (intelligence, logistics, and medical personnel) that would be necessary, leading to a second, mini escalation.[14] The leak only added to these dynamics.

Among other factors that influenced the president's fall war policy change were the disastrous Afghan elections and Democratic Party politics at home. The Afghan elections, held on August 20, were marred by UN allegations of fraud. Over one million votes were thrown out.[15] Afghanistan's election commission canceled a runoff scheduled for November 7 between the top two candidates, Hamid Karzai and Abdullah Abdullah, when the latter withdrew a week before.[16] Meanwhile, Obama was facing stiff opposition to escalating the war among his fellow Democrats.[17] After his initial escalations in the spring, his supporters saw no reason for continued escalation at the potential cost of what they deemed higher priority needs in the United States. Obama feared backlash from his support base in the Democratic Party if he escalated too much in Afghanistan and likely feared being labeled as "weak on national security" by Republicans if he concluded that the war was unwinnable.[18]

AIMS

> The aims were to prevent a renewed Al Qaeda safe haven and to reassure Pakistan of U.S. counterterrorism commitment regionally.
>
> —Denis McDonough and Thomas Donilon

President Obama aimed to prioritize the fight against al-Qaeda, prevent them from having safe havens in either Afghanistan or Pakistan, and ultimately eliminate the threat they, the Afghan Taliban, and like-minded terrorist groups posed. He also sought to stabilize Pakistan by signaling to its leaders America's commitment to counterterrorism and helping them address the terrorism threat against their own country that existed within their borders.[19] These aims informed the fall 2009 decision-making process, but they were not new. "He [Obama] argued repeatedly in the campaign that while the Bush administration was pursuing phantom enemies and nonexistent weapons of mass destruction in Iraq, we had lost our focus on the organization which had attacked the United States."[20] Obama's multiple escalations in Afghanistan during his first year in office were tangible manifestations of his campaign promise to reorient the fight against terrorism to there from Iraq. There were two additions to these publicly communicated aims. During the fall decision-making, Obama communicated privately to the military leaders on the ground in Afghanistan that he wanted to pursue a war policy that would ensure a stable, democratic Afghanistan—a more ambitious objective, and one potentially divergent from the others.[21]

The chapter utilizes the same research questions as the other case study chapters to examine President Obama's decision to escalate and implement counterinsurgency for a given time period. First, it explores why this situation qualifies as a sunk cost trap—or a no-win situation. Second, it addresses the options the commander in chief and his advisers considered. Third, the chapter examines the role played by historical lessons and fear, and whether those matched expectations. Fourth, the chapter investigates the degree of consistency between Obama's private rationale for and public justifications of his decision. It concludes with a brief discussion of one emergent lesson.

1. WHY WAS THIS A SUNK COST TRAP THAT REQUIRED A MAJOR POLICY PIVOT?

> We were not on a path to reach our objectives there [in Afghanistan].
>
> —Michèle Flournoy

> The United States is not losing in Afghanistan, but it is not winning either.
>
> —Stanley McChrystal

The situation in Afghanistan was a sunk cost trap because, as the undersecretary of defense for policy at the time, Michèle Flournoy, said, America's trajectory did not portend policy success. Journalist John Barry summarized the situation in a comparable manner upon Obama taking office. "The situation in Afghanistan is bad and getting worse."[22] In fact, assessments of this type were prevalent throughout Obama's first year in office. By the fall, both the new military commander on the ground, General McChrystal, and the American people agreed that the situation was serious. McChrystal wrote in his initial *Commander's Assessment* that "neither success nor failure can be taken for granted. . . . Many indicators suggest the overall situation is deteriorating."[23] Popular support, as depicted in public opinion graphs later in this section, exhibited growing discontent with Obama's handling of US policy in Afghanistan, the direction of American foreign policy in general, and the president's overall job performance. Thus there was an urgent need for a meaningful change to US war policy.

Obama faced significant sunk costs before his major change in war policy. The government and military had invested eight years in the war effort. This represented significant temporal and manpower sunk costs, marked by becoming America's longest war six months later.[24] Nearly 950 US military members had lost their lives in Afghanistan at the time of decision.[25] The year 2008 had been the "deadliest year of the war [so far] for American forces."[26] Yet, the first year of Obama's presidency saw casualties increase even further, doubling 2008 levels.[27] Senior military officials acknowledged that some of McChrystal's new directives, instilled to protect Afghan civilians, placed US troops at greater risk, seemingly confirmed by the spike in casualties.[28] The rise in casualties increased concern among military families and Congress while causing average Americans to doubt the prospects for success.[29] Financially, the nation had spent an estimated $230 billion on the war,[30] which was important considering the recession the country was experiencing. The first three categories of table 6.1 list these sunk costs, and the last two briefly describe their relevance to the president and the nation.

SUNK COST SALIENCE

The sunk costs increased pressure on the Obama administration. The war was "not perceived to be generating a level of benefits that can be convincingly described as proportionate to the costs."[31] "Increasingly the war in Afghanistan, like the Vietnam War, ha[d] become highly unpopular and politically costly."[32] During the span from the inauguration on January 20 until right before the December 1 West Point speech announcing the escalation, there was a steady decline in public approval across Obama's job approval on his handling of Afghanistan, his job approval on foreign policy, and his overall job approval.

TABLE 6.1
Obama's Afghanistan Sunk Costs (2009)

Time	8 years, 2 months (October 7, 2001–December 1, 2009)
Casualties	667 KIA; 262 wounded[1] (October 7, 2001–November 30, 2009)
Financial Investment	230 billion[2] (FY2001–FY2009)
Personal Credibility	An 11% decline in approval of Afghanistan policy and a 21% decline in job approval as measured by popular opinion from the time of the inauguration up until the December 1, 2009, speech. Obama held responsibility to uphold his campaign promise to increase US focus on the war in Afghanistan.
National Prestige	Defeat at the hands of a weaker enemy in Afghanistan would diminish national credibility and prestige.

[1] iCasualties, "Operation Enduring Freedom," accessed July 17, 2015, http://icasualties.org/OEF/ByMonth.aspx.
[2] Anthony Cordesman, "The US Cost of the Afghan War: FY2002-FY2013," Center for Strategic and International Studies (CSIS), 2012, 4–7.

This reflects the domestic political environment in which Obama was operating. Across these categories, the president's approval-disapproval ratings were converging—and not in a good direction for him. The downward slide from mid-50 percent to mid-60 percent approval ratings to 35 percent to 49 percent is a proxy for the change in Obama's personal prestige that had occurred since taking office, as it related to Afghanistan and foreign policy. Along with the human and financial investments already made, these public opinion ratings contributed to the sense that he was facing a no-win situation. The prolonged time commitment also contributed to the sunk cost element of national prestige. The longer the conflict lasted, the more it showcased that the United States, the global superpower, was unable to defeat a far weaker enemy.[33]

2. WHAT WERE THE PRESIDENT'S OPTIONS AND WHAT STRATEGY DID HE IMPLEMENT?

I don't think it was true that the military was trying to box in the president. I just think there were a lot of people that thought that was happening.

—Vikram Singh

IMPORTANT DECISION FACTORS LEADING UP TO OBAMA'S DECISION

Friction between the administration's civilian policymakers and military leaders mounted during the decision-making partially because Obama felt the military did not provide enough choices. He also felt that they sought to make the decision preestablished.[34] This perception, right or wrong, raised civil-military discord[35] earlier fueled by McChrystal indicating—while deliberations were still ongoing—that he did not believe that a counterterrorism strategy, such as the one favored by the vice president, would work.[36] Given all this, Obama asked tough questions and sought a variety of options.[37] During the formal policy review period, Obama pushed his national security team on strategic matters. He questioned assumptions undergirding the request for more troops. He reexamined America's core interests in the region and sought creative ways of achieving them.[38]

Obama's reticence to embrace another escalation in Afghanistan so quickly was due to a Clausewitzian instinct that the country's effort there might not be worth that much effort.[39] The president and some of his team had a light bulb moment in which they realized that the real threat to America, which stemmed from al-Qaeda's core leadership, was in Pakistan. These terrorist leaders were not in Afghanistan where the United States was, with the surge, going to have one hundred thousand troops and would be spending $113 billion a year.[40] The United States was investing, and preparing to invest further, in substantial ways in Afghanistan, but that was not where the majority of al-Qaeda and its senior leaders were.[41]

Civilian and military intelligence analysts and leaders in Afghanistan in August 2009 estimated that al-Qaeda did not have more than two hundred to three hundred fighters in Afghanistan. The rest were in Pakistan or other areas around the world. Those who were in Afghanistan were among the lower-level ranks, not the senior leadership responsible for the most significant terrorist plot planning or execution.[42] This sanctuary problem raised the specter of whether US military intervention was properly addressing core national security interests and whether success was possible. This debate echoed a similar debate during the Vietnam War. It also relates to a discussion near the end of the chapter about discrepancies between the private rationale for the decision (focused on stability in Pakistan) and its public justification (tied to security interests in Afghanistan).

Despite Obama's instincts toward a critical evaluation of McChrystal's request, key factors complicated his decision, opening him to an escalation.

Most of the president's principal advisers, both civilian and military, supported an escalation and counterinsurgency strategy. Alongside McChrystal, Secretary of Defense Robert Gates, Secretary of State Hillary Clinton, Chairman of the Joint Chiefs Admiral Michael Mullen, and Central Command Commander General David Petraeus backed the proposal. Moreover, summarily dismissing McChrystal's recommendation would have taxed an already fragile relationship with the Pentagon. It would signal that the president viewed the situation in Afghanistan differently than the military's leadership. Some could also interpret this as Obama losing confidence in his own judgment. Since he had recently instilled McChrystal as his top commander in Afghanistan and directed him to turn the situation there around, a failure to follow McChrystal's recommendation would appear inconsistent. Additionally, counterinsurgency was hard to argue against in the fall of 2009 because of its apparent success in Iraq.

"The reason we went from September to the West-Point Speech in the December of 2009, 'dithering,' as some have claimed, is that the President refused to consider one option alone, and the Pentagon refused to give him any [significantly different] choices."[43] The commander in chief did get some alternatives from other advisers, as described later in this section, but the choices were stark. If Obama refused the military's recommendation, he would be ignoring a catastrophic mission failure warning. If he accepted the plan, he would be committing to a revitalized effort in Afghanistan that could end up in a quagmire. A compromise could leave him with the worst results of either possibility, with a halfhearted attempt lacking the means to show any worthwhile progress.

OPTIONS CONSIDERED

> Additional resources are required, but focusing on force or resource requirements misses the point entirely.
>
> —Stanley McChrystal

This excerpt from McChrystal's *Commanders' Initial Assessment* is ironic because, despite its advocacy to the contrary, the war policy debate devolved into a discussion largely focused on the number of additional forces one alternative would provide versus another. Although Option 1 (Status Quo) was a possible course of action, Obama did not give it much consideration, nor did he appear to consider withdrawal. The military characterized McChrystal's three options, all involving more troops, by the residual risk they carried. This,

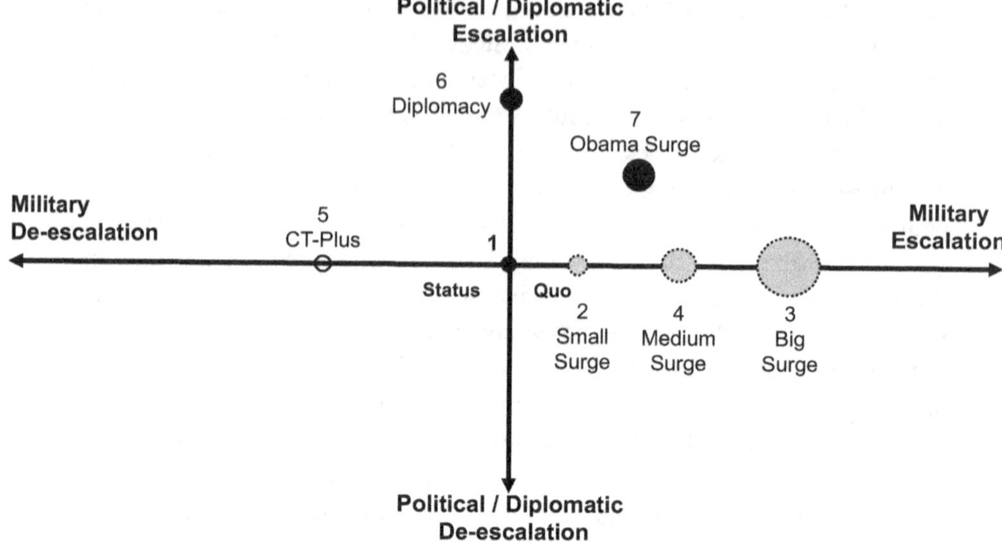

Figure 6.1. Potential presidential policy options in Afghanistan in 2009.

in turn, was based on the likelihood of failure given the number of new soldiers entering the fight (Options 2, 3, and 4)—portrayed, along with the other options, in figure 6.1.

McChrystal's high-risk alternative (Option 2: Small Surge) entailed an additional troop request of ten thousand. While this would provoke the least political opposition of McChrystal's options, it would do relatively little to reduce violence and provide time for political and economic development to occur.[44] On the other end, the low-risk course of action (Option 3: Big Surge) asked for the deployment of eighty thousand US troops. It would facilitate the protection of Afghans through the pacification of the Taliban and terrorist threats. This was viewed as a ridiculously high number, however, especially coming on the heels of the spring escalations, which were yet to be fully implemented. That left Option 4 (Medium Surge), which would include forty thousand more troops. It was the medium-risk option because it provided significant forces to address the enemy's growing strength but without additional margin to address contingencies.[45]

Special Envoy for Afghanistan and Pakistan Richard Holbrooke had foreshadowed this framing of options by the military. The experienced envoy predicted that the military would present three options, framing all in terms of the level of additional troops requested. Further, Holbrooke indicated that the military's use of this method was to point the decision-maker, President Obama, to the middle option—which is what the military really wanted. The other two were essentially throwaways designed to make the president feel that the middle alternative was not so bad. Just by including the two extreme courses, that alternative would appear more practical. By selecting it, the president might imagine that he would be taking the compromise approach, something Obama was purportedly keen to do.[46] As such, he could avoid the political pitfalls of either overextending the United States by sending too many troops or appearing to do too little.[47]

Biden proposed a fifth option that refocused on counterterrorism rather than undertaking a broader counterinsurgency mandate (Option 5). The vice president argued that counterinsurgency would require an extensive military and diplomatic effort over many years and further involve the United States in Afghanistan, without guaranteeing mission accomplishment.[48] As an alternative, Biden's CT-Plus option would utilize drones and Special Forces to target the enemy, cutting the estimated costs entailed in another counterinsurgency campaign.[49] This strategy focused on the enemy instead of protecting the civilian population, which was the first priority of McChrystal's population-centric counterinsurgency strategy. The "plus" portion of Biden's policy sought an increased diplomatic push to leverage Pakistan to take more effective action against al-Qaeda, Taliban, and other groups conducting terrorist attacks in Afghanistan, such as the Haqqani network.

Holbrooke and US Ambassador to Afghanistan Karl Eikenberry championed greater diplomatic efforts (Option 6), which would refocus efforts on Pakistan.[50] They concluded that the United States should refocus away from Afghanistan to Pakistan because that was where the senior terrorist leaders were and because Pakistan was the more pivotal country.[51] Pakistan had nuclear weapons. Pakistan had a history of instability, both in its tensions with its larger neighbor, India, and as evidenced by a string of military coups since the 1990s. Eikenberry advocated in a cable that "the better answer to our difficulties could well be to further ratchet up our engagement in Pakistan."[52] In it, Eikenberry bluntly noted the corruption and unreliability of a Karzai-led Afghanistan. Just like the McChrystal report, someone leaked this communiqué. That strained diplomatic relations with the Afghan leader but provided the other notable alternative for Obama, emphasizing diplomatic rather than military escalation. Option 6 attracted less attention than McChrystal's alternatives, but its support was not merely among Eikenberry and Holbrooke; it had collective appeal.

GRAPHICAL PORTRAYAL OF THE OPTIONS

Figure 6.1 portrays these options in terms of escalation and de-escalation, both militarily and politically/diplomatically. The two-dimensional chart is designed to capture the differences between alternatives in these terms. The closer the options are positioned to the middle of the graph, where the two axes intersect, the less change they propose and the more they resemble status quo efforts. The inverse is also true. The farther away from the center an alternative is, the more change it would involve and the less it resembles the status quo.

Figure 6.1 shows a graphical comparison of the options across diplomatic and military factors. Conceptually, presidents can manipulate options in the number of additional troops deployed or those withdrawn. They can change the type of mission those forces conduct. They can adjust the intensity of diplomacy undertaken and the breadth of its focus bilaterally, regionally, or globally. They can modify the amount of political capital expended on domestic politics to secure popular and congressional support. They can determine the pace at which those changes will be implemented, within the constraints of the US military's available lift capacity. They can also determine how long to apply these measures. Figure 6.1 shows that Obama considered options with different degrees of military and diplomatic escalations. Only one or two involved a likely or possible drawdown (Option 5: CT-Plus and Option 6: Diplomacy, respectively). In addition, the military's options varied little, other than in the number of additional forces added and, congruently, what those forces could accomplish.

STRATEGY IMPLEMENTED

Obama announced his decision on December 1, 2009, at West Point. He decided on forty thousand additional troops, but not all from the United States. Obama went with Gates's proposal to deploy thirty thousand US soldiers and seek contributions of ten thousand others from the North Atlantic Treaty Organization (NATO) and other partners.[53] Nor was the surge to be permanent, or conditions-based. Troop manning would return to presurge levels beginning in the summer of 2011. The military could use a counterinsurgency strategy, but the president's intent was not to conduct a fully resourced counterinsurgency mission.[54] The strategy Obama implemented involved a midrange degree of military escalation, along with increased diplomacy. Diplomacy was necessary to secure greater troop contributions from NATO or other partner nations. It was also necessary to push Pakistan to do more or at least allow America to do more on Pakistan's territory, despite the latter's concerns about territorial sovereignty and domestic politics.

This was a hybrid solution. The policy involved vertical military escalation and officially embracing a limited counterinsurgency strategy but also setting a time limit for the surge. The military would have the number of forces it wanted, but in recognition of the arguments made by those who opposed another escalation, the military must make progress relatively quickly and one-fourth of the force increase had to come from allies. Critics argued that the decision "caused confusion among allies and sent the wrong signals to the region. It seemed to say to the Taliban that they need wait only for the Americans to leave before re-emerging and seizing control."[55] So, while the surge showed that America had set out to "finish the job" in Afghanistan, it would be doing so for a limited time, attempting to avoid an open-ended commitment.[56] McChrystal was concerned that a set withdrawal date would give the Taliban "a sense that if they survived until the [withdrawal] date, they could prevail."[57]

Still, this component of Obama's decision leveraged NATO members, International Security Assistance Force partners, and other troop-contributing nations to share the burden and develop "skin in the game." It also forced McChrystal and other military leaders to join the administration in asking their counterparts to escalate military (and later fiscal) contributions. Indeed, Admiral James Stavridis, the NATO commander, went to extraordinary lengths to obtain this buy-in from international partners. He traveled to approximately sixty countries and logged a million miles in an exhaustive effort to garner troop and other contributions from partner nations.[58] Finally, it sent notice to the military that future requests would not necessarily be approved wholesale or without critical analysis.

3. WHAT ROLE DID HISTORICAL LESSONS AND FEAR PLAY IN AFGHANISTAN DECISION-MAKING?

From the beginning of Obama's presidency, for the cabinet and senior military leaders, the dominant lessons were gleaned from 9/11 and the Iraq War. The 9/11 lesson was that the United States must remain on the offensive, proactively engaged in an overseas war against international terrorists to avoid suffering another major terrorist attack at home. The Iraq War lesson was that lasting results in the United States' major contemporary military campaigns would come via counterinsurgency.[59] For the president, the 9/11 lesson was important, as evidenced by his campaign promises to refocus on "the good war." It mattered to him that the war on terrorism originated from the al-Qaeda leaders harbored in Afghanistan by the Taliban.[60] However, Obama was leery of the Iraq War lesson because he was skeptical of the efficacy of robust American nation-building efforts and more interested in building the US economy.[61] Vice President Biden, a former chair of the Senate Foreign Relations Committee, reinforced this skepticism for Obama by making the connection between the wars in Afghanistan and Vietnam explicit. Biden indicated that within a year, they might be able to determine that the surge was *not* working. At that point, as in 2009 and Vietnam, the generals would *again* ask for more troops in a never-ending incrementalism. In response to this gloomy, historically based prediction, the president assured Biden that he understood and would follow the Vietnam War lesson of avoiding a quagmire by setting a clear timeline for departure.[62]

The following subsections further discuss the impact of lessons from 9/11, Iraq, and Vietnam on Obama's decision regarding Afghanistan. They divide Obama's decision into three parts. First is the decision to escalate. Though it would have been difficult in his first year and because of his campaign rhetoric,[63] the president could have turned down the military's request for additional forces.[64] He could have deferred the decision since not all of the additional twenty-one thousand soldiers and marines Obama had ordered to Afghanistan in February and March—also in response to a Pentagon request—had yet made it into the fight.[65] Yet Obama did neither. Thus, the first subsection below discusses the president's decision to escalate. The second looks at the decision to utilize aspects of counterinsurgency as part of the strategy for the surge troops. The third examines the decision to limit the infusion of additional troops to eighteen months.

DECISION TO ESCALATE

The seeds of Obama's decision to escalate out of his sunk cost trap were laid before assuming office. He drew a distinction during the campaign between the ongoing wars. Afghanistan was the good war; Iraq was the bad war—a war upon which the United States should not have embarked. Obama contended that by opening an "unnecessary war" in Iraq, George W. Bush had taken his eyes off al-Qaeda.[66] Bush had failed to prioritize US efforts appropriately. Obama was determined to reverse that trend.[67] A lesson gleaned from 9/11 was foundational to this distinction. Afghanistan and especially Pakistan were the true sources of the threat to the United States.[68] According to Obama's assessment as a presidential candidate, the surge of forces to Iraq had had a negative impact on the resources available for and outcomes obtained in Afghanistan. Moreover, Obama argued that "the central front in the war on terror is not Iraq, and it never was." He promised to send "additional combat brigades to Afghanistan" and "seek greater contributions—with fewer restrictions—from NATO allies" to take "the fight to al Qaeda in Afghanistan and Pakistan."[69] The aim was to prevent a renewed al-Qaeda safe haven and to reassure Pakistan of US counterterrorism commitment regionally.[70] Once in office, key members of the president's national security team shared this understanding of Obama's prioritization of the war efforts. In a phone interview with the author, Obama's number three at the Defense Department, Michèle Flournoy, explained how the president viewed the priority for military action and why. "Obama came into office with the premise that Iraq was a war of choice, but Afghanistan was a war of necessity. Afghanistan had become an economy of force mission under the Bush administration after the Iraq invasion. Obama came in with the view of turning that around because he believed Afghanistan was a war we needed to win. He believed we needed to stay on the offensive against terrorists where they actually lived and operated."[71] Obama's director of central intelligence, Leon Panetta, shared Flournoy's understanding. "He [Obama] was convinced that the war in Iraq had distracted the United States from the genuine threat to our security—that of terrorism generally and Al Qaeda specifically. . . . For the new president, nothing was more symbolic of that misdirection than bin Laden himself, who had killed more Americans than any terrorist in history, was actively attempting to kill more, and yet was still at large."[72]

Obama's inclination during the campaign that a more robust effort was necessary—and the linkage of that determination to 9/11 lessons—was critical. His disposition left open the possibility of escalating when McChrystal and company made the case that the war was not going well.[73] This was, in fact, an argument Obama himself had made during the campaign.[74]

Moreover, the apparent success of the Iraq surge in reducing violence was a model whose replication promised similar success in Afghanistan—at least on the surface. Because it was so recent, and key military and defense leaders advising the president about Afghanistan (Gates, Petraeus, and McChrystal) were heavily invested in Iraq's surge, it was a natural archetype. Yet, while history can be helpful, it can also present a trap apart from careful distinctions among situations. Instead of treating Afghanistan as its own conflict, otherwise discerning leaders were captured by their experiences. They believed a surge would provide Afghanistan, like Iraq, time for social and political reconciliation that would produce lasting stability.

DECISION TO UTILIZE A COUNTERINSURGENCY STRATEGY

> We were trying to capture for the [Afghanistan] project that we want to repeat that [Iraq surge] success, and I believe it was a success.
>
> —Joseph Collins, Frank Hoffman, and Nathan White

> If one ghost hovering over the discussion of Afghanistan was that of Vietnam, where an earlier Democratic president had come to grief by escalating a war in Asia, another ghost was that of the "surge" in Iraq.
>
> —Peter Bergen

There were plenty of differences between Afghanistan and Iraq.[75] From 2009 onward, Afghan president Hamid Karzai proved a less cooperative partner than Iraqi prime minister Nouri al-Maliki during the Iraq surge. Afghanistan lacked the developed state institutions that Iraq had. In Afghanistan, American efforts were starting from a much more rudimentary basis for developing national and provincial-level leadership. The Afghan population was more fragmented, less educated, and much more rurally based.

Nor were there the same type of galvanizing events in Afghanistan as occurred in Iraq to win the locals' support away from the insurgency and terrorists. In Iraq, this came in the form of sectarian violence. The bombing of the sacred Shia Al-Askari ("Golden Dome") Mosque in Samarra by Sunni extremists on February 22, 2006, was a particularly egregious act and a turning point in the war. It led Sunnis to abandon al-Qaeda and align themselves with the United States and the Iraqi government. There was no similar event in Afghanistan, however. So "the problem with exporting the Sunni Awakening approach to Afghanistan is that there was no analogous group."[76] All these differences made success via a cut-and-paste approach difficult.[77]

Yet if these important differences were overlooked, Iraq and Afghanistan's similarities seemed significant on the surface. They included a mix of terrorism and insurgency against the coalition and host nation, US aspirations of democracy and stability, a lengthy previous effort, and perceptions of high stakes. They also included similar options to go heavy with a counterinsurgency strategy or do a lighter counterterrorism-only footprint. These similarities influenced the options recommended to the president. For leaders with limited time, facing uncertainty, high stakes, and options that all seemed bad and had potential negative trade-offs,[78] the Iraq policy afforded a handy heuristic. Michèle Flournoy indicated, "The Iraq counterinsurgency model was certainly on everyone's mind during the fall 2009 decision making about Afghanistan."[79] A similar policy against a similar threat seemed to promise a similar positive outcome.[80]

The Iraq's surge success validated in the minds of important principals the Iraq War lesson that robust forces using a counterinsurgency strategy was the formula for success.[81] This included Generals McChrystal and Petraeus and Admiral Mullen. This represented the top three relevant military officers: the commander on the ground (McChrystal), the Central Command commander (Petraeus), and the chairman of the Joint Chiefs of Staff (Mullen). Support was strong on the civilian side as well, namely with Secretaries Gates and Clinton. "Clearly, the surge's apparent success in Iraq circa 2007–08 influenced some senior military officers' thinking about Afghanistan. . . . It understandably became the template to adopt."[82] Not everyone, however, was convinced. Vali Nasr explains where Holbrooke's skepticism of the surge and counterinsurgency strategies originated: historical lessons. "Holbrooke was convinced that such an effort would fail, and that in trying to avoid that outcome, America would deepen its military commitment, doubling down on a failing strategy in what might turn into a dangerous repeat of the Vietnam debacle that Holbrooke had witnessed as a young Foreign Service officer."[83] Despite a few skeptics, such as Ambassador Holbrooke, Lieutenant General Douglas Lute,[84] and Rahm Emanuel,[85] who expressed their views in private, "all the heavy hitters in the war cabinet were in favor of one course of action:"[86] escalation and counterinsurgency.[87]

The principals favored the surge and counterinsurgency approach in Afghanistan because they credited the Iraq surge with reducing violence between 2007 and 2009. The weekly attacks had gone from nearly 1,800 in June 2007 to less than four hundred in July 2008, and civilian deaths per month had plummeted from almost four thousand in November 2006 to five hundred in July 2008.[88] This success was still fresh in leaders' minds, and many of them were the same individuals who had been most responsible for the Iraq surge.[89] Even Leon Panetta, though not involved in the Iraq surge decision of 2007, reflected, "I was determined not to repeat [in Afghanistan] what I regarded as the essential mistake of the transition in Iraq—an abrupt departure that left the United States without any presence to continue exercising influence." As a result, counterinsurgency advocates, nicknamed "COINistas," had gained inroads with think tanks, journalists, military officers, and civilian officials, leading many to believe it was the ideal option in the United States' low-intensity wars—like Afghanistan.[90] It is not surprising, then, that those who were so invested in implementing the Iraq surge would look at a similar problem a couple of years later and propose an analogous solution.

The Iraq War model not only influenced Obama's key national security advisers; it also made the president contemplate the possibilities of a similar approach in Afghanistan. As Flournoy said, "The fact that the Iraq War surge and Sunni Awakening seemed to be stabilizing things in Iraq and turning the security situation around made Obama open to the notion that a surge in Afghanistan might be what was needed."[91] As respected counterterrorism journalist Peter Bergen recalled, "Obama said, 'I'm not saying it'd be the exact same plan as Iraq, but I am looking for something that is a surge to create the conditions for a transition.'"[92] As in Iraq, the military goal involved creating time and space for political and social reconciliation to occur.

What most did not realize was how much different other dynamics between the two countries were. There was no equivalent to the Sunni Awakening or a Maliki-like leader to provide at least occasional nationalist leadership. There was a different topography, which led to terrorist safe havens in the mountains and across the border that was even more problematic than that faced in the Iraq War. More than in Iraq, there was a history and culture of tribal, decentralized governance and stiff opposition to foreign invaders. There was a robust system of shadow governance enforced by the Taliban, both within Afghanistan and by senior leaders across the Pakistan border in Quetta. They considered themselves the Afghan government in exile and were awaiting the opportune moment to resume the mantle of leadership. This exceeded similar efforts in Iraq. Policymakers understood these matters individually and in the abstract. What they did not understand was how significant these factors were in the aggregate. They did not grasp that policies deemed successful in Iraq would not translate, even with slight modification, into success in Afghanistan.

Although Obama had internal tension about a surge, it was not necessarily because he recognized these differences between Iraq and Afghanistan.

Instead, he had an aversion to robust military operations that lacked an international consensus, did not address a definitive threat to the United States, or did not have clear prospects for success.[93] In a fall 2002 speech against the Iraq War (before it began and before he was even a senator), Obama communicated this viewpoint. He expressed his opposition to a war in Iraq because it would "require a U.S. occupation of undetermined length, at undetermined cost, with undetermined consequences." Moreover, a war "without strong international support" would create regional problems and "strengthen the recruitment arm of Al Qaeda."[94] Obama brought that perspective with him to the White House and the Afghanistan policy review in the fall of 2009. For the vice president, who was widely regarded as a foreign policy expert, a similar perspective came from the Vietnam War–era lesson that without real caution and limits in place, presidents can find themselves trapped in a cycle of incremental escalations, each promising, but not delivering victory.[95]

DECISION TO LIMIT THE SURGE TO EIGHTEEN MONTHS

> I don't want to make an open-ended commitment.
>
> —Barack Obama

> This is Vietnam all over again.
>
> —Helen Thomas

Obama went to Afghanistan with two other senators while on the campaign trail. They discussed the Vietnam War and the parallels with the war in Afghanistan on the flight. For all their differences, the US military interventions in Afghanistan and Vietnam shared several important similarities as one journalist pointed out early in Obama's presidency.

> All American interventions after Vietnam have been potential "quagmires." . . . The war in Afghanistan is shaping up in all-too-familiar ways. The parallels are disturbing: the president, eager to show his toughness, vows to do what it takes to "win." The nation that we are supposedly rescuing is no nation at all but rather a deeply divided, semi-failed state with an incompetent, corrupt government held to be illegitimate by a large portion of its population. The enemy is well accustomed to resisting foreign invaders and can escape into convenient refuges across the

> border. There are constraints on America striking those sanctuaries. Meanwhile, neighboring countries may see a chance to bog America down in a costly war. Last, there is no easy way out.[96]

Obama was concerned about possible Vietnam parallels while reading Gordon Goldstein's *Lessons in Disaster: McGeorge Bundy and the Path to War in Vietnam*. The parallels prompted him to address Vietnam War analogies repeatedly during the fall 2009 war policy review, starting with the first NSC meeting. Unlike his understanding of what had happened during the Vietnam War when President Lyndon Johnson repeatedly escalated, Obama wanted to apply a thorough process to decision-making. He wanted assumptions questioned. He wanted to determine which analogies were germane and which were not.[97] At one point, Obama emphasized that Afghanistan was not another Vietnam, but the administration was unable to dismiss the quagmire comparison.[98] Obama could have ignored the parallels that Congress and the press were making but instead felt compelled to address them because he did not want Afghanistan to become his Vietnam.[99]

Marvin Kalb thought this was because Obama was haunted by the Vietnam War's length and outcome and wanted to avoid similar outcomes in Afghanistan, despite it being the better of the two wars he inherited.[100] Flournoy added, "President Obama was determined not to get bogged down in a forever war—an open-ended commitment," and, in an effort to avoid a similar quagmire, read a lot about the Vietnam War.[101] Obama's director of central intelligence and later secretary of defense, Leon Panetta, confirmed that similar to the war in Vietnam, "the war in Afghanistan, [although] launched to roust Al Qaeda, had by 2009 become mired in debates over nation building, [and] the reliability of Karzai."[102] This was similar to how America had faced challenges with the competence, trustworthiness, and indigenous support for its partner in South Vietnam, as well as debates about how much effort the country should apply there. Obama recognized that these debates about Afghanistan, unchecked, could lead to a seemingly endless war—an outcome reminiscent of the Vietnam War. He was not going to let that happen. The surge's time limit would force US military and diplomatic efforts, as well as Afghanistan's, to achieve results by the summer of 2011 before the president pulled the plug. Obama had multiple audiences in mind when determining to limit the surge's length. Both for the international audience (Karzai) and Obama's domestic audience (the Democratic Party and American citizens more broadly), he wanted to signal that American commitment was not going to be indefinite.

Vice President Biden reinforced this thinking. He warned Obama that he had to take firm, definitive steps with the national security team—cabinet members and senior military leaders—to ensure Afghanistan did not turn into Obama's Vietnam. At a critical NSC meeting in late November 2009, Obama was to tell his team what he had decided. This was a few days before announcing it to the public. At the meeting, Obama was going to give his leaders a five-page terms sheet. The memorandum had the number of troops the escalation would entail, the mission and their military objectives, how long the surge would last, and what it would cost financially.[103]

Before that Sunday, November 29 meeting, Biden offered unsolicited advice to the young president, drawing on a key lesson from the Vietnam War. "If you give the military everything they want, the 40,000 [additional troops] and kind of unlimited counterinsurgency—fully resourced counterinsurgency, you're going to . . . go down the escalation trail."[104] Biden continued, referencing the terms sheet for the principals that outlined the new strategy. "'This is an order.' If he [Obama] didn't stick to [i.e., enforce] those orders, there was no exit. Without them—and this was his main argument—'We're locked into Vietnam.'"[105] Moreover, the war policy change would require reevaluation down the road. Biden told the president, "It [the surge] might not work, and by next December it might be clear. 'You may get to the point where you've got to make a really tough [expletive] . . . decision.'"[106] Obama replied, "I'm not signing on to a failure. . . . If what I proposed is not working, I'm not going to be like these other presidents and stick to it based upon my ego or my politics—my political security."[107] "I'm not doing Vietnam."[108] This exchange demonstrated the clear impact of the Vietnam War lesson to avoid a lengthy quagmire. This lesson and the five-page memorandum are what Obama used to get everyone's agreement that it would not be a forever war.[109]

This evidence demonstrates first that lessons were "very much on the minds of the central decision makers" and that they were "used at important junctures in the policy process." The second goal has been to provide an empirically based analysis of which lessons mattered most and to show that those lessons were "consistent with the option chosen."[110] Together, these measures constitute political science scholar Yuen Foong Khong's two-pronged test for arguing that historical lessons influenced Obama's decision. Another aim of this section has been to provide a partial explanation of why these lessons were important. The "why" so far has been because leaders saw the lessons as useful past examples that they believed offered helpful policy prescriptions to the contemporary problem, given the conditions in Afghanistan and the broader international context. Another element of the "why" was that Obama thought escalation would result in less remorse.

FEAR OF ANOTHER 9/11 AND ANOTHER VIETNAM

> To abandon this area now—and to rely only on efforts against al Qaeda from a distance—would significantly hamper our ability to keep the pressure on al Qaeda, and create an unacceptable risk of additional attacks on our homeland and our allies.
>
> —Barack Obama

As his speech announcing the surge indicates, Obama was more concerned about the potential outcomes associated with de-escalation than those of escalation. Since he was not excited about any of the options, however, it became important to minimize the potential fallout of a war policy shift gone awry.[111] As Obama saw it, if he de-escalated, the risk of suffering new attacks would increase as American military pressure against al-Qaeda lessened. If escalation were ineffective, the war effort could become a quagmire, but it offered a greater likelihood of keeping the American people safe than did pursuing the status quo or de-escalating.[112] This led to Obama's escalation. Nonetheless, the strength of Obama's fear about creating his own Vietnam-like quagmire also led to the surge's time limit.

The thought of boundless escalation, without predetermined and achievable goals, increased administration fears of Afghanistan becoming a Vietnam-like quagmire, lacking popular support and an exit strategy. After all, the stalemate President Obama faced in Afghanistan was seen as having many parallels with those confronting previous presidents during the Vietnam War. Dr. Gordon Goldstein explained some of these. "Afghanistan and Vietnam are small powers that have been historically extraordinarily resistant to the efforts of large powers to impose order." Both had "corrupt and ineffectual regimes." Both have "contiguous border countries, through which support and sanctuary for an insurgency flows and fortifies that insurgency." "But most importantly, the parallel, really, that drives Afghanistan and Vietnam is in the realm of military strategy. In Vietnam [for the last few years of the war under General Creighton Abrams], it was a strategy of 'counterinsurgency and clear and hold.' In Afghanistan, General McChrystal had called for a strategy of 'clear, hold and build.'"[113] The similarities appeared stark, raising fears that the wars might share a similar, humiliating outcome.[114]

One way to address the president's concerns, other than denying the similarities with the Vietnam War,[115] would be to limit his aims in Afghanistan. Another approach would set a time limit to US commitment. The administration communicated as if they were doing the former but really only implemented the latter. The administration and the military attempted to limit goals by saying that all they sought was an "Afghan good enough."[116] They also shied away from referring to the policy as a fully resourced counterinsurgency. Yet the lines of effort sought considerable progress not only with security but also in the political, development, and diplomatic realms—only the latter of which was narrowly scoped. Understanding the dangers of an open-ended conflict that lacked an exit strategy, however, Obama did make a strong attempt to limit the surge's length to eighteen months. This was a hybrid solution to balance his twin fears of suffering another catastrophic terrorist attack and Afghanistan becoming his own Vietnam.

The following passage illustrates Obama's challenge in learning from US failures in the Vietnam War and applying the corresponding lessons in Afghanistan decision-making. "During Obama's first term, Democrats were still tainted with weakness by the long shadow of Vietnam. Determined to escape those ghosts and make the Democrats seem strong on national security, President Obama judged counterinsurgency to be the least bad option available during two separate rounds of White House deliberations over Afghanistan strategy in his first year. He nearly tripled U.S. forces committed to the war but simultaneously imposed a definite deadline of summer 2011 as the endpoint of the Afghan surge."[117] Thus, President Obama's "reading of the Vietnam War had a powerful effect on the . . . 'surge' and subsequent drawdown of U.S. forces in Afghanistan."[118] The Vietnam War's Avoid a Quagmire lesson influenced Obama's decision to withdraw surge troops after eighteen months.

Like Obama's decision to limit the surge's duration, fear fueled by historical lessons led to the president's escalation in the first place. This is where 9/11 and Iraq War lessons—that a military war footing and counterinsurgency were necessary for success—were paramount. After 9/11, it was more difficult for presidents to fully withdraw from military conflicts against terrorists abroad. While the sunk costs piled up and presidential foreign policy approval steadily declined, new terrorist developments were still enough to justify military action. And from Obama's perspective, unlike other post-Vietnam conflicts, the war in Afghanistan posed a serious threat to American civilians and national security.[119]

What is interesting about the president's decision is that it was a deviation both from his reputation as a candidate and from what later became his modus operandi on questions of force. Obama consistently sought ways to solve foreign policy problems other than with robust military engagement. He was not afraid to use force, but he preferred diplomatic, economic, and selective military strikes supported by allies over large, conventional, unilateral wars. This approach was seen in his approach to Iran, North Korea, Libya, and counterterrorism efforts writ large. However, Obama felt that George W. Bush and Lyndon Johnson, among others, had been too quick to reach for robust military answers to intractable foreign policy problems.[120]

Throughout his two terms, Obama remained unconvinced that major escalations of military power held much efficacy in many instances.[121] Obama was careful, therefore, not to repeat the mistakes he perceived his predecessors had made. The president's escalation in Afghanistan was a notable aberration from this "Obama Doctrine," later described by Jeffrey Goldberg in the *Atlantic*.[122] That it was a departure from his modus operandi highlights that Obama's fear of suffering another major terrorist attack after a de-escalation was a powerful motivator for escalation. That fear was significant enough to overcome his usually strong desire to minimize US military engagement.

> Assessment 2 (Never Again on My Watch): In post-9/11 sunk cost traps, new lessons taught that proactive counterinsurgency abroad was more effective in protecting America from another major homeland attack than reactive counterterrorism, influencing presidents' escalation decisions to avoid that regret.

In this assessment, I did not account for the extent to which Vietnam's shadow was still influential during post-9/11 sunk cost traps. Instead, I focused on the impact of 9/11 and Iraq War lessons, but Obama drew important lessons from Vietnam and the post-9/11 environment. So, consistent with my assessment, lessons from 9/11 and the Iraq War shaped Obama's fundamental decision for escalation and counterinsurgency. Inconsistent with the Never Again on My Watch assessment, Vietnam's lessons were more explicit in verbal discussions during decision-making and led to the surge's eighteen-month time limit.[123]

4. DID INTERNAL ADMINISTRATION RATIONALE DIFFER FROM THE PUBLIC JUSTIFICATIONS?

> These wars [including the one in Afghanistan] have likely led policy makers to describe ongoing operations as Counter Terrorism efforts rather

> than as counterinsurgency campaigns, even though the latter more accurately captures the comprehensive nature of what is required to defeat [the terrorist organizations we face].
>
> —David Petraeus

> There is not an obvious military victory anywhere in sight. . . . The US and its allies have to be candid that this will not be the "win" on its terms that it hoped for.
>
> —Nick Patton Walsh

The public justifications for the new war policy demonstrated a mixture of consistency and inconsistency with the private logic for the decision's three elements: to escalate, to utilize a counterinsurgency strategy, and to limit the surge to eighteen months. The private rationale for these three aspects of the decision stemmed largely from lessons learned from 9/11, the Iraq War, and the Vietnam War, respectively. The public justification for the first component, escalation, was the threat related to the 9/11 attacks, consistent with the private rationale.[124]

The public justification for the decision's second component, employing a counterinsurgency strategy, was inconsistent with the private rationale. The Iraq War model of success influenced Obama's advisers and opened the president to the idea of an Afghanistan surge.[125] Publicly, however, the president sold it in a way consistent with his campaign promises to refocus military action away from Iraq and against al-Qaeda and in Afghanistan.[126] As this section's quotation from General Petraeus indicates, Obama did not fully embrace counterinsurgency.[127] This was because it could have signaled a greater nation-building effort abroad, which he was keen to avoid, in favor of nation building at home.[128]

Third, Obama also attempted to distance his war policy from that pursued by Lyndon Johnson in Vietnam. The public justification for the third component of the decision, limiting the surge to eighteen months, was that the Afghans would be ready to begin accepting responsibility for their own security at that point.[129] The time limit was likely made with Afghan president Hamid Karzai in mind to signal that American commitment was not going to be indefinite. Afghans would have to assume the leadership of their own security and determine their fate in the not-too-distant future. Like with the counterinsurgency element of the war policy shift, this also differed—in part—from the underlying private reasoning, which was to avoid a quagmire like Vietnam by limiting the time horizon, setting a reevaluation date, and attempting to establish clear, limited objectives.[130]

Obama distanced his war policy from Johnson's by highlighting several distinguishing features of the contemporary war. He pointed out that al-Qaeda attacked the United States from Afghanistan, while the North Vietnamese did not attack the American homeland. Obama also noted that America still faced a threat emanating from Afghanistan but had not during the Vietnam War, and that the threat in Vietnam was not an insurgency with broad-based support. The United States had a "broad coalition" with whom it was fighting alongside in Afghanistan, conferring legitimacy on its efforts, unlike in Vietnam.[131] Obama began making these distinctions while running for president and continued them in his speech announcing the new war policy.[132]

While Obama tried to distance his "good war" from the US military experience in Vietnam, doing so was confirmation of its impact on private deliberations and public comparisons. Obama emphasized the differences among the conflicts in an attempt to justify the national security need in Afghanistan as opposed to that faced in Vietnam and, in turn, to justify his escalation decision.[133] Despite his public articulation of the differences he saw between the wars, Obama was privately concerned that Afghanistan might turn into his own Vietnam.[134] He wanted a victory but was committed to avoiding a similar, Vietnam quagmire outcome. He would not allow incremental escalations to back him into a policy trap, with no good end in sight.[135] Obama would avoid that at all costs. The shadow of America's most traumatic conflict was long indeed.

The largest discrepancy between private deliberations and public justifications was the extent to which the threat from Pakistan was the driving force behind the decision and would be a focus of its implementation. At the NSC meeting just before Obama's West Point address, Vice President Biden and President Obama explained the escalation decision to the principals and revealed this inconsistency. They stated that the "main pillar" of the new policy "would be top secret and not be made public. That pillar was that safe havens for al Qaeda in Pakistan or elsewhere would no longer be acceptable. . . . He [Obama] wanted to . . . address the real threat to the homeland and U.S. interests," which emanated from Pakistan—not Afghanistan.[136] The president would be dramatically increasing the number of drone strikes against enemy targets in Pakistan.[137] Obama wanted to keep that quiet because of the sensitivity surrounding Pakistani sovereignty. In addition, the use of unmanned aerial vehicles as lethal platforms from which to launch kinetic strikes and wage modern war was controversial.[138] If the public soured on his increased drone campaign, it might limit the tools at his disposal, increasing risk to US interests and American forces in Afghanistan.

CONCLUSION

> Obama invoked historical analogies, narratives, and insights in choosing or justifying policies.
>
> —Hal Brands and Jeremi Suri

> Like Vietnam—our most famous quagmire—we win all the battles but are unable to win the war.
>
> —Elliot Ackerman

The story of the Afghanistan surge is one influenced by lessons from two traumatic wars and the single-most casualty-producing attack on US soil. Lessons from the Vietnam War, 9/11, and the ongoing war in Iraq each played important roles in Obama's decision to escalate commitment. Like in the Gulf and Iraq Wars, historical lessons were influential directly with the president, changing his risk calculus, and as a filter for which arguments were most persuasive. As occurred during past conflicts in Lebanon, the Persian Gulf, Somalia, and Iraq, Vietnam analogies were also present. They mattered to the president and were among those to which policymakers in the executive and legislative branches referred.

The dominant lessons and accompanying fear that most shaped Obama's propensity for escalation were from 9/11 and Iraq.[139] They were the prism through which he and his national security team came to favor an increased focus on Afghanistan.[140] The Vietnam War lesson against sunk cost inclusion and incremental approaches—because they ensnare a president—was also important. It led Obama to limit the surge's duration.[141]

The impact of 9/11 had the largest effect on Obama's new policy. It influenced the primary component of the change—the decision to escalate further than he already had twice earlier that year.[142] The fear of suffering another spectacular 9/11-style attack changed how presidents reacted to wartime sunk cost traps. The strategy for these situations was no longer de-escalation but escalation. September 11 taught presidents that they could no longer pursue the defensive, reactive, and law enforcement-centric approach to counterterrorism that previous presidents had employed. Instead, a new proactive, military-centric strategy that sought to kill terrorists overseas was necessary. Persistent efforts to decapitate terrorist organizations and degrade their other capabilities were imperative. America must disrupt its social media narratives, bomb-making, recruitment, radicalization, training, and plot planning. It was the only way to prevent another 9/11. Thus, a more recent tragedy (9/11) and stalemate (Iraq)—with their own lessons, antithetical to the "let sunk costs be sunk" lesson gleaned from the Vietnam experience—replaced the earlier lesson as the most powerful. Nevertheless, as the last chapter on the Iraq surge revealed, the Vietnam War ghosts had not disappeared.

The thought of escalating without limit and without predetermined and achievable goals increased administration fears of Afghanistan becoming a Vietnam-like quagmire, lacking popular support and an exit strategy.[143] After all, the sunk cost trap President Obama faced in Afghanistan was seen as having many parallels with those confronting previous presidents during the Vietnam War. During both conflicts, enemy sanctuary combined with incompetent and corruption-racked governments had made positive outcomes elusive.[144] In both cases, the US military had implemented similar counterinsurgency approaches after years of trying other strategies that had proven ineffective. In both cases, commanders in chief found that their initial escalation decisions "set in motion a series of events that fostered unrealistic expectations of what could be achieved."[145] Presidents Lyndon Johnson and Barack Obama failed to narrow their goal sufficiently and followed their initial decisions with subsequent escalations of greater magnitude. They expressed skepticism about military troop requests and the viability of success and had advisers who warned them against the likely perils of doubling down on their respective conflicts with the secondary escalations.[146] Despite all of this, sunk costs and loss aversion made the decisions difficult. The risks of action versus the risks of inaction weighed heavily, muddied by the investments already made. In the end, for Obama, traumatic lessons from 9/11 and Iraq had caused fear of inaction (de-escalation) to overtake fear of action (escalation)—just as it had for Johnson.[147] These dynamics, defining characteristics of sunk cost traps, complicated the presidents' cost-benefit calculus.

Given the challenges associated with these vexing dilemmas in the middle of wars, one lesson of the Afghanistan War is to wisely apply the lessons of the past. This means knowing when to mirror past strategies and when not to. Discernment grounded in a deep understanding of the similarities and differences between past and present circumstances is imperative. It also requires a prescient anticipation of how various strategies will play out in an uncertain future. Obama tried hard, implementing a comprehensive decision-making process of ten NSC meetings to determine the problems, question assumptions, and craft a new policy.[148]

The Afghanistan decision-making followed a deliberate and thorough process, but the eventual outcome on the ground did not serve the nation well.

Military leaders once reluctant to endorse the surge and counterinsurgency strategy in Iraq, had become committed to it in Afghanistan as a means to win the war and preserve their institutional legitimacy.[149] Despite Petraeus's professed recognition as early as 2005 that Afghanistan did not equal Iraq and that Afghanistan was more challenging in some ways, key civilians agreed that escalation and counterinsurgency were necessary.[150] The commitment to this model as a war-winning strategy was myopic, based on faith that what had worked in Iraq would work in Afghanistan. Michèle Flournoy said, "The Iraq counterinsurgency model was certainly on everyone's mind during the fall 2009 decision making about Afghanistan." During the surge implementation, General Petraeus regularly made comments like "This is how we did it in Iraq."[151]

The commitment to the escalation and counterinsurgency paradigm for winning a war was predicated on a false assumption.[152] The assumption boiled down to believing that the surge and counterinsurgency approach were the requisite components of success in Iraq. They were not the only essential elements, however. Without the changes—albeit temporary—of Prime Minister Nouri al-Maliki to work with the United States and to adopt a national versus a sectarian approach, and of the Al-Anbar tribes to side with the American military instead of al-Qaeda, the new Iraq War policy would not have been as effective in reducing violence. In Afghanistan, however, there was no Al-Anbar Awakening or a Hamid Karzai version of Maliki's support of the British against a revolt of his own Shia at Basra in the military operation "Charge of the Knights." Nor was there even a catastrophic failure event like the bombing of the Al-Askari Mosque that might trigger something similar to the Al-Anbar Awakening and the partnering of the Sons of Iraq with US security efforts.

After eight years of war in Afghanistan, key leaders other than Ambassador Karl Eikenberry should have recognized these differences. As Eikenberry pointed out,

> The revised [Field Manual 3-24 Counterinsurgency] doctrine placed high confidence in the infallibility of military leadership at all levels of engagement (from privates to generals) with the indigenous population throughout the conflict zone. . . . Modern COIN doctrine stresses the need to protect civilian populations, eliminate insurgent leaders and infrastructure, and help establish a legitimate and accountable host-nation government able to deliver essential human services. *Field Manual 3-24* also makes clear the extensive length and expense of COIN campaigns: "Insurgencies are protracted by nature. Thus,

> COIN operations always demand considerable expenditures of time and resources." The apparent validation of this doctrine during the 2007 troop surge in Iraq increased its standing.[153]

This made it even more difficult for Obama to opt in favor of an alternative strategy. If more policymakers had fully realized the implications of these dynamics, perhaps they would have been more successful in crafting an appropriate and cost-effective strategy to address vital US national security interests within the limits of what was achievable.

Success in securing and reshaping Afghanistan, even before the departure of US troops and the Taliban's takeover was limited. The greatest success came in terms of a negative, or unproven, counterfactual. Success achieved is best measured in the prevention of another 9/11-type spectacular attack in the United States. The level of effort applied, however, may not have been necessary to achieve that end. As a result, many policymakers and average Americans alike now "recoil at the thought of another operation that might be of the size—and cost—of Iraq or Afghanistan."[154] Moreover, the haunting Vietnam quagmire legacy now extends to and is strengthened by what happened in Afghanistan.[155] The battles were won, and yet there was a failure to accomplish political aims and win the war.[156]

Chapter 7, however, explores an all too rare situation: one in which the president and country achieved their goals and had the chance to go for more. It was a sunk cost opportunity instead of a sunk cost trap. The so-called tables were turned. When the president had the chance to throw good money after good money, historical lessons derived from past conflicts again shaped presidential decision-making.

7

Gulf War Endgame

A Sunk Cost Opportunity and Fear of Another Vietnam

> If you would understand America's victory in the Persian Gulf War you must first understand America's defeat in Vietnam.
>
> —Harry G. Summers

INTRODUCTION

Greater than anticipated success during the Persian Gulf War presented President George Herbert Walker Bush with a sunk cost opportunity. The rapid success of coalition forces and the minimal casualties they sustained meant that by the end of February 1991, Bush had the opportunity to add regime change to the list of political objectives. America had already incurred the sunk costs of deploying half a million troops and military equipment to the Middle East. Given those sunk costs, perhaps it made sense to take care of the Saddam Hussein problem once and for all at that time. This was an opportunity, not a sunk cost trap, as in the other conflicts. The endeavor was not failing but experiencing catastrophic success that presented new opportunities. Despite recognizing the opportunities afforded by the sunk costs already invested, Bush opted for the exits instead of adding regime change as a policy objective.[1]

President George H. W. Bush ended the Gulf War when he did because he feared the outcome that would result from an escalation of commitment to remove Iraqi president Saddam Hussein from power. Several factors drove his fear. First, Bush had learned from the Vietnam War.[2] One of that conflict's lessons that he most often cited was that a clean exit was important.[3] Bush perceived the Vietnam War as having concluded after multiple incremental escalations; much investment of lives, money, time, and prestige; and without successful accomplishment of American political goals.[4] That did not represent the type of clear conclusion Bush sought.[5] Similar to civilian and military advisers who shared the view[6] reflected in the Weinberger-Powell Doctrine,[7] Bush thought removing Hussein from power would complicate the American exit strategy. Extraction of US forces would be much more difficult if the coalition collapsed, a power vacuum emerged in Iraq, and sectarian conflict was on the rise—all as a result of a push to Baghdad. Second, Bush believed the coalition that he and his administration had tirelessly constructed would collapse if he added that objective.[8] This would delegitimize the United States' effort and leave it with few friends to share the financial costs, which to that point had largely been met by allied contributions ($53.7 billion donated to offset the $61.1 billion cost).[9] Moreover, Bush believed that the military had already achieved his political aims.[10] America had routed Hussein's military—or so it seemed when Bush was making the decision.[11] Bush's generals assessed Hussein's most loyal and capable forces, the Republican Guard divisions, such that Hussein would no longer be a regional threat.[12]

The Gulf War is an interesting situation in that the operation was experiencing substantial success, and yet the president did not invest further by adding more objectives. In business, that would be akin to not investing further in a project providing a significant return on investment. The rationale, consistent with acting independently from sunk costs, was based on the Vietnam syndrome and followed the Weinberger-Powell Doctrine.[13] George H. W. Bush sought a clear victory and a clean exit—two things not realized during the Vietnam War.[14] He would not allow other opportunities to put those objectives at risk. In other words, Bush acted based on past lessons and future fear rather than on the investments already made.[15] The decision was also in line with a Clausewitzian perspective of the "value of the political object." Carl Von Clausewitz argues for stopping as soon as you reach the point of diminishing returns. Clausewitz said it like this: "Once the expenditure of effort exceeds the value of the political object, the object must be renounced and peace must follow."[16] In other words, the mission must be abandoned immediately once the level of effort exceeds the value the decider places on its accomplishment.

CASE SUMMARY (PERSIAN GULF WAR)

Iraqi president Saddam Hussein invaded Kuwait on August 2, 1990, after deploying a large number of troops along the border during the final week of

July. Much has been made of the late July meeting between Hussein and the American ambassador to Iraq, April Glaspie. The US envoy's lukewarm message indicated, in part, that America did not concern itself with Arab territorial disputes.[17] Yet this was not the critical determinant in Hussein's strategic calculus.[18] He invaded after failing to peacefully resolve territorial and oil disputes with the Kuwaiti government, despite third-party intervention such as negotiations facilitated by Saudi Arabia and US diplomatic engagement.[19] In addition to invading Kuwait, Hussein massed his military in an offensive formation just across the Saudi border within a couple hundred kilometers of massive Saudi oil fields.[20] The Iraqi military posture led Saudi Arabia to invite America to send troops to ensure Saudi security.[21] The United States began sending forces to Saudi Arabia and planning for its defense immediately after the Saudi request.

President George H. W. Bush outlined American policy objectives in the Gulf in National Security Directive (NSD) 45, approved on August 20, 1990. The aims were fourfold. The first goal was "the immediate, complete, and unconditional withdrawal of all Iraqi forces from Kuwait." Second, America would ensure "the restoration of the Kuwait's legitimate government." Third, the United States would pursue "the security and stability of the Persian Gulf." Fourth, Bush wanted to protect "the lives of American citizens abroad." Bush later affirmed these same four goals in NSD 54 on January 15, 1991.[22] The United States also mobilized the international community through a series of United Nations Security Council Resolutions (UNSCRs). The twelve UNSCRs condemned Iraq's invasion, enacted economic sanctions, demanded Iraq withdraw its military, and authorized the use of force to restore the legitimate Kuwaiti government if Iraq did not comply by January 15, 1991.[23]

During an October 30, 1990, meeting with National Security Adviser, Lieutenant General (Ret.) Brent Scowcroft; Secretary of Defense Richard (Dick) Cheney; and Chairman of the Joint Chiefs of Staff, General Colin Powell, President George H. W. Bush approved a request for two hundred thousand additional troops. He delayed making the decision public until a couple of days after the midterm congressional elections, on November 8.[24] The force bump effectively doubled the American military presence in the Gulf.[25] It reflected a growing consensus among Bush's national security team that removing Iraqi forces from Kuwait would require military action. It was a big commitment for President Bush to grant the military's request since (1) the additional deployment order meant there would not be enough forces left in garrison to rotate deployed units out, (2) many forces had to come from Germany where they were poised to deter the former threat from the Soviet Union, and (3) much of the equipment had to be repainted in desert camouflage pattern from the woodland green camouflage.[26] The deployment of additional troops transitioned the US-led coalition from primarily a defensive orientation to having offensive capability and developing offensive war plans.[27]

Secretary of State James Baker's efforts to build a robust international coalition also proved effective not only for passing UNSCRs and enacting sanctions but also for receiving troop and cash contributions.[28] America provided most of the ground combat force, but other coalition states supplied "nearly half the total allied force." Troop contributions included Kuwait, 7,000; Pakistan, 10,000; France, 10,000 plus three aircraft fighter groups and an aircraft carrier; Syria, 20,000; Egypt, 35,000; Saudi Arabia, 40,000; and Britain, 45,000. International contributions were financial as well as human. Germany provided about $6.5 billion. Japan donated $10 billion to the cause, and Saudi Arabia and Kuwait each chipped in $13 billion. In total, Baker secured $48 billion and military assistance from thirty-six countries. America received help in other ways from other nations. For instance, to increase the economic pressure on Hussein, Turkey stopped importing oil from Iraq.[29] These developments did not, however, portend an end to diplomatic overtures to resolve the crisis peacefully.

Even at the eleventh hour, in early January 1991, George H. W. Bush wrote a letter to Hussein urging him to understand that America and the rest of the international community were serious. Secretary of State James Baker delivered the letter to the Iraqi foreign minister, Tariq Aziz, at a diplomatic meeting in Geneva, Switzerland, on January 9, 1991. The message was clear.[30] If Hussein did not immediately, completely, and unconditionally withdraw his forces from Kuwait, in compliance with UNSCR 660 and the eleven other UN resolutions, the coalition would deliver on its threats. The consequences for the Iraqi military and people would be grave. The diplomatic effort was for naught, however. Aziz refused to deliver the letter to Hussein.[31]

To further demonstrate the unity and commitment of the American people and their representatives, Bush insisted on asking Congress for a joint resolution supporting the use of force to compel Iraq to withdraw from Kuwait.[32] Bush sought this congressional approval despite the very real possibility of it not passing.[33] Despite some significant concerns, Congress passed the resolution on January 14, one day before UNSCR 678's deadline to Hussein.[34] The vote was "the closest in U.S. history on a decision to go to war": 250–183 in the House, but only 52–47 in the Senate.[35]

The deadline came, and Hussein still had not begun a withdrawal. Bush had the requisite military force necessary to force Hussein's hand as well as domestic and international support. And "in certain respects, war had become preferable to peace" because it would enable the United States to destroy key elements of the Iraqi armed forces, restoring a favorable regional balance of power.[36] It might also precipitate Hussein's fall.[37]

Demonstrating the same decisive commitment to enforce US and international aims that he would later show in his February escalation and de-escalation decisions—but only to initially agreed-on objectives—George H. W. Bush gave the order to free Kuwait. NSD 54, dated January 15, 1991, directed the military to do just that while also proscribing key tasks to support the ultimate political goal.[38] Among the critical tasks was to "eliminate the Republican Guard as an effective fighting force." Further (and contrary to his future de-escalation decision), Bush stated that "should Iraq . . . destroy Kuwait's oil fields, it shall become an explicit objective of the United States to replace the current leadership of Iraq."[39] Under this guidance from the commander in chief, air strikes began two days later.

The air war began to take a toll on Iraq right away. During a meeting on January 18, 1991, a day after air strikes began, President Hussein commented that he wished the coalition air strikes would shift from targets of economic value to military ones because of the pressure that the air war was placing on Iraq's already strained economy. Hussein told his advisers that if the Security Council asked for a ceasefire, they would not reject it, but they would not agree either.[40] Hussein went on to inform advisers that Iraq would launch missile attacks against Israel's main cities, including Tel Aviv, that day. Revealingly, an adviser identified only as "Adil" asked him whether the missiles would be conventional ones. Hussein answered in the affirmative, saying that Iraq would utilize the same type of weapons in retaliation for those "they" (the coalition) were using. Further, Iraq's next target would be Saudi cities. These response measures would ensure that "the battle will be a bit exciting" and test Israeli mettle. Moreover, Hussein's design was to inflict maximum casualties on Middle Eastern states aligned with the West.[41] Hussein's ultimate intention, not explicitly stated during his war meeting with the Iraqi Revolutionary Command Council, was to divide the coalition by provoking an indiscriminate response—especially from Israel. The "scud" missile attacks against Israel were Hussein's way of trying to do this.[42] Moreover, after being captured during another war between America and Iraq twelve years later, Hussein acknowledged that he believed "the United States would stop the war if Israel was 'hurt.'"[43]

Internationally, although Iraq and the Soviet Union agreed on a peace proposal involving a twenty-one-day withdrawal in mid-February, the world's most powerful country dictated different terms for a cessation of hostilities. The coalition held the advantage because of the tremendous success they were experiencing on the battlefield. Military might, properly leveraged, yielded diplomatic fruit. Mikhail Gorbachev emerged from his multiple phone calls with President George H. W. Bush between February 21 and 23 with a clear understanding that time to avoid a ground war was short, if not entirely in doubt.[44] Gorbachev recommended that Hussein announce and complete a withdrawal within a week and a half. Yet Bush gave Hussein a one-day ultimatum on February 22 to commence his withdrawal by noon Washington time on the twenty-third—or face a ground war.[45] When Saddam did not comply, Bush initiated what would become a one-hundred-hour ground war.

President George H. W. Bush wanted to accomplish his policy aims without going too far in his offensive attack. Inverting the favorable regional balance of power might invite mischief by other powers against Iraq. American leadership wanted stability in the Middle East. Hussein had been a destabilizing presence in the region: first by attacking Iran, which led to an eight-year war, and then by invading Kuwait. Iran, though, had also been guilty of such malfeasance, especially through its cultivation and use of proxy terrorist forces to export its revolutionary brand of Islam. Leaving the right amount of Iraqi military elements intact was a strategic, and delicate, US consideration: not enough to threaten its neighbors, but enough to deter retaliatory adventurism against Iraq. Thus, Bush shifted priorities among his aims over time from the restoration of the status quo (Kuwait's sovereignty under its legitimate rulers) to a rebalancing of power in the Middle East. This required a greater level of destruction of the Iraqi war machine and was designed to prevent Iraq from further threatening its neighbors.[46] It is ultimately why Bush rejected the last-minute Soviet-sponsored peace initiatives and did not immediately call an end to hostilities when elements of the Iraqi Army began retreating back across the Kuwait border.[47]

George H. W. Bush also had strong domestic support during the war. Although many in Congress had initially questioned the wisdom of war versus allowing more time for sanctions to work, and the vote to authorize the use of force was the closest in American history, war success rallied support.[48] Figure 7.1 below illustrates Bush's approval ratings for the war effort and overall. In both cases, Bush's ratings dropped during the first few months of the buildup but rebounded as war neared and military action broke out.[49] Large-scale participation of the National Guard and Reserve, having an international coalition, congressional authorization, the "rally-around-the-flag" effect, and the "halo effect" resulting from rapid success contributed to popular support.[50]

As they transitioned from an air-centric campaign to a ground war, Bush and his generals continued calibrating the appropriate destruction level of the

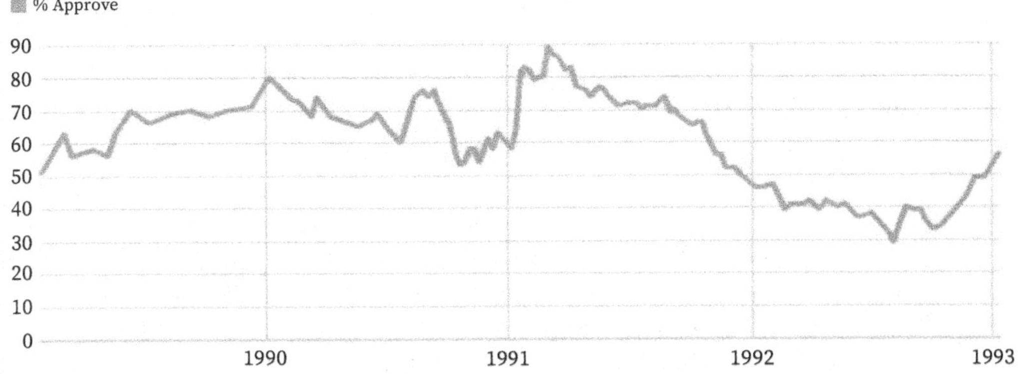

Figure 7.1. President George H. W. Bush's approval rating over time (Courtesy of Gallup, https://news.gallup.com/poll/116677/presidential-approval-ratings-gallup-historical-statistics-trends.aspx).

Iraqi military, particularly the elite Republican Guard.[51] Iraqi air defenses and air force were not a factor, and its army in Kuwait was substantially degraded. Iraqi forces fleeing Kuwait along the one main highway that connected the country with the southern Iraqi city of Basra surrendered en masse to coalition forces. This stretched the ability of US-led forces to manage tens of thousands of war prisoners, which entailed transporting them to the rear and housing and feeding them.[52] It was in this context that Bush made his decision to end the war.

1. WHY WAS THIS A SUNK COST OPPORTUNITY THAT CONSTITUTED A MAJOR POLICY PIVOT POINT?

The lopsided success the American-led coalition experienced and the speed at which the Iraqi military collapsed once the ground war started presented President George H. W. Bush with a unique sunk cost situation. Bush had already deployed more than half a million troops to the region. This presence and the success already experienced presented Bush with an opportunity. He could increase his political aims to accomplish another objective: removing Hussein from power. Hussein had been a destabilizing presence in an area in which the United States had important national security interests, through his invasions of both Iran and Kuwait and by gassing fellow Iraqis. Removing Hussein could be a foreign policy triumph and might lead to a more stable and peaceful Middle East. It could thereby facilitate America and the world's ability to focus on bringing the Israelis and Palestinians together, another major foreign policy objective in the Middle East.[53]

The sunk costs, from this perspective, seemed to have worked to Bush's advantage. Instead of being in a sunk cost trap, he had a sunk cost opportunity. His critical midwar decision point was characterized by unanticipated, rapid success rather than by losses or a prolonged stalemate. Instead of considering whether to escalate commitment to a failing effort, Bush had to decide whether to escalate commitment to a winning endeavor. Secretary of Defense Richard (Dick) Cheney described the sunk cost opportunity this way: "We were faced with an unexpected situation—the prospect of the war coming to an end much sooner than we anticipated. Our forces had moved with much greater speed than we had predicted . . . it was a very sudden shift, after three days of ground operations."[54]

Critics might question the inclusion of the Gulf War as a midcourse de-escalation decision instead of a war termination move. Bush's decision qualifies as a midcourse decision by virtue of the tangible opportunity to extend the war, add to the initially stated aims, and capitalize on the already experienced success to seek more. That success presented opportunities and pressures that a Commander-in-Chief and advisers forged by an education rooted in something other than the Vietnam "avoid a quagmire" lesson would have found hard to ignore. Absent this opportunity to continue and the sunk cost framing, Bush's decision would appropriately be viewed simply as a war termination decision. However, given the context of costs already expended and the potential to decide differently—not just determine when and how to end the war but the possibility to pursue regime change in addition to booting Hussein's army from Kuwait—Bush's decision is best seen as a de-escalation, not a traditional war termination decision. Moreover, war termination decisions are often dependent on negotiations with and actions undertaken by one's enemy, while de-escalations can be done unilaterally, as Bush did.

SUNK COSTS QUANTIFIED AND SALIENCE

Table 7.1 quantifies the sunk costs in time, casualties suffered, money spent, President Bush's personal credibility, and national prestige at risk. Compared to the expected casualty count, which some experts had predicted to number as many as ten thousand, the losses were very minimal.[55] Accordingly, losses were not relevant as an argument to double down on the conflict to prevent those who had been killed from having died in vain—as in the other conflicts. Rather,

TABLE 7.1

George H. W. Bush's Gulf War Sunk Costs (1990–1991)

Time	Desert Shield: 6 months (August 2, 1990–January 16, 1991) Air and ground wars: 6 weeks (January 17, 1991–February 28, 1991)
Casualties	148 battle deaths; 235 other deaths; 467 wounded[1]
Financial Investment	$61 billion in 1990–1991 dollars[2] $102 billion in inflation-adjusted 2011 dollars[3]
Personal Credibility	The president's overall approval ratings were above 60% in the initial stages of the deployment phase beginning in August 1990. However, they began to dip below 60% in late October, hitting their lowest point of 49% in early November before steadily rising again to the low 60% range. Once military action started, his approval rating increased to a high of 89% during the war.[4] As a proxy, that reflected a 40% increase in Bush's political capital from his lowest approval rating during the crisis. Similarly, support specifically for the president's handling of the war fell during the deployment phase from a high of 80% in August to 54% in November. It then climbed slowly until the war's start, again reflecting increased presidential capital.[5]
National Prestige	Bush had to weigh the risks to national prestige of greater action (a potential quagmire yet with the possibility of removing Hussein), versus those of war termination and its inverse risks (a clean exit but continued challenges from a Hussein regime).[6]

[1] Nese F. DeBruyne and Anne Leland, *American War and Military Operations Casualties: Lists & Statistics* (CRS, 2015), 3, https://www.fas.org/sgp/crs/natsec/RL32492.pdf.

[2] "The United States received $53.7 billion to offset costs of $61.1 billion." Richard B. Cheney and Liz Cheney, *In My Time: A Personal and Political Memoir* (New York: Simon & Schuster, 2011), 228. "The incremental costs for the period October 1, 1990, to March 31, 1991 (plus redeployment and return) total nearly $40 billion plus the incremental costs of combat, which cannot be definitively estimated at this point." "Daily Press Releases," February 22, 1991, box 17, White House Press Office, George Bush Presidential Library; "Statement by Press Secretary Fitzwater on Incremental Costs for Operation Desert Shield," Public Papers of the Presidents of the United States: George H. W. Bush, January 11, 1991, Book 1, 31, http://www.gpo.gov/fdsys/pkg/PPP-1991-book1/html/PPP-1991-book1-doc-pg31.htm.

[3] Stephen Daggett, "Costs of Major U.S. Wars, Congressional Research Service (CRS)" (current year figures), 2010, 2, http://cironline.org/sites/default/files/legacy/files/June2010CRScostofuswars.pdf.

[4] "Presidential Approval," Roper Center for Public Opinion Research, Roper Center Public Opinion Archives, accessed October 12, 2015, http://www.ropercenter.uconn.edu/polls/presidential-approval/.

[5] Joseph Carroll, *Like Father, Like Son? Bush on Iraq*, Gallup, 2002, http://www.gallup.com/poll/7000/like-father-like-son-bush-iraq.aspx.

[6] Frank Newport, David W. Moore, and Jeffrey M. Jones, *Special Release: American Opinion of the War*, Gallup, 2003, http://www.gallup.com/poll/8068/special-release-american-opinion-war.aspx; Gallup Poll Organization, "Gallup Poll Finds Public Highly Supportive of War in the Gulf," *Baltimore Sun*, January 20, 1991, http://articles.baltimoresun.com/1991-01-20/news/1991020034_1_war-job-approval-americans.

the potential decision in this case was whether to capitalize on the sunk costs of the military buildup and leverage the success already experienced toward a new aim. Would it be worthwhile to remove Saddam Hussein from office while the military force was still in place? Heading home while allowing Hussein to remain in power might result in more trouble down the road. Why let that happen? Why redeploy forces a number of years later for a second "Gulf War"? That may not be strategically wise in the long term.

2. WHAT WERE THE PRESIDENT'S OPTIONS AND WHAT STRATEGY DID HE IMPLEMENT?

President George H. W. Bush had four real options. The first option was the status quo, the continuance of military operations for another day or more (beyond February 28). This would ensure adequate destruction of the Iraqi military, especially Hussein's loyal and most capable units, the Republican Guard divisions. The second alternative was to push to Baghdad to remove Saddam (i.e., escalate vertically by adding a new political aim, per tab. 7.2), requiring significant diplomatic escalation to keep the Coalition together. The third possibility was to continue the war through proxy forces, also with the goal of removing Hussein. The fourth option was to end the ground war unilaterally. Unilateral de-escalation meant stopping the firing apart from a bilateral agreement with Iraq. A bilateral ceasefire agreement, a carryover from the preground war ceasefire proposals Gorbachev had proffered, was not a part of the discussion among the Bush team or foreign policy leaders beyond the first hours of this period (February 24). Figure 7.2 graphically portrays these options, using the political/diplomatic and military escalation/de-escalation categories in table 7.2.

During the February 25–27 window, it increasingly became clear that getting the Iraqi military out of Kuwait would not necessitate as long or as difficult

TABLE 7.2
Escalation Options

	Vertical	Horizontal
Political	Increased number/type of aims	Seeking/gaining more allies; increased diplomatic activity
Military	Using more lethal weapons or more troops	Attacking other countries/sanctuaries

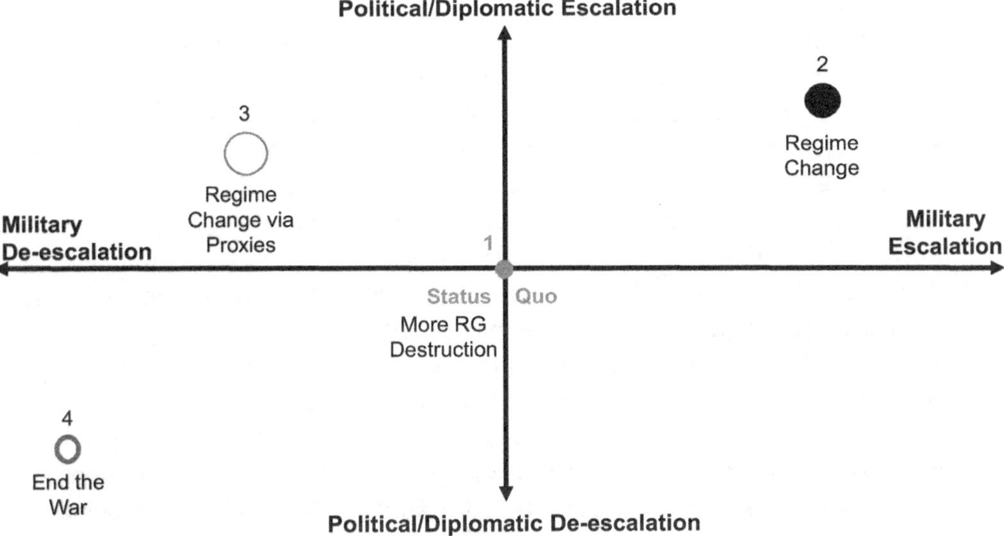

Figure 7.2. Potential presidential policy options in the Persian Gulf in 1991.

a ground war as initially expected, rendering it feasible to consider regime change.[56] Hussein had invaded two countries and had gassed his own people. He had seized Kuwait's massive oil reserves, affecting global oil markets. Additionally, Bush had indicated his desire, both privately[57] and publicly,[58] for Saddam to be ousted.

RATIONALE FOR OPTIONS CONSIDERED

On the evening of February 25, principals debated how long to continue the ground war. Iraqi Foreign Minister Aziz had requested a ceasefire. Aziz contacted the Soviet ambassador in Baghdad, asking him to relay this request through Gorbachev to the UN. The request emphasized that Iraqi leadership had agreed to comply with UNSCR 660 by agreeing to the Soviet peace proposal.[59] Importantly, however, Hussein had not publicly and unequivocally agreed to abide by all of the UNSCRs.

This led George H. W. Bush to reject the Aziz proposal. The key question was whether to let Iraqi units withdraw unhindered at their own pace, retaining their armor, and declare victory, or to continue to attack their retreating formations. Scowcroft believed that it was necessary to continue fighting until Hussein personally and publicly agreed to comply with all the UN resolutions.

Bush concurred.[60] They recognized the corresponding challenge, though, of differentiating between unarmed soldiers and retreating Iraqi formations that might intend to reestablish defensive positions and continue fighting later, from within Iraq.[61] It was an important part of the discussion during that time because Generals Colin Powell and Norman Schwarzkopf, Secretary Baker, and the president realized that continuing the war much longer could result in America being portrayed in the media as wanton killers due to the Iraqi Army's Kuwait exit along the "highway of death."[62] Indeed, there was the "troubling (but accurate) impression that U.S. forces were attacking a retreating enemy."[63]

During the four-day ground campaign, only the precise timing of de-escalation was a serious question. The Bush administration did consider continuing the ground war for another day or two to destroy more of Iraq's Republican Guard and other armor and mechanized infantry units.[64] They did not consider pursuing the status quo as a long-term (weeks or months) option. The other options—unilateral escalation or transition to a proxy war through Shia and Kurd support—were likewise not part of the discussion.[65]

THE DECISION

President George H. W. Bush made the decision to end the ground war on February 27, just hours before reaching the one-hundred-hour milestone. During the afternoon, after a meeting with Douglas Hurd, the British foreign secretary, the president and his advisers discussed coalition progress.[66] "Ground operations had gone far better than the most optimistic of us had dared to hope—with respect to both successes achieved and casualties suffered."[67] Powell and Bush concluded that they were "in the endgame."[68] Enemy strength estimates indicated that "only two or three Iraqi divisions in the combat theater" remained "sufficiently organized to fight as units." Further, Powell stated that "the Basra 'gate' [of encircling coalition forces] would be completely closed by the end of the next day at the latest, cutting off the remaining Iraqi units." Moreover, the "impressions being created in the press about the 'highway of death' from Kuwait City to Basra" was of growing concern to Bush and his advisers as well.[69]

President Bush directed that the coalition ceasefire occur the next morning, February 28, 1991.[70] Bush's de-escalation initially came in the form of a unilateral cessation of hostilities. It followed consultation with civilian and military members of his national security team as well as allies and partners of the coalition. After a unilateral ceasefire, General Schwarzkopf met with Iraqi leaders at Safwan to arrange the details of a prisoner of war exchange and Iraqi compliance with coalition demands and UNSCRs. Although Saddam demonstrated early compliance, including the full withdrawal of his forces from and repudiation of Iraq's claim to Kuwait as its nineteenth province, he soon faced internal uprisings from Iraq's two other major ethnic groups. The Kurds and the Shia both challenged his right to rule. Saddam's grasp on power had been weakened by the Gulf War, both through the loss of military might and through the resulting loss of political legitimacy. To reassert his control, Saddam brutally suppressed both rebellions. At that point, post-war, Bush implemented no-fly zones in both the northern and southern portions of the country. US pilots enforced the no-fly zones for years. These escalations, however, were separate from the de-escalation decision that resulted from the evaluation window of interest in this book—the period at the end of February 1991.

3. WHAT ROLE DID HISTORICAL LESSONS AND FEAR PLAY IN GULF WAR DECISION-MAKING?

> That war [in Vietnam] cleaves [to] us still. . . . I have learned from Vietnam.
>
> —President George H. W. Bush

> Ironically, while Saddam was wrong in thinking that America's Vietnam and Lebanon hangovers would save him from war, the painful lessons learned by U.S. policy makers from those conflicts might have saved Saddam himself from capture [during the Gulf War].
>
> —James A. Baker

THE SHADOW OF THE VIETNAM WAR

As these topline citations indicate, Vietnam War lessons influenced President George H. W. Bush's decision-making regarding how to wage the Persian Gulf War—and when to end it. The Vietnam War had taught American policymakers that they should avoid incremental escalation, instead applying decisive force from the outset. Moreover, they should narrow policy aims to only those that were realistically achievable and essential to accomplish clear US interests.

In addition to the preoccupation with lessons learned from the Vietnam War for the buildup and conduct of the war, Vietnam-era lessons also exerted their influence on the war's ending. In fact, they did so before the war even began. The lesson that a decisive war and rapid exit were paramount influenced the objectives determined in NSDs 45 and 54. Those policy aims, outlined above, forsook any occupation of Iraq, save for contingencies in which

Hussein utilized weapons of mass destruction against US forces, supported terrorist attacks against America or its allies, or destroyed Kuwaiti oil fields.[71] Yet despite the Iraqi destruction of Kuwaiti oil wells, Bush and his team did not consider a march to Baghdad once the war began. He deliberately avoided actions that might contribute to a drawn-out or stalemated endeavor. "Bush feared a march into Baghdad or armed support to the Kurds and the Shiites to overthrow Saddam Hussein would embroil America in an extremely messy civil war, just as Vietnam was."[72]

The Vietnam War lessons that massive force should be used from the start and that civilian leaders should provide clear objectives, but not interfere unnecessarily with the military's conduct of wars, were central to Bush's approach to the Gulf War. Bush's national security adviser, Lieutenant General (Ret.) Brent Scowcroft journaled at the time of Iraqi president Saddam Hussein's invasion of Kuwait, "We should immediately begin marshalling 'a massive force' in the Gulf. As justification, I [Scowcroft] wrote: 'New world order—have to be principled and stand up to aggression. Don't make same mistakes we did in the 30s; *nor* the same as in Vietnam—uncertain, tentative, etc.—if we go in[,] we have to have *massive* force.'"[73] General Powell shared a similar view, later asking for another couple hundred thousand forces, because "we cannot put the United States through another Vietnam" must have enough to accomplish the job quickly.[74]

As the United States assembled a robust coalition to confront Hussein, Bush's rationale—as codified in Scowcroft's early journal entry and Powell's request and later reflection—became readily apparent: "As President Bush and his administration set out to mobilize national opinion in support of a possible new war, a key part of that effort, from the very beginning, was a conscious, explicit campaign to free the country, and its leaders, from the legacy of that earlier conflict in Vietnam. Indeed, it was hard to escape the impression that laying the Vietnam syndrome to rest was itself a major administration goal, perhaps even equal in importance to the goal of defeating Iraq."[75] This objective was remarkably similar to President Ronald Reagan's unsuccessful effort to rid the country of the Vietnam syndrome a decade earlier during the Lebanon intervention.[76]

During the Gulf War, President George H. W. Bush focused more than Reagan did, however, on keeping the military intervention short. Toward this end, he ensured the coalition stuck together, which required accomplishing goals quickly and leaving immediately thereafter.[77] Policy success was due both to the military overmatch established on the battlefield as well these policy determinations in the White House. A seemingly simple decision to capitalize on unprecedented success for other purposes (Iraqi regime change) may have seemed smart in the short term. Having over a half million American troops in the region presented a sunk cost opportunity to address so-called root problems by adding Hussein's ouster to the list of policy goals midcourse. Vietnam lessons, however, suggested that might lead to a barren outcome.[78] Bush deplored mission creep and the precedent set during the Vietnam War of presidents falling prey to the sunk cost effect.[79] President Lyndon Baines Johnson and others repeatedly doubled down on previous commitments, despite a lack of success, always claiming that the next set of reinforcements, policy, or military strategy would make the difference.[80]

Avoiding this sunk cost effect was a vital influence of Vietnam's shadow on Bush's decision-making regarding how and when to end the Gulf War. He was determined to ensure a short war, focused on limited policy aims, that concluded when the US-led coalition had accomplished them.[81] Incremental escalation, underestimation of the enemy, overestimation of the South Vietnam government's capacity, as well as micromanagement and constraints imposed by the White House, contributed to the Vietnam War's length and crippled America's chance to accomplish its policy objectives.[82] Bush and his administration would have none of that. As Cheney later wrote, "Vietnam had shaped the views of America's top generals. They had seen loss of public support for the Vietnam War undermine the war effort as well as damage the reputation of the military. There was a view in the Pentagon, for which I had a lot of sympathy, that the civilian leadership had blown it in Vietnam by failing to make the tough decisions that were required to have a chance at prevailing."[83]

When making those tough decisions during the Gulf War, facing catastrophic success and contemplating how and when to end the conflict, the Vietnam lesson to end wars quickly and on a successful note to avoid a quagmire was the dominant lesson shaping presidential policy. Military leadership reinforced the commander in chief's predilections. "Under the influence of Gen. Colin Powell, . . . the military was determined that U.S. forces should, above all, avoid any prolonged entanglement . . . 'Americans would enter the enemy's territory in force and leave as soon as possible, with no entangling occupation duties or alliances with Iraqi insurgents who might take up arms against the Iraqi dictator.'"[84] The ultimate goal was that "the stain of Vietnam would be removed by a rapid victory, and American forces would exit swiftly. Anything else was a potential snare."[85] So, when the ground war went exceedingly well and the administration faced the opportunity to escalate and continue a bit longer with an added objective, or end the war abruptly, it chose the latter. Bush and "U.S. commanders seem to have been mainly interested . . . in making sure that the war would be concluded in the shortest possible time and that U.S. forces would avoid any entanglement in subsequent events."[86]

Despite the Iraqi destruction of Kuwaiti oil wells, George H. W. Bush and his team did not consider a march to Baghdad at the end of February because they had already eschewed that aim. They avoided the inclusion of regime change as a goal because they suspected it would become a "barren" occupation and result in a lengthy war rather than one ended decisively.[87] Such an outcome was inconsistent with one of the most significant lessons the Bush administration and its generals had learned from US military intervention in Vietnam, and it was therefore one they feared and intensely wanted to avoid. The barren outcome would be a long and messy quagmire that failed to accomplish all the intended policy aims. The lesson to avoid such an outcome was to scope objectives narrowly, mass force and use it decisively, and then end the war rapidly—while things were going well, rather than pursue incremental escalation for expanded goals.[88]

Thus the legacy of the Vietnam War heavily influenced Bush's decision to end the war before it dragged on and lacked a decisive conclusion.[89] He said he would never put US troops "into a military situation that we do not win—ever. And there's not going to be any drawn-out agony [like] Vietnam."[90] Toward that end, Bush stuck to the limited goals he outlined in NSD-45 and NSD-54, pursuing a "no-more-Vietnams" policy.[91] "Both lessons of 'no more Vietnams'—the Vietnam syndrome and the massive force syndrome—may have informed the Bush administration at different points in the war. One lesson played a role in influencing the choice of 'overwhelming force,' and the other lesson played a role in the quick termination of the war."[92]

FEAR OF ANOTHER VIETNAM

> It would not be a Vietnam situation . . . it could be short.
>
> —George H. W. Bush

> We promised this would not be another Vietnam and we kept that promise. The specter of Vietnam has been buried forever in the desert sands of the Arabian Peninsula.
>
> —George H. W. Bush

George H. W. Bush recognized the challenges inherent in finding Hussein, removing him from power, and facilitating the development of a new Iraqi government. The prospect of being "an occupying power in a bitterly hostile land . . . (with) a dramatically different—and perhaps—barren outcome" stemmed any appetite Bush and his administration might have had for going after Hussein.[93] The administration and the military feared the lengthy, messy quagmire that might result from pursuing regime change. A long and arduous occupation without a clean exit ran contrary to Vietnam-era lessons and was therefore an outcome the Bush administration and its generals took action to prevent.[94]

Had Bush not considered the opportunity costs (or trade-offs) involved in a march on Baghdad, the prospect of having a new Iraqi leader in place may have been more appealing. The upside could be a more friendly regime and a more stable Middle East, benefiting America—as well as the world's oil flow and price predictability. The downside of a post-Saddam Iraq was the costs of making it happen. The possibility of and costs associated with coalition collapse, initial governance responsibilities, standing up a nascent Iraqi government, and a messy exit outweighed the potential benefits of installing a more friendly regime.[95] When ignoring the sunk costs of forces already deployed to the theater, the future price tag of installing a more friendly government outweighed the benefits in Bush's eyes.

President George H. W. Bush's decision to end the Gulf War at the end of February was consistent with my "avoid a quagmire" assessment.

> Assessment 1 (Avoid a Quagmire): In the sunk cost traps/opportunity between the Vietnam War and 9/11, Vietnam lessons influenced presidents' de-escalation decisions, having taught them that success in a lengthy war via incremental escalation was doubtful and likely to be regrettable.

The administration and military leadership's reaction to Vietnam as contrasted with Bush's World War II experience necessitated a clear victory and clean exit.[96] Bush and his team purposefully crafted narrow aims well aligned with feasible ways of accomplishing them—such as decisive force and a unified coalition—to increase the chances of rapid success and avoid "another Vietnam."[97] In line with my expectations, the Vietnam-era lesson to avoid a quagmire drove Bush's de-escalation in his sunk cost opportunity—just as it did for Presidents Reagan and Clinton during their sunk cost traps.

4. DID INTERNAL ADMINISTRATION RATIONALE DIFFER FROM THE PUBLIC JUSTIFICATIONS?

> The same words ["this will not be another Vietnam" that were central for Bush and his senior aides] rang in the minds of the country's military leaders, who almost seemed more preoccupied with avoiding a repeat of Vietnam than with achieving the country's objectives.
>
> —Arnold R. Isaacs

Public justifications were consistent with internal administration rationale. In fact, just as they were privately concerned with repeating Vietnam War mistakes,[98] publicly "Bush and his senior aides incessantly promised that war against Iraq would not be 'another Vietnam.' . . . [In fact,] in one press conference in December [1990], . . . the president managed to say it no fewer than three times in the space of seven sentences: 'We are not looking at another Vietnam. . . . This is not another Vietnam. . . . It is not going to be another Vietnam.'"[99]

After the war, the administration responded to some critics who argued that George H. W. Bush ended the war prematurely. To avoid another Vietnam, the Weinberger-Powell Doctrine had urged clear, narrow goals; decisive force; and ending conflicts quickly, victoriously, and without entanglements.[100] Some critics made the case that this had led Bush to end the war earlier than he should have.[101] Continuing the war at least a few days longer to destroy more of Iraq's military might, they said, would have resulted in a better outcome.[102] Others claimed that removing Saddam was necessary for lasting political victory—whether done with the coalition or by supporting the Kurds and Shia in rebellions against the Iraqi dictator.[103] Had America actually removed Saddam from power, critics claim the United States could have remedied past grievances, for which he was the culprit,[104] and avoided subsequent challenges—like the 2003 Iraq War.[105] Critics also claimed that Bush gave the Kurds and Shia false hope by indicating that there was another way for Hussein to be overthrown.[106] The unstated, but often assumed presumption was that Bush meant that the United States would support any Iraqi attempt to overthrow Hussein. He did not.[107]

Even Arab leaders thought the war, despite its brevity and apart from further US action, would be too much for Saddam to survive. On Tuesday, February 26, in the middle of the ground campaign, Egyptian president Hosni Mubarak encouraged Bush to wait two to three days to see how things would play out.[108] The inference was that the path for Hussein's departure might become clearer in short order. Hussein might be toppled as a second-order implication from the coalition's military efforts, or he might flee the country. If he remained in Iraq, his fellow citizens or his military might seize the opportunity to overthrow him because the war had so weakened his grip on the country. When Saddam did not lose his grip on power and it became apparent that the war had not crippled him as much as originally thought, American pundits seized on this critique. In response, Bush and his team publicly made the case for ending the war when they did. Despite the significant debate about these issues since then, however, they were not the focus of internal administration deliberations at the time.[109]

Debate after the war questions whether Bush ended military operations at an appropriate time but fails to address the lack of administration discussions about whether to extend the war. By February 27, the national security team had developed "an unspoken consensus" that it was time to end the war, having met the military objectives and UN resolutions.[110] "There was no dissent" in response to President George H. W. Bush's question of "whether it was time to stop."[111] Powell checked with Schwarzkopf to get the field commander's view. A few more days would have led to greater destruction of important Iraqi military units, but not to the extent of completely preventing them from reinforcing the Hussein regime against the Iraqi people after the war.[112] Moreover, the American military thought it had destroyed sufficient levels of the Iraqi Republican Guard to keep Hussein from threatening his neighbors in the future, which was the real concern at the time.[113] So Schwarzkopf had no objections. He simply asked for time to confer with his subordinate commanders to ensure they could disengage safely from the enemy by 8:00 a.m. Iraqi time on February 28.[114] Following Cheney and Powell's briefing to congressional leaders on Capitol Hill, they reconvened at around 6:00 p.m. Checking again with Schwarzkopf at that time, the field commander indicated that his subordinates had confirmed his tentative approval of the timeline for ceasing hostilities. Bush told Americans three hours later that they had enforced "the line in the sand" and erased the Vietnam syndrome.[115]

A cursory review might leave readers to conclude that Bush and his team stopped military operations simply because they had achieved their objectives. While partially true, that is not the whole story. Vietnam had taught them to take an appetite suppressant and stop while ahead. Recognizing this while still in the planning stages of a potential military operation, and during the decision time, proves Vietnam was the overriding factor in ending the war when Bush did.[116] Hence, despite later debates about the war's conclusion, the desire to avoid another "Vietnam" was at the root of the internal rationale for ending the war when Bush did—consistent with his repeated use of it publicly to justify his decision.[117]

CONCLUSION

> Ultimately, the Persian Gulf crisis would establish in rather convincing fashion that our country's long and oftentimes debilitating post-Vietnam hangover had at least temporarily run its course. In large measure, because Desert Storm was such a resounding success, the American people and their elected representatives now appear more willing to endorse the application of military power under clearly defined circumstances when vital national interests are at stake.
>
> —James A. Baker

As this section's topline quotation suggests, Gulf War success healed some of the nation's psychological wounds from Vietnam, restoring confidence in military and governmental leaders. Even so, some have argued that the Weinberger-Powell Doctrine contributed to a premature closure to the war because of its emphasis on achieving a decisive outcome and ensuring a clean exit.[118] "Rather than overcoming the Vietnam syndrome, Wolfowitz and other like-minded officials believed that Bush and Scowcroft had succumbed to it in their fear of taking on the job of ousting Saddam and transforming Iraq, and had settled on a passive policy of containment that did not solve the fundamental problem America faced from the Baath regime."[119] Despite no permanent resolution to the menace of Saddam Hussein's Iraq, America came away with what President George H. W. Bush wanted most: the achievement of stated policy goals and an entanglement-free exit.

Amid today's mounting US debt, worsened by the 2008 bank bailouts, the COVID-19 pandemic, and stimulus spending, understanding the manner in which presidents think about and respond to sunk cost dilemmas during military conflicts has growing fiscal relevance. Unexpected military success presents a different type of pressure than does failure or stalemate. However, sunk cost traps and opportunities both lead to critical junctures in which presidents make difficult decisions to cut losses, maintain the status quo, double down on their efforts, or develop a hybrid approach. These conflicts raise the question of what, if any, lessons future presidents can learn and apply from past decision-making when in their own wartime sunk cost dilemmas. Chapter 8 addresses this topic.

8

Winning the Next (versus the Last) War

INTRODUCTION

> Sometimes changing objectives is portrayed as mission failure, when in fact in a protracted campaign the likelihood of renegotiating objectives is 100 percent.
>
> —General Martin Dempsey

> Conflict makes us. History makes us. . . . Hangovers from another period can affect what's going on in this period.
>
> —John Lewis Gaddis

The conflict decisions examined in this book reveal that historical lessons act as a filter for strategic calculations among policy elites, ultimately influencing decision outcomes. Between the Vietnam War and 9/11, the Vietnam lesson to avoid quagmires by treating sunk costs as sunk and avoiding incremental escalation was dominant. The fear of their own Vietnam created de-escalatory pressures on presidents, demonstrated in the exits from Lebanon (1984) and Somalia (1993–94). Even in the Persian Gulf War (1991), despite tremendous success, Vietnam lessons shaped President George H. W. Bush's decision to limit his war aims and the conflict's length despite additional, success-driven opportunities.[1] After 9/11, the logic flipped due to new lessons learned, including the need for proactive counterterrorism overseas and counterinsurgency strategies. This created escalatory pressures in Iraq (2007) and Afghanistan (2009) because of presidents' desire to avoid another 9/11 on their watch.

Table 8.1 summarizes my framework's application to the cases. It gives a sense of how lessons triggered fear in each case, together influencing the

TABLE 8.1

Historical Learning and Fear—Applicability across Cases

President (Case)	**Dominant (and Other Operative) Historical Lesson(s)**	**Primary Fear**	**President's Decision**
Reagan (Lebanon)	**Vietnam:** Sunk costs are sunk. Avoid a quagmire by cutting losses when prospects for success are low.	Escalation's potential: A quagmire	De-escalate
George H. W. Bush *(Persian Gulf)*	***Vietnam:*** *Sunk costs are sunk. Avoid a quagmire by cutting losses when prospects for success are low.*	*Escalation's potential: A quagmire*	*De-escalate*
Clinton (Somalia)	**Vietnam:** Stop digging when conflict is going poorly. Lebanon: Reelection after de-escalation is possible.	Escalation's potential: A quagmire	De-escalate (w/ hybrid elements)
George W. Bush (Iraq)	**9/11:** Hunt terrorists proactively abroad. Iraq: COIN is necessary. Vietnam: US must win its wars.	De-escalation's potential: Another 9/11	Escalate (until conditions permit a change)
Obama (Afghanistan)	**9/11:** Hunt terrorists proactively abroad. Iraq: COIN can be successful. Vietnam: US must limit commitment.	De-escalation's potential: Another 9/11	Escalate (for ~18 months)

president's decision. The historical lessons can be thought of as underlying causes, and fear as the proximate cause. The dominant lesson is in bold in the lessons column. It indicates the prime contributor to the president's base decision for de-escalation or escalation (or a hybrid approach). Vietnam lessons influenced de-escalation in the top three, pre-9/11 cases. In the bottom two cases, 9/11 lessons influenced escalation. The Gulf War, the only sunk cost opportunity, is in italics.

My assessments, as initially stated in chapter 2, stood up well under scrutiny. Assessment 1 pertains to the pre-9/11 period, dating from the end of the Vietnam War until 9/11. Assessment 2 applies to the period from 9/11 to the present—until another traumatic lesson supplants 9/11's lesson as dominant for midcourse conflict dilemmas.

Assessment 1 (Avoid a Quagmire): In the sunk cost traps/opportunity between the Vietnam War and 9/11, Vietnam lessons influenced presidents' de-escalation decisions, having taught them that success in a lengthy war via incremental escalation was doubtful and likely to be regrettable.

Assessment 2 (Never Again on My Watch): In post-9/11 sunk cost traps, new lessons taught that proactive counterinsurgency abroad was more effective in protecting America from another major homeland attack than reactive counterterrorism, influencing presidents' escalation decisions to avoid that regret.

The relevant assessment held in all five cases, though it did not account for all the nuanced influences. Older lessons from Vietnam had tremendous resiliency, even beyond 9/11. Other conflicts, including ongoing ones, sometimes played supporting roles. As expected, 9/11 replaced Vietnam-era lessons as dominant predictors of presidents' base policy response, either for de-escalation or escalation. While Vietnam and 9/11 lessons shaped the commander in chief's decision-making, each case's outcome then left lasting shadows of their own—though none (so far) quite as long and dark as that from Vietnam.

ALTERNATIVE EXPLANATIONS

In fairness, determining *the* most significant causal variable is complicated. Given this complex tapestry, presidents' fears often have multiple causes. For instance, eroding public opinion presents presidents with political ramifications. Those matter partly because of the Vietnam War dynamic and the subsequent lesson that public opinion tends to fade as casualties rise.[2] Several competing theories are worth a brief examination to compare their ability to explain presidents' decisions during military sunk cost dilemmas with the analysis my explanation offers.

The rationalist approach to sunk cost theory holds that rational leaders do not include sunk costs in their determinations over whether to continue investments.[3] Instead, they conduct an objective assessment of future costs and benefits and do whatever that analysis indicates will be most fruitful. A second explanation argues that the reason many investors, leaders, and deciders do not act like this but instead include sunk costs in their calculations is that they were responsible for the initial investment or intervention decision.[4] Those making midcourse decisions are more likely to double down on the effort if they were responsible for the initial investment. Their personal involvement makes them more inclined to gamble for success than cut losses.[5] A third explanation is prospect theory.[6] Presidents in a domain of losses will be more risk-seeking, while those in a domain of gains will be more risk-averse.

In each sunk cost trap case, the rationalist theory would predict that the commander in chief would cut losses. The commanders in chief faced difficult continuation decisions because the nation had expended (i.e., sunk) much treasure, effort, lives, and time into the endeavor and was not currently experiencing success, and the prospects of future success looked bleak. However, the rationalist theory would have expected that Bush would have gone to Baghdad to remove Saddam Hussein given the positive prospects of success. Therefore, the rationalist theory accurately explains two of these five cases correctly (Ronald Reagan in Lebanon and Bill Clinton in Somalia).

The theory of personal responsibility for the initial decision would expect that Reagan would double down, as he was responsible for the initial intervention decision (as well as the decision to reintervene with Multinational Force II). It would expect that Clinton would cut losses (not culpable for the initial intervention decision), that George W. Bush would double down (responsible for the initial Iraq intervention decision), and that Barack Obama would cut losses (did not send troops to Afghanistan in the first place). This theory accurately explains two of these five cases correctly (Clinton in Somalia and Bush in Iraq) and does not address how presidents would address sunk cost opportunities, such as the Gulf War case.

Prospect theory would predict that presidents will be more risk-seeking and thus double down on efforts when in a position of losses. That is, when having experienced a recent setback (all four of the sunk cost traps), commanders in chief will be more willing to double down on conflicts (than in a sunk cost opportunity). It is true that there are risks associated with both escalation and de-escalation. Related work from both prospect theory and the sunk cost literature, however, treats additional investment as the riskier commitment.[7] In contrast, prospect theory would predict that presidents will be more risk-averse and therefore cut losses when in a position of gains, when they have recently experienced success (as with the Gulf War). Thus, prospect theory accurately explains three of five cases, including the Gulf War and the post-9/11 surges.

Contrasted with these explanations, my framework is able—with caveats—to explain all five cases accurately. It is able to do so because it uses lessons as the primary explanatory variable rather than prospects for success (cost-benefit analysis), personal responsibility, or the domain of gains or losses. The caveats include that Vietnam-era lessons remained applicable after 9/11, although they were no longer the primary motivator. For Bush, Vietnam's key lesson to "win" wars to avoid "breaking" the military[8] reinforced his 9/11 lesson. For Obama, the Vietnam imperative to avoid a quagmire convinced him to put a timeline on the surge,[9] while 9/11 and Iraq persuaded him, respectively, to surge and implement a counterinsurgency strategy as the main policy components. For George H. W. Bush, Vietnam limited his aims and increased his means before the war started. He then "stuck to his guns" when things went swimmingly well.

Andrew Payne offers a complement to my explanation regarding the timing and implementation behind Bush's and Obama's decisions.

> In both [the Iraq and Afghanistan] cases, electoral constraints clearly had an impact on the nature and timing of key decisions regarding military strategy, with both Bush and Obama seeking to offset the political risk of preferred courses of action in a manner strikingly consistent with the demands of the domestic political calendar. More specifically, both episodes highlight the increasing reluctance to approve and implement plans that entail a prolonged or an increased level of military commitment to a conflict as an election approaches. Elected leaders may deem such proposals strategically beneficial, but the likelihood and timing of their adoption appears to be conditional on the stage of the electoral cycle.[10]

Bush did wait until after the 2006 midterms to announce his decision to bring a new secretary of defense on board. Bush then gave Robert Gates a chance to make his own assessment about the best way forward and offer his advice before Bush finalized his decision and announced it. Yet, according to numerous accounts from his administration's officials, retired flag officers' public admonition to change secretaries of defense convinced Bush that waiting six months minimum was necessary to reinforce civilian control of the military. Hence, it was not the election cycle per se that led to this delay.[11] Nor was it historical lessons, though. Rather, it was considerations related to civil-military relations.

Similarly, the length of Obama's surge did have political undertones, consistent with Payne's election timing argument—but the baseline decision went against his party. Obama limited his surge duration to eighteen months, timed for completion before the 2012 elections.[12] However, his decision in favor of a third large escalation during his first year in office—despite his Democratic colleagues' domestic focus[13] defied political expectations. A key conversation just before Obama's final decision was with his vice president, Joe Biden, who used a Vietnam War vignette—not domestic politics or election cycles—to argue that Obama must be prepared to end the war effort if escalation was not successful.[14] Thus, even while politics and election cycles influenced decision timing and implementation to some degree, those considerations do not negate the central impact of traumatically learned lessons in shaping the decisions themselves. Moreover, without the traumatically learned lessons from the American military experiences during the Vietnam War, 9/11, and subsequent counterterrorism operations—which were shared among executive and legislative branch leaders (as well as the military itself and the American people)—domestic politics would not have had the same influence. Nonetheless, domestic and bureaucratic politics provided venues for lesson-based discourse to occur and amplified their impact. The post-Vietnam cases then produced shadows of their own.

LINGERING SHADOWS

> [In the future, unlike in Vietnam and Lebanon,] the President will not allow our military forces to creep . . . [because] the tests . . . can, if applied carefully, avoid the danger of this gradualist incremental approach . . . [and] help us to avoid being drawn inexorably into an endless morass.
>
> —Caspar Weinberger

> Policy makers and average Americans now "recoil at the thought of another operation that might be of the size—and cost—of Iraq or Afghanistan."
>
> —David Petraeus

Faced with significant dilemmas during overseas military operations, presidents from Reagan onward have wrestled with the shadows of the Vietnam War and 9/11. When operational realities replaced prewar expectations and the status quo was no longer tenable, presidents had to make major policy changes. Rather than individual battles or events, policy decisions—shaped by historical lessons—were the critical factors influencing these operations' eventual outcomes.

When stakes were high and time was short, traumatically ingrained lessons pointed the way out—whether toward withdrawal or doubling down.[15] Those lessons formed a decision filter through which presidents, advisers, and congressional leaders interpreted analytical arguments. The expectation—*not* always accurate—was that similar decisions would yield comparable results in the current scenario. Moreover, fear of a similar outcome as in past failures steered presidents toward another course.

Each of the cases—like Vietnam—has its own shadow.[16] Lebanon's shadow is the codification of the Weinberger-Powell Doctrine encouraging military force only after prudent reflection to ensure it met six tests. Force must be a last resort and US vital national interests must be at stake. Moreover, America must "have clearly defined political and military objectives," apply sufficient resources to ensure it wins, match appropriate resources to the ends sought, and have popular and congressional support.[17] Somalia's shadow precluded intervention in the Rwandan genocide less than a year later.[18] It also led US policymakers to ensure that American troops only serve under US military leadership, not the UN, in future operations.[19] These were the aftermath consequences stemming from the Clinton administration's determination "not to have another Somalia."[20] After 9/11, and in the words of General (Ret.) David Petraeus, as captured in the last of this section's top-line quotations, the shadow of counterterrorism wars is that Americans wanted to avoid future participation in large or expense overseas military endeavors.[21]

The Gulf War's shadow is twofold. First, its success led to a partial and temporary erasure of the Vietnam syndrome and buoyed Americans' confidence in their power and ability to wield it successfully. Second, it convinced other powers, including China, Russia, Iran, and North Korea, to pursue options to win without fighting—at least not fighting symmetrically against American conventional military strength.[22] The persistent shadows from Vietnam and other previous conflicts highlight the ongoing relevance of lessons in shaping policy and the need for strategic approaches for presidents facing major military sunk cost dilemmas.

POLICY PRESCRIPTIONS

The enduring, haunting shadows also mean that we should expect new (or reobserved—if not *learned*) lessons to emerge from these cases, just as they did from the Vietnam War. The next section captures common policy prescriptions emerging from these five conflicts. They are as follows: (1) past performance is no guarantee of future results: presidential engagement throughout is essential; (2) be a prairie dog, not an ostrich: conduct regular war policy reviews to question assumptions and reevaluate progress; (3) follow the Goldilocks principle: align ways and means with ends; (4) heed the cardinal rule of Special Forces selection: do not be late, last, or light; and (5) what you say can and will be held against you: given intended and unintended audiences will use your words for good and ill, prioritize the signals you send.

The most surprising observation, though, may be that presidents fight the last war—just as generals are often blamed for doing. That is, they shift policy during conflicts based on perceptions of what would have produced the best outcome in the last conflict. This is what we saw in each of these cases—the most major operations in the wake of the Vietnam War.

Some lesson-based policy prescriptions were initially implemented poorly or not at all, but later improved on, such as increased presidential engagement over time. Many lessons were repeatedly encountered, evidence that they were not learned by presidents ahead of their own dilemmas but instead had to be relearned the hard way, such as aligning means with ends—or changing those ends. All the cases illustrate the limits of American military power and will.[23]

Presidents' course corrections during the sunk cost traps took between four months (Clinton) and three and a half years (George W. Bush) from the time of plausible realization to announcement. The sunk cost opportunity decision occurred much faster. In one sense, George H. W. Bush made his decision on the evening of February 27, 1991. In reality, and as discussed in chapter 7, Bush made his decision before the war ever began. He did so based on and because of Vietnam's lessons, thereby avoiding the lengthy incapacitation experienced by the other commanders in chief.

While the others lacked an understanding of the war they were in and were paralyzed with indecision about how better to wage it, George H. W. Bush did not suffer these ills. Nor was he tempted to deviate from these policy prescriptions by outstanding success. Bush's lesson-based leadership shows that presidents need not be prisoners to wartime policy paralysis. Five policy prescriptions, taken from Bush's leadership and supplemented by those of other presidents, help presidents prevent and mitigate sunk cost traps. They help commanders in chief determine whether to double down on an intervention or "stop digging" to get out of a sunk cost dilemma.[24]

1. PAST PERFORMANCE IS NO GUARANTEE OF FUTURE RESULTS: PRESIDENTIAL ENGAGEMENT THROUGHOUT IS ESSENTIAL

> [George W.] Bush made crises through neglect and then resolved crises through courage[ous engagement].
>
> —David Frum

Being engaged from beginning to end involves active and critical participation in decisions regarding if to deploy troops *and* the macro-level decisions about how to employ them. It involves influencing the crafting, implementation, and modification of war policy from before committing troops to after bringing them home. It requires critical questions and continually relooking at assumptions. It involves providing matériel and political support to the effort. Presidents must ensure that military strategy supports policy aims, and they must hold commanders responsible for achieving the military successes necessary to support political goals. Being engaged enables changing course in a timely manner to be successful or prevent greater loss. Being engaged means commanders in chief—not generals—are ultimately responsible for the war effort and its outcome, while the military must execute operations and tactics that match presidential policy.

Being engaged enables recognizing and admitting the extent of the problem sooner rather than later. It also enables an accurate understanding of the art of the possible based on the nature of the war and presidents' aims.[25] In my cases, presidents except for Obama recognized, admitted, and addressed the problem only after multiple indicators that problems existed had passed. Presidents Reagan, Clinton, and Bush experienced unfavorable war developments longer than was necessary because they were not actively engaged from the beginning. Reagan long refused to resolve the debate between his two principal cabinet members, Secretary of State George Shultz, who favored American intervention in Lebanon, and Secretary of Defense Caspar Weinberger, who did not. Despite the massacre of UN forces four months before the Battle of Mogadishu, raids that yielded nothing, repeated requests for heavy armor and aircraft support, and a downed helicopter the week prior, Clinton did not direct a clear change in war policy—not one that made it to the troops on the ground.[26] Despite a sectarian war that increased over time and bordered on full-blown civil war, Bush took three years from the completion of major combat operations to swing the policy review into high gear.

Being engaged and willing to make a major policy change is difficult for several reasons, including a preoccupation with other priorities or holding tightly to original aims. Reagan held to his aspiration of stemming Soviet influence in the Middle East and continuing the peaceful solution initially implemented with Israel's exit from Lebanon. Clinton was engrossed with his domestic agenda and learning to govern rather than the intervention in Somalia. George W. Bush deferred to his generals' thoughts about how to conduct the Iraq War. Obama sought change in Afghanistan but also thought he had already embarked on it. Meanwhile, he was focused on domestic rather than overseas nation building as he sought to bring the United States out of a recession.

Ambiguity of other parties' aims, third-party intervention, apparently temporary circumstances, shifting alliances, and other complicating dynamics also cloud reality. These factors led these presidents to continue with the status quo much longer than they should have. Reagan faced uncertainty about how Lebanese militia groups, the Syrian military, and Russia would respond to forceful American actions. Clinton and his administration balanced an evolving United Nations mandate, their own aspirations, and military requests for heavier equipment. To Bush and his team, the Iraqi political situation always seemed close to turning the corner, which they thought would facilitate national reconciliation and decrease violence. Obama did not know how many additional troops the North Atlantic Treaty Organization (NATO) and other partners would contribute or the full effects of his first two escalations, as those forces had not all arrived in theater at the time of his surge decision.

Despite the challenges, presidents can change the seemingly unchangeable—but not always to mission accomplishment. Presidents can change priorities and hence the resources allocated for a mission. They and their principal advisers can question foundational assumptions, direct a zero-based review, redefine the problem, and prod the development of creative solutions that utilize all applicable elements of national power. Sometimes presidents use these measures to adjust course by cutting losses or by doubling down or conducting a hybrid strategy. Reagan and Clinton determined that they could not achieve their aims at a price they were willing to pay and withdrew forces, though Clinton escalated to facilitate a six-month withdrawal. After review, Bush and Obama decided they might achieve at least a version of what they were after if they increased the means they were employing.

The contrast in results *can* be significant when a president is engaged. Among my cases, this is seen most clearly once George W. Bush decided on a new war policy for the Iraq War. He eventually got engaged after prodding from multiple fronts, including by *Supreme Command* author Eliot Cohen. Cohen argued that presidential leadership in crafting and adjusting war policy leads to better outcomes.[27] Following Bush's reevaluation and change in Iraq War policy, Cohen's thesis played out, and the contrast in results was stark. Population support went up. Control of territory increased significantly, and violence went down remarkably.[28]

Presidential engagement can facilitate the development of a successful war strategy, but its implementation also requires presidential attention. In

America, one of the requirements for successful war policy implementation is that the commander in chief also be the rallier in chief. The democratic election cycle attunes presidents to the political winds related to their policies. Ultimately, they require popular support for reelection and successful policy. Thus, presidents' rationale for war is important because it can help build and maintain public support. When Americans are war-weary or the importance of US involvement is not clear, this becomes especially critical.

The commander in chief must explain the objective and the stakes clearly. The rallier in chief must make a strong case that the benefits are worth the costs and that the strategy employed has good prospects for success.[29] Bush rallied the American people and Congress by stating his case, changing his commander on the ground, changing strategies, levying more resources to the effort, and bringing his general and ambassador home periodically for congressional hearings. Making these decisions and going to this effort when other priorities beckon is not easy. However, it can maintain a president's freedom of maneuver, preventing a foreclosure of options due to souring public opinion.

Presidential engagement is a necessary but insufficient condition for the development and implementation of a successful war policy. The necessity of regular reassessments facilitates presidential engagement and necessary adjustments.

2. BE A PRAIRIE DOG, NOT AN OSTRICH: CONDUCT REGULAR WAR POLICY REVIEWS TO QUESTION ASSUMPTIONS AND REEVALUATE PROGRESS

> Predictions and assumptions about war should never be trusted uncritically.
>
> —Colin S. Gray

> All armies get it wrong at the beginning . . . the question is who adapts fastest.
>
> —Michael Howard

In each of the sunk cost traps, presidents pursued their aims for too long without questioning or addressing the underlying assumptions. This is typical, as "leaders attempt to impose prewar conceptions on the war they are fighting, rather than adapt their assumptions to reality."[30] However, "we rarely win wars with the same force or the same strategy [that we started them with]. Wars . . . require leaders to assess progress, recognize shortfalls, and resolve gaps in strategy or operational method as the conflict evolves. This assessment and adaptation function is often overlooked."[31] This was true for too long during the four sunk cost traps examined herein. The Iraq War presents an especially rich example. The following paragraphs provide an example of policy prescriptions 1 and 2 at work in that case. They also provide a cautionary tale of challenges to navigate while conducting war policy reviews.

One of the reasons that it took the George W. Bush administration so long to determine how badly the Iraq War effort was going was that it hesitated to question the judgment of commanders in the field. This was especially true of someone like General John Abizaid, a Lebanese American and Middle East expert who spoke Arabic fluently and understood the region as well as anyone in government.[32] Another reason was due to lessons learned from Vietnam and George W. Bush's attempt to avoid the perceived mistakes President Lyndon Johnson had made in micromanaging the military and determining targets from the White House.[33] Eliot Cohen tried to disabuse Bush of this Vietnam lesson during a December 2006 session with other outside experts.[34] "Cohen rebutted Bush's Lyndon Johnson analogy, saying the failure in Vietnam was not micromanagement but a failure to force a serious strategic debate."[35] Another reason it took a long time to do a zero-based review was because of Iraqi political developments (constitution ratification, elections, and seating of the government) that led US officials to believe that the current strategy might work with more time. Unfortunately, events had to spiral deeply out of control before it was clear to the administration that a significant policy adaptation was necessary.[36]

Regular war policy reviews should examine and address problems of bad assumptions and misapplied lessons as well as rigid strategic approaches unfit to the war. Leaders must adapt to reality instead of being wedded to the plan. General George Casey and Ambassador Zalmay Khalilzad did not. They should have recognized that the Iraqis would not be ready to take control of security according to the timelines under which President Bush was operating. By the summer of 2006, Casey should have recognized that US politics required strategy adjustments, that his commander in chief wanted a military change, and that the situation required it. Instead, he insisted on minimal changes to the status quo.[37]

Regardless of how one judges the effectiveness of the Iraq War surge, George W. Bush addressed these deficiencies. He and his advisers realized that they must be more engaged[38] (policy prescription 1) and that some of their assumptions were incorrect. They recognized that the coalition could not be effective in achieving its objectives without first establishing security.[39] They came to believe that protecting the Iraqi populace should replace killing the enemy as task one.[40] And they came to these realizations through a thorough review process (hence this policy prescription).

Reviews can offer opportunities for engagement on many levels that facilitate such realizations. Presidents can engage with their ambassadors and field commanders in preparation for and following congressional hearings. Relevant intelligence and other agencies can intentionally update and coordinate their policy approaches with those of the State and Defense Departments based on threat evolution or changes in the domestic and international contexts. This can affect the Office of National Intelligence, the Central Intelligence Agency, the Federal Bureau of Investigation, and the Departments of Justice, Treasury, Energy, and Commerce. Congress can exercise its oversight role. The press can cover the unclassified portions of the hearings, and the American people can provide their input to their representatives. Thus, these reviews present natural opportunities to reevaluate the level of effort that the operation is worth. That calculation should include trade-offs in time, casualties, money, and anticipated outcomes. Presidents should opt for war continuation only when the benefits that *may* be accrued exceed the costs that *will* be incurred.[41] They should follow Clausewitz's injunction to stop waging war as soon as the cost exceeds the objective's value.[42]

Policymakers—like generals—should not fight the last war. They cannot "assume that past successes can be replicated merely by performing past actions."[43] Contexts vary. The current war will require different approaches and adaptations than did the last. Conducting regularly scheduled war policy evaluations, involving Congress and the press, would be a forcing function to recalibrate ends or ways, bringing them into alignment (policy prescription 3). Even if policymakers do not identify the likely challenges before a war's onset, reevaluations that include regular visits to the war's front lines may uncover them. For this to happen, though, presidents and their advisers must undertake visits for that purpose—not just for troop morale. Such consistent, systematic azimuth checks can facilitate the determination of mistaken assumptions and misguided policies. This is what eventually occurred during the Iraq War once the administration undertook a wholesale reassessment. Yet an earlier determination would be better. And even if a war is going relatively well, reappraisals can determine better ways to attack the enemy and accomplish US goals.

Reviews are not a silver bullet solution. They will not always produce change, nor will change always lead to victory. However, they are more likely to produce needed change than conducting wars without regular reviews. While relevant changes are not an end unto themselves, they are a potential means toward successful war outcomes.

Whether in a sunk cost trap or progressing toward national goals, if the aim warrants military action, it is important enough to conduct reevaluations of progress, policy, and strategy. If the approach is failing to achieve policy ends, the military strategy can be changed, the policy goals modified, or the effort abandoned. Semiannual reassessments would allow for course corrections no more than six months after straying down the wrong direction. This would improve on the more than ten months it took in Lebanon, the three and a half years in Iraq, and the eight years in Afghanistan before presidents acted to review war policy.

In their war policy reviews, presidents would do well to consider various options. The status quo can be one—but not the only—course explored. Alexander George's "multiple advocacy" can be helpful in avoiding groupthink, recognizing and avoiding biases, and reaching optimized decisions. Rather than one "devil's advocate," this approach utilizes advocates for each potential course of action. In addition, ensuring adequate time for discussion and debate surfaces the assumptions, advantages, and potential disadvantages associated with each proposed course and may even lead to the adoption of a hybrid option. Advocates should identify the assumptions underlying suggested courses of action. Presidents should query both the potential policy's adherents and nonadherents regarding the probability of success and what that assessment is based on.[44] Reevaluating and adjusting war policy regularly in this manner—before it unmistakably constitutes a sunk cost trap—can help ensure that future US warfighting accomplishes presidents' aims as quickly as possible and at the least possible cost.

3. FOLLOW THE GOLDILOCKS PRINCIPLE: ALIGN WAYS AND MEANS WITH ENDS

Alignment between ends and means occurs when presidents exercise means commensurate with the ends they want to achieve. Misalignment occurs when that is not the case. If a president's aims are significant but the means he is applying are insufficient to achieve them, his war policy lacks ends-means alignment. The same is true if his objectives are small but he employs significant resources toward their achievement.

Almost by definition, the latter category—narrow ends and robust means—is not a problem in sunk cost traps. That situation is more likely to lead to the successful accomplishment of ends rather than shocking battlefield tragedy, failure, or a prolonged stalemate. War policy in the Gulf War followed that approach. President George H. W. Bush assembled a massive coalition to oust Iraqi forces from Kuwait. He accomplished that aim quickly, convincingly, and with relatively few casualties.

George H. W. Bush's rapid success during the Gulf War presented the opposite dilemma—that of widening ends without sufficient means. Given the sunk costs of deploying half a million troops to the region, Bush could have added another objective: removing Iraqi president Saddam Hussein from power. He decided, however, not to widen his goals to include Iraqi regime change, a move that would have changed the war from a limited to an unlimited one. Interestingly, just as with the pre-9/11 sunk cost traps, Vietnam War lessons influenced that decision-making. In the Gulf War, it was Vietnam's lesson to keep a narrow objective, use overwhelming force, and ensure a clean ending versus a drawn-out quagmire that led to President George H. W. Bush's decision.[45]

The Gulf War is an example of how presidents can have a disparity between ends and means without experiencing battlefield failure. Nonetheless, the application of more resources than are needed to accomplish an aim is an opportunity cost issue. It may impact other policy priorities. The attention required to prosecute a war affects presidents' focus on the rest of their policy agenda. An over-resourced war may rob these other issues of time and attention.

On the other hand, executing a war with robust ends and insufficient means often becomes a *real* problem. It was an issue during each of the four major sunk cost traps America has faced since the Vietnam War. Despite the significant goals the United States sought in Lebanon, it did not match its means to its ends. Given the ambitious aims to secure Lebanon, restore peace, and counter Soviet influence in the Middle East, one might have expected that President Reagan would have applied robust means to accomplish them. He did not. The marine peacekeeping force was relatively small. Moreover, they lacked the requisite training and authorities. And Reagan did not conduct punitive strikes against those responsible for bombing US facilities. Where he did use force, it backfired. Ostensibly, American involvement was as a neutral third-party power enforcing the peace between the Israeli military and Lebanese militias. Firing naval guns at positions held by the militia groups in September 1983 (before the barracks bombing) violated the perception of US neutrality, complicating mission accomplishment. Using continued US engagement as a bargaining chip to persuade combatants to achieve a better peace would have been a more effective alignment of ends and means.[46] It would have leveraged American military strength and ongoing involvement to achieve a diplomatic solution.

Before the Battle of Mogadishu, Clinton's ends were also out of proportion with his means. Clinton's aims had evolved from a humanitarian assistance focus to include man hunting and political stability. Yet he was not applying the requisite resources diplomatically, politically, or militarily to accomplish those robust aims. Reflecting on the Black Hawk Down tragedy, Clinton determined that national interests did not warrant expanded or indefinite commitment.[47] His main adjustment, therefore, was to decrease his aspirations, which I address further below.

During the first part of the Iraq and Afghanistan Wars, Bush and Obama did not apply enough forces, assets, civilian expertise, diplomacy, or political capital to the war effort. Bush's aims were significant. He wanted to rid Iraq of weapons of mass destruction, conduct regime change, and bring democracy and stability to Iraq. The number of troops in Iraq, operating from large bases, were unable to provide a secure environment for political reconciliation and economic reconstruction. With violence out of control, the resources Bush applied and the ways he utilized them were not sufficient to accomplish his goals.

A couple of years later, Obama sought to correct what he saw as his predecessor's undue economy of force effort against America's real enemy in Afghanistan: al-Qaeda and the Taliban.[48] His concern was that Bush had used too few resources to go after what he thought should be a major policy effort. Al-Qaeda was the source of the 9/11 attack, its leaders were still at large, and violence across Afghanistan was increasing. These were facts that constituted a threat worthy of significant effort in Obama's eyes.[49] These examples show that unbalanced ends and means cause dilemmas when the aims are great and the means utilized to achieve them are too limited. A major war policy change is necessary to realign them by cutting losses and de-escalating, or by doubling down on the conflict to provide more realistic odds of success.

Successfully navigating the United States out of these sunk cost traps required presidents to realign their means with their policy aims. To realign his ends and means, a president can adjust either his objectives (ends) or the strategies (ways) and the resources (means) utilized to accomplish his ends.[50] In a sunk cost trap, a president adjusting his ends narrows his objectives, making them less ambitious. This is what Reagan did in Lebanon when he chose to pull forces out. He lowered his policy aims to what had already been achieved (initial peace settlement and Israel's withdrawal from Lebanon). Meanwhile, he dropped that which had proven elusive (Middle East peace and a stable Lebanon). It is also what Clinton did in Somalia. He claimed success by focusing on the humanitarian assistance provided to the Somalis while eschewing nation-building efforts and the hunt for warlords that continued to ransack the country and prevent the political stability Clinton had sought.[51]

Clinton decreased his aims to support reconciliation among Somali clans while securely withdrawing troops and transitioning to UN-led efforts. His hybrid approach, though, involved more than decreasing his aims. Initially, Clinton nearly doubled the military assets in and off the coast of Somalia. He escalated to de-escalate. He applied the resources necessary to disengage safely and turn over the mission to the United Nations and the Somalis themselves. That was an example of decreasing aims and temporally increasing means. Together, these steps brought Clinton's ends and means in alignment and led to the successful execution of his policy.

A president keeping his ends constant would have to change his ways or increase his means to align the two and improve prospects for success. This is what Bush did in Iraq and what Obama did in Afghanistan. Bush surged forces and civilians, embraced counterinsurgency strategy, and installed new leadership. With this policy change, he aimed to correct the ends-means misalignment caused by too few forces (means) and an inappropriate strategy of hunkering down on a few big bases (ways) that he had been using to achieve ambitious aspirations (a stable, democratic Iraq that was a counterterrorism partner). Similarly, Obama escalated troop levels, sent more civilians, conducted regional diplomacy, took up a counterinsurgency approach, and reached out to allies to contribute more military forces. His changes also addressed a lack of balance between ends and means. Both war policy changes rectified ends-means misalignment through increased means instead of decreased ends.

War policy appraisals (policy prescription 2) facilitated these realignments of ends and means. In the pre-9/11 cases, the actual decision process appeared extremely short. In the Lebanon case, this involved a short phone call between Reagan and his vice president, George H. W. Bush. In the end, Reagan approved a withdrawal from Lebanon. This decision came after publicly endorsing the mission just the day prior. In the Somalia case, Clinton's decision followed a few days of deliberation prompted by the Blackhawk Down tragedy. In both cases, however, the sequence of incidents leading up to these distinct decision periods led to reflection on American military involvement.[52] So Reagan's and Clinton's decisions had been brewing longer than might have been revealed at first glance. Bush's and Obama's decisions were deliberate and lasted months. In all cases, adjustments of ends, ways, or means brought them into balance.

4. HEED THE CARDINAL RULE OF SPECIAL FORCES SELECTION—DO NOT BE LATE, LAST, OR LIGHT: RAPIDLY IMPLEMENT CREATIVE, DECISIVE, AND HOLISTIC POLICY CHANGES—BEFORE THE BAD GUYS

During selection for the US Army Special Forces (more commonly known as the Green Berets), it is important never to be late for a formation, never to be last in completing an event, and never to pack less weight than required for events. Likewise, presidents must not be late to implement necessary policy changes, continually trail the enemy's actions, or take indecisive, half measures. Failure to anticipate, learn, and adapt during armed conflict and peacekeeping missions can prevent strategic success.[53] Only by anticipating, learning, and adapting can presidents emerge from their sunk cost traps and wrap up their wars. Although the particulars of wars' developments are impossible to presage, presidents can be assured that they will face difficult and unexpected decisions midcourse. These should not be completely unexpected, but they sometimes appear to be, as with Clinton and his administration being very surprised by the Blackhawk Down tragedy despite an American helicopter having been shot down the week prior.[54] The previous policy prescriptions address the concept that sustained military operations will require adaptation, or a new definition of success.[55] This policy prescription furthers that discussion by urging comprehensive and creative solutions to sunk cost traps, including steps to help prevent them. This is important since, as the section's topline citation indicates, unintended and unexpected consequences make finishing wars more challenging than starting them.

Before an intervention, presidents could identify preconditions under which either side might escalate significantly and then attempt to prevent those from happening. Inherent in that process would be understanding the enemies' objectives and expectations, as well as their own, and preventing the "sense of a closing future" in which only the "worst possibilities" remain.[56] Based on that analysis, presidents could credibly communicate "redline" thresholds or a "golden bridge" to adversaries for deterrence and conflict "exit ramps," respectively.[57] Presidents in my cases eventually pursued exit ramps that sometimes included versions of redlines or a golden bridge, but they were not quick adaptations to unexpected developments. In a December 1983 press conference, a year and a half after the initial intervention, Reagan indicated that a collapse of the Lebanese government—though unanticipated—could lead to an American departure. This happened less than two months later. That was not a golden bridge or a redline, but it was an exit ramp. In Somalia, Clinton used a redline to communicate clearly to Mohamed Farrah Aideed (through Envoy Robert Oakley) that the United States would stop hunting Aideed if he returned Chief Michael Durant immediately. Clinton did this four months after forces purportedly linked to Aideed ambushed a UN force. In Iraq, after three and a half years of sectarian violence, Bush forced Iraqi prime minister Nouri al-Maliki to publicly align himself with US policy intentions before Bush would send additional troops. This was neither a redline nor a golden bridge toward an adversary. It was part of Bush's decision criteria. It was also part of what would be his eventual exit ramp through persuading partner policy alignment. In Afghanistan, eight years after 9/11, Obama required partner contributions to fill out the US escalation. He also sought an exit ramp with an eighteen-month surge time limit and a plan for security transition to Afghans.

Presidents should also understand the rigid ways in which governmental departments often respond to problems—rigidity that can preclude effective solutions. Standard operating procedures generally lack nuance and can lead to decision-making during national crises that is too decentralized and that does not meet the commander in chief's intent. Presidents need to remember that their cabinet officials and agencies have their own bureaucratic agendas and that those may work at cross purposes with each other or with his aims.[58] The policy differences between Reagan's secretary of state George Shultz and his secretary of defense Caspar Weinberger illustrated this dynamic during American involvement in Lebanon from 1982 to 1984. Shultz favored US intervention; Weinberger increasingly became opposed to it. Further, use-of-force preference differences[59] may bias generals' advice in favor of "going heavy" to "win" to improve their institutional legitimacy and perceived effectiveness.[60] This rationale influenced the military chain of command during decision-making about the war in Afghanistan.[61] In fact, military leaders' preferences and actions caused President Obama to feel like the military was attempting to box him in.[62] That happens when advisers do not present a full array of options to the president. Instead of having options that span the four quadrants shown in figure 8.1, they may all be in one quadrant, with minimal differences, and focused solely on troop levels instead of multiple levers of national power.

Figure 8.1 showcases the differences between the pre-9/11 de-escalations (in the bottom-left quadrant) and the post-9/11 escalations (in the top-right quadrant). It portrays presidents' sunk cost dilemma decisions in terms of escalation and de-escalation, both militarily and politically/diplomatically. The

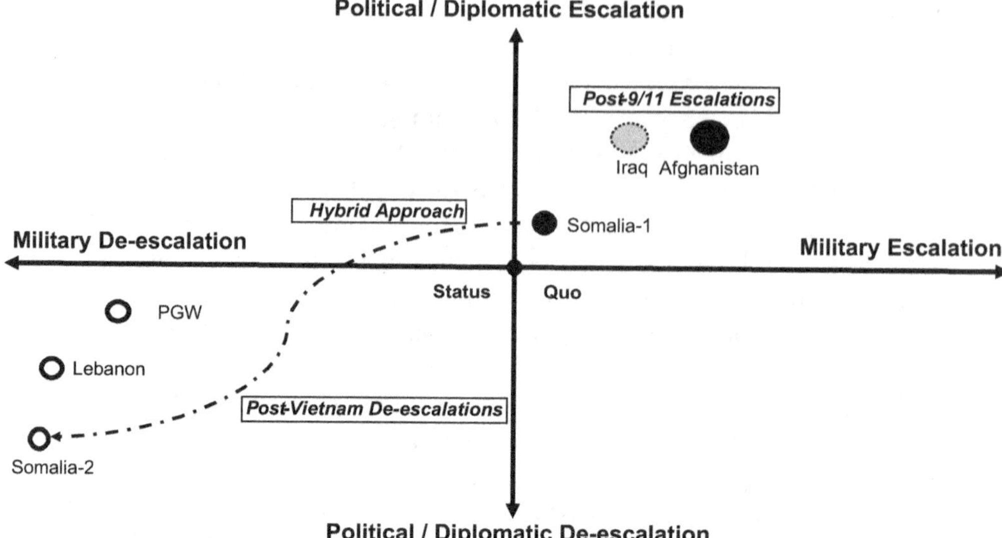

Figure 8.1. Potential presidential policy options for all the military conflicts examined in *When Presidents Fight the Last War.*

closer the decisions are positioned to the middle of the graph, where the two axes intersect, the less change they proposed and the more they resemble status quo efforts. The inverse is also true. The farther away from the center a decision is, the more change it involved and the less it resembled the status quo.

As portrayed, presidents considered options with different degrees of military and political/diplomatic de-escalations and escalations. However, in some cases, several options varied little, other than in the number of additional forces added and, subsequently, what those forces could accomplish militarily. Those options reflected a gravitation to military options instead of more broadly conceived solutions. The need for creativity and unconventional, balanced, or nonmilitary-generated strategies has served presidents well—such as during the Cuban Missile Crisis—and presidents should keep it as a paramount consideration during major national security decisions. Graphically, the military-heavy focus in the decision making during these cases sometimes resulted in options that consisted of a close grouping of dots along the x-axis. Yet the four quadrants emphasize that a range of options exist, supporting policy prescriptions 4 and 5: creative, holistic approaches to policy changes and robust strategic communication to various audiences.

For creative presidents, the options are much more diverse than those belied by a recent, simplistic focus on force levels—such as in debates over surges in

Iraq and Afghanistan.[63] As figure 8.1 shows, presidents can manipulate options in the number of additional troops deployed or those withdrawn. But they can also change the type of mission those forces conduct. They can adjust the intensity of diplomacy undertaken and the breadth of its focus bilaterally, regionally, or globally. They can modify the amount of capital expended on domestic politics to secure popular and congressional support. They can determine the pace at which changes will be implemented, within the constraints of the US military's available lift capacity. They can also determine how long to apply certain measures and their sequencing.

Presidents' combination of these elements involves creativity, and they can tailor their approach based on the specific situation they face. Different adjustments will be necessary in different circumstances. It is a strategic calculation to determine which levers to pull, in what order, and for what period to achieve the desired outcome. Which allies, overseas and at home, are critical? What type of military strategy should they pursue, and which generals are best to lead the war? How can economics, politics, diplomacy, and interagency elements contribute? It is the presidential advisers' responsibility to develop cogent answers to these questions and to develop options across the escalation spectra (most/all four quadrants).

It does the president and the nation a disservice when options instead focus only on troop levels. When options are close together or all in a single quadrant, it demonstrates that the president's team did not exhibit creativity in developing options or that circumstances, combined with presidential direction, narrowed the scope of serious options. In most cases, even if he had not been actively involved in directing the intervention up to the time of decision, the commander in chief chose a course that varied from the presented options. Presidents often do not accept an option in its recommended form but modify it based on their own ideas.

Despite the relative congruence of options presented to them (only differing in military force levels and what they could achieve), Presidents Clinton, Bush, and Obama implemented creative responses. President Clinton conducted a hybrid approach: immediate escalation to enhance force protection for the transition to the United Nations. President George W. Bush made a very tough decision during the Iraq War to double down on a war that had long been going poorly and despite a war-weary public.[64] President Obama made a similar decision in that he escalated and adopted a counterinsurgency strategy, and he did so in the face of a war-weary public. This was different from Bush's response in that Obama required a fourth of the surge to come from other nations, placed a time constraint on its length, and made his fall 2009 decision after two escalations just months prior. Both Bush's and Obama's decisions coupled the military surges with civilian ones. They both utilized civilian, interagency elements to join military members on Provincial Reconstruction Teams. Finally, they both conducted regional diplomacy—against Iran and with Pakistan, respectively. The administrations crafted these policies after deliberate reassessment and by incorporating elements of policymakers' proposals along with the military's options.

Even so, there is room for improvement—namely in rapid adaptation when reality diverges from expectations. In the Iraq War case, if civilian policymakers had a better understanding of what the military could accomplish and exhibited less deference to military leaders, they might have changed war policy earlier, bridging the gap between means and desired outcomes. In the Afghanistan War case, Obama did not act in a way that demonstrated he understood that Afghanistan was not Iraq. He and his national security team did not realize that a similar template would not work because of the different tribal dynamics, different (mountainous) terrain, greater al-Qaeda (and Taliban) sanctuary problems, and no enemy catastrophic failure mechanism. The Golden Dome Mosque bombing was such a mechanism in Iraq. It contributed to the Sunni Awakening and realistic prospects of success against al-Qaeda in Iraq. There was no such opportunity for enemy overreach in Afghanistan because of its population's greater diversity. Had Obama truly grasped all this, he could have ratcheted down his aims, as Vice President Joseph Biden proposed. Instead, Obama pursued ends-means alignment by increasing means and changing the strategy employed.

The key to prevent, mitigate, or work one's way out of a wartime sunk cost trap is to follow the policy prescriptions laid out here. They involve early and consistent presidential engagement; regular reassessments and adaptations; ends-means alignment; rapid, creative, and holistic responses to the unexpected; and strategic communication. I have covered the first four thus far. The fifth is the subject of the last policy prescription arising from my cases.

5. WHAT YOU SAY CAN AND WILL BE HELD AGAINST YOU: GIVEN INTENDED AND UNINTENDED AUDIENCES WILL USE YOUR WORDS FOR GOOD AND ILL, PRIORITIZE THE SIGNALS YOU SEND

Effective communication across multiple audiences is critical during wartime sunk cost traps. A couple of these audiences include the American people and

Congress. Clinton and his administration failed to engage sufficiently with Congress and to inform the American people about the changing nature of the intervention from the spring to the fall of 1993. Following United Nations Security Council Resolutions 814 and 837 in March and June, respectively, the mission shifted from one solely addressing the humanitarian crisis to one that included Task Force Ranger's deployment to hunt Mohamed Farrah Aideed. When Black Hawk Down happened, the American people awoke to find a much different and expanded mission from that initially embarked on. The result was a domestic push to cut losses, sensing that whatever the administration had been up to in Somalia was not worth the costs it entailed.

On the other hand, regular and clear engagement facilitates support for an administration's war policy amid setbacks. The administration, and specifically the president, must confer regularly with congressional leaders and the public about what the mission is, why it is important, what criteria must be met before bringing troops home, and what the prospects for success are. Clear communication on these topics offers the best chance of gaining and maintaining support. This type of engagement in sunk cost traps is most important if a president wants to continue a policy that goes against the current of domestic political opinion—as President George W. Bush did during his Iraq War sunk cost trap. It is *relatively* less so if a president wants to change his own policy in the direction of majority sentiment—as President Reagan did after the Beirut bombing or President Clinton did after Blackhawk Down.

Another facet of communication is that actions can have different effects on multiple audiences. President Reagan's decision to withdraw marines from Lebanon in February 1984 sent different signals to different audiences. The American people were generally in favor of freeing the country of an overseas entanglement. Moreover, voters did not hold the departure against Reagan later that year when they went to the polls in his reelection bid. Reagan trounced Walter Mondale, winning forty-nine states and 58.8 percent of the popular vote.[65] In this, the Lebanon situation revealed that the American public could forgive a sitting president for a military setback—that is, leaving an operation on a sour note after a shocking tragedy. Therefore, Lebanon provides a powerful example that presidents can let sunk costs remain sunk and that a military loss does not necessarily condemn their reelection prospects.[66]

Future terrorists interpreted Reagan's exit from Lebanon differently; rather than illustrating strength by reprioritizing efforts toward more fruitful endeavors, they saw it as demonstrating US weakness. Osama bin Laden referred to the United States' failure to respond to the Beirut embassy and marine barracks bombings in his 1998 declaration of war against America.[67] Bin Laden thought that the lack of an American response meant that terrorists could strike the United States with impunity and that doing so could contribute to a major change in US foreign policy. Thus, in some ways, Lebanon set the stage for the beginning of America's current war on terrorism.[68]

The Blackhawk Down tragedy in Somalia offers another example where the president's response and messaging during a sunk cost trap had varying impacts on different audiences. Clinton's consultation with Congress and a hybrid strategy pacified the legislature and satisfied the American public. Yet some believe the United States sent a signal of weakness through its response to the Black Hawk Down tragedy.[69] Among those with this view were members of the American military establishment. Others who shared this view included non-state actors that would declare war on the United States in the coming years.[70] Like with the US intervention in Lebanon, al-Qaeda saw the American departure as premature. Contrary to Clinton's professed aim,[71] the six-month window between the Battle of Mogadishu and the American exit from Somalia did not negate Osama bin Laden's and al-Qaeda's view that it was a "cut-and-run" strategy.[72] Rather, they believed that two superpowers had been defeated in less than five years by nonstate actors. First, mujahedeen (albeit with American support) forced Soviet withdrawal from Afghanistan in 1989. Second, a Somali warlord pushed America from Mogadishu in 1993.

Obama's decision to limit the surge in Afghanistan's duration, announcing its end time along with the escalation strategy itself, also sent divergent signals to different audiences. Domestically, it signaled to a war-weary country that he wanted to prioritize nation building at home versus abroad. To the military, it signaled that their requests for additional troops would not be met wholesale and without caveat. Many in the military viewed it as an imprudent move because it set a timeline for the withdrawal of the additional forces instead of deciding that based on improved security conditions. This was perceived as signaling to American enemies—the terrorists the country was fighting in Afghanistan and Pakistan—that they only needed to wait out the United States. To the Afghan government, Obama intended to signal that American commitment had its limits, so they needed to act quickly to increase their security and governance capability and capacity. To the international community, it communicated that the end was within sight. Foreign leaders could point to the US president's timetable as not too far off if pressured by their domestic constituencies to abandon the coalition sooner.[73]

Three of these cases—Lebanon, Somalia, and Afghanistan—demonstrate the challenges associated with communicating intent during wartime sunk cost dilemmas. The actions one audience interprets a certain way are often seen in another light by others. No clear right or wrong exists in these situations, but the trade-offs are critical. Reagan, Clinton, and Obama prioritized the audiences and arguments favorable to de-escalating, a hybrid strategy and one offering an endgame timeline, respectively. Other presidents would likewise do well to consider the trade-offs and decide accordingly.

Finally, it is worth noting that in most cases there were differences between the private rationale and public justifications for the policy change decisions. Presidents and their administrations sought to spin things in one way to sell it, but the factors mentioned to the public were not always the primary influencers behind closed doors. For instance, in the Lebanon case, the Reagan administration publicly characterized as "redeployment" what it recognized privately as a "withdrawal" of the marines offshore. Since "Reagan had been reluctant to admit failure in Lebanon," referring to the move as a "redeployment" suited him more than the term "withdrawal."[74] Discrepancies between these private rationales and public justifications showed things were going poorly and the administrations knew it but did not want to acknowledge it openly. Instead, they put the best possible spin on it.

A prescient assessment of which policy levers to pull to navigate wartime sunk cost dilemmas is deceptively difficult. As elementary as the prescriptions in this chapter seem, Carl von Clausewitz, the esteemed Prussian strategist, indicated that even the simplest things in war can be exceedingly difficult to implement successfully. This is due to enemy actions, third-party interventions, the nonlinear nature of war, and its "fog" and "friction."[75] Thus, although seemingly basic, the policy prescriptions offered here will require significant expertise for future presidents and their advisers to pull off. As shown in the Gulf War case, when followed faithfully, these policy prescriptions help prevent a sunk cost trap. As shown in the other cases, once embraced, they help presidents steer out of one. Moreover, they become baked into the Washington discourse, so commanders in chief, legislators, and other aspiring policymakers ought to apply them well.

HOW DO HISTORICAL LESSONS INFLUENCE PRESIDENTS' SUNK COST TRAPS?

> History offers no manual of instructions that can be applied automatically; history teaches by analogy, shedding light on the likely consequences of comparable situations.
>
> —Henry Kissinger

> History is the principal way in which argumentation is made, and therefore it can be an effective way to explain and defend your policies, either positively . . . or negatively.
>
> —Ash Carter

Presidential sunk cost traps in Lebanon, Somalia, Iraq (twice), and Afghanistan show that historical lessons are inherently part of presidents' decision calculus, forming a decision filter through which analytical arguments are interpreted. The baked-in nature of these lessons means that they influence presidents' decision calculus—whether or not explicitly discussed—by affecting perspectives about risk, trade-offs, and fear of making various war policy changes. Presidents and advisers usually make decisions while expressly recognizing the linkage to historical lessons. This happened to a lesser or greater extent in every case.

Even if presidents do not consider the lesson directly, some of their officials do, impacting the pros and cons upon which presidents subsequently weigh the various options presented to them. The risks and trade-offs that advisers highlight come from examples of how decisions in similar situations have played out in the past. That reinforces decisions with positive results and weakens those with poor outcomes. The expectation is that similar decisions will yield comparable results in the current scenario. Fear based on past failures steers presidents toward the course they least anticipate regretting. This influence can be direct or through advisers and is sometimes supplemented by (or despite) opposition in Congress.

Presidents and advisers may think they are basing their decisions simply on the tapestry created by a host of complicated decision factors—a cost-benefit calculus.[76] What they do not always realize, however, is that historical lessons have already been baked into the psyche of executive branch elites, military leaders, members of Congress and senators, popular opinion, and the media. These lessons affect the operating context and influence which analytic arguments are most persuasive, causing some to be more convincing than others. Thus, even if subconsciously or under a different pretext, lessons are often the fundamental rationale for advice given and decisions taken.

Traumatic wars and events in our history indelibly impact current and aspiring leaders, creating shared understanding. Although there is variance in how they interpret and apply these lessons to contemporary conflicts, there is enough similarity that collective understanding exists. Without it, lawmakers or the media could not effectively utilize short-form monikers such as "Iraq: Bush's Vietnam." Colloquial terminology demonstrates that these analogies, with corresponding lessons, become baked in.

CONCLUSION

> Thinking historically is the most important practical tool used by everyone from presidents, legislators, and judges to thoughtful members of the media.
>
> —Ash Carter

In sum, this book shows that for midconflict policy decisions during the post–Vietnam War period, both continuity and change were at work. In all cases, the most recent and traumatic lesson, along with the regret it engendered, shaped presidents' responses to sunk cost dilemmas. As long as the primary lesson and associated regret remained the same, there was continuity of sunk cost trap/opportunity decision-making across Republican and Democratic administrations during major military engagements. When the operative lesson and accompanying regret changed, the analytical dividing line proved to be not pre- and post–Cold War, but pre- and post-9/11. When the lesson and type of regret changed, so, too, did the sunk cost response, changing from de-escalation to escalation.

The pendulum swung, but not because of reactions to the previous president's policies, as the media sometimes portrays as the rationale. Nor was it driven by other alternative explanations such as domestic, bureaucratic, or international politics. Rather, it was because of the fear of potential policy options' implications, a derivative of lessons learned from traumatic events. If presidents most feared a quagmire (a Vietnam War lesson), they de-escalated. Admittedly, in President Clinton's Somalia case, the de-escalation followed an escalation, but that was a very fleeting response, and it served only to facilitate an orderly exit. If presidents most feared another spectacular terrorist attack at home, they escalated force abroad. These dynamics suggest that the key to the prediction of policy adaptations in future sunk cost traps is understanding the lesson that most resonates with the president and the corresponding fear it induces.

Biden's Afghanistan withdrawal decision in 2021 was a notable symptom, not a driver, per se, of current (preconflict) de-escalatory policy headwinds, a shift from the Bush Doctrine of preventive war and regime change.[77] The potential for a crisis with China or Russia, which both stole the march on future warfare while the United States was preoccupied with counterterrorism, triggered this *preconflict* move toward retrenchment and military modernization among the defense establishment even before the Afghanistan withdrawal.[78] The US response to China is not *directly* related to a recently learned traumatic lesson.[79] It is tied, though, to lessons of avoiding the tragedy of great power politics,[80] power transitions,[81] and history.[82] If the two nations become embroiled in a future armed conflict, it is not yet clear what lesson will steer presidential *midconflict* policy changes. That will depend on the dominant lesson at such a *future* decision point.

Russian president Vladimir Putin's attack against Ukraine will not change US presidents' intrawar escalation calculus for a future conflict. US military conflicts' lessons are most influential in doing that—just as the cases throughout this book demonstrate. The Russia-Ukraine War will, however, yield many tactical and operational lessons for future warfare. Its influence on the types of midconflict decisions examined here will be marginal at best, though, unless Russia attacks NATO territory—triggering a NATO Article V collective defense response—or uses nuclear weapons, or the American military becomes directly involved in a shooting war against Russian forces.[83] Russia's onslaught against Europe's second-largest country is a "European 9/11" in that it is awakening European countries to their vulnerability and the need for hard power.[84] It is *not* a uniquely American war, however, and, as of this writing, it is not resulting in American military deaths. Thus, while the strategic implications of how the war in Ukraine will influence China and the rules-based international order are not fully known, it will leave a strategic wake—as have the cases herein. We will see what I refer to as the "Reverse Las Vegs Principle: What Happens in Ukraine will not Stay in Ukraine." It may impact Chinese designs on Taiwan, as well as calculations by rogue states such as North Korea. Exactly what that impact is will depend on how the war ends and who is seen as the victor—a matter on many minds as I write this, and the United States is negotiating an end to the war. What is already clear is the impact of past military conflicts.

Each major post-Vietnam conflict—like the Vietnam War itself—has a persistent shadow of its own.[85] Lebanon's shadow is the codification of the Weinberger-Powell Doctrine recommending the use of force only if doing so meets six tests.[86] Force must be a last resort, and US vital national interests must be at stake. Moreover, America must "have clearly defined political and military objectives," apply sufficient resources to ensure it wins, match appropriate resources to the ends sought, and have popular and congressional support.[87] Somalia's shadow reinforced the Vietnam and Lebanon perspectives on limiting the use of force. It emphasized careful intervention selection, clear objectives, US forces serving under US commanders, and avoiding casualties.[88] In the words of General (Ret.) David Petraeus, Iraq's and Afghanistan's shadows are that policymakers (and average Americans) now "recoil at the thought of another operation that might be of the [same] size—and cost."[89] These lingering shadows demonstrate the ongoing relevance of traumatic lessons in shaping policy shifts during major conflicts.

The most surprising revelation from all these cases may be that presidents, like generals, have fought the last war. Pundits often blame generals for fighting the last war at the operational and tactical levels.[90]

These cases demonstrate that presidents have done this at the strategic level. That is, commanders in chief changed policy during conflicts based on perceptions of what would have produced the best possible outcome in the last conflict. This parallels how generals are thought to employ the tactics and operational art they think would have led to military success during the last war.

Presidents in the cases described throughout this book experienced sunk cost traps not because they *initially* fought the last war, but because they initially failed to follow the fundamental policy prescriptions described in this chapter. Presidents before 9/11 *did*, however, act during their sunk cost dilemmas based on the most traumatic lesson from *the "last" (big) war*: "Avoid a Quagmire—No More Vietnams!" Presidents after 9/11 acted on the most traumatic lesson from *the last spectacular attack* against the homeland: "Never Again on My Watch." In all cases, presidents fought "the last war" when adjusting policy mid-course. With a notable exception in the Persian Gulf, and a debatable case in the Iraq War, this usually resulted in outcomes that left bitter aftertastes for Americans.

EPILOGUE

> It's a lot easier to start wars than it is to finish them.
>
> —Leon Panetta and Jim Newton

President Joseph (Joe) Biden's 2021 Afghanistan withdrawal decision has echoes of his 1975 vote limiting continued Vietnam War involvement and funding. Both place Biden at the center of the debate. In the first, he was a thirty-two-year-old freshman senator and against funding anything other than withdrawal of our military—not prolonged US involvement or extraction of South Vietnamese who had assisted the American war effort. After his April 2021 announcement, Biden defended the decision with another speech on July 8. In the question-and-answer session, he unequivocally rejected any similarities between the retrograde from Afghanistan and the humbling withdrawal from Vietnam. Biden said there were "none whatsoever. Zero."[91] Yet there are parallels.

Chapter 6 covered the similarities in the wars' nature, but US departures and the wars' legacies also resemble each other: the two longest wars in American history. Aims not fully met. A war-weary public. Insufficient capacity to extract US interpreters and other partners. Questions about the competence of our host nations. US supported government collapse soon after the American military departure. Questions about America's moral responsibilities and foreign policy wisdom.

During the Afghanistan withdrawal, it was Biden himself who orchestrated an end to the US military intervention and provided his rationale as commander in chief. Biden had had a strong allergic reaction to the American military experience in Vietnam. He had learned the lesson of "avoiding a quagmire" and convinced Obama to put a time limit on the 2009 surge decision as a result.[92] Yet, when Biden became president, the war was still ongoing. When it was Biden's turn twelve years after Obama's surge decisions, he closed the American military endeavor in Afghanistan. Biden was unwilling to commit another generation of America's sons and daughters to the long-standing conflict without greater national interests at stake and better prospects of success.[93]

Despite the similarities, there are differences between the Vietnam and Afghanistan withdrawals. The tragic end to the Afghanistan War and the lack of a tangible positive outcome (other than the prevention of another 9/11) haunt some, as does the inability to bring all the Afghanis who supported the US effort out. However, the war in Afghanistan lacks the Vietnam War's pervasive and traumatic impact on the American psyche. After the Afghanistan withdrawal, as contrasted with the post-Vietnam period, the questions about the efficacy of US power—while still important—are not as penetrating or as crippling to foreign policy. Additionally, Americans do not have the intense sense of betrayal caused by their leaders' deceitfulness in prosecuting the Vietnam War.[94] So far, there has not been a wholesale wiping of the slate, a replacement of the 9/11 shibboleth.[95]

Yet from the end of Obama's tenure and continuing under Trump and Biden, the proverbial pendulum had largely begun swinging from escalatory to de-escalatory pressures. Both Trump and Biden advocated for a smaller US military footprint in current conflicts and for ending "forever wars."[96] Biden's Afghanistan withdrawal decision is the most tangible expression of that in action. Yet it was the potential for a crisis with China or Russia, as much as any other factor, that triggered this *preconflict* refocus on military modernization. Biden's support for Ukraine during its war with Russia, on the other hand, sent mixed signals. Willingness to provide robust security assistance while initially limiting the types of munitions and other support signaled a willingness to exercise force through proxies but a desire to avoid overly aggressive actions against a great power that has repeatedly rattled its nuclear saber. Whether the de-escalation push will continue when the next iteration of the Islamic State emerges, another Middle East crisis arises, or during a great power conflict is not clear.

Whether that change results in de-escalation during a *midconflict* sunk cost trap depends on the dominant lesson at a *future* decision point, just as has been true in the *past*. It depends on what lessons the country and president in office at the time have taken away from two decades of counterterrorism efforts, including the shadows of Iraq and Afghanistan, and whether we suffer a new traumatic lesson in the intervening period. If an interpretation based on the sunk cost fallacy wins out, the inclination will be to escalate. Such a narrative "says if we can just stay a little longer, fight a little more, maybe do another surge, maybe try a new strategy, maybe hire a different commander, maybe vote in a new president, maybe drop bigger bombs, maybe this, maybe that, maybe the long promise of 'disorder curbed, democracy promoted, human rights advanced, terrorism suppressed' . . . will finally be fulfilled."[97] The reality is that in some situations, US intervention *has not*, and likely in the future *will not*, secure those outcomes. That realization, on the other hand, pushes toward de-escalation or even non-intervention in the first place.

Finishing wars—whether through de-escalation or escalation—is almost always difficult. This will *not* change in the future. This matters because the stakes in future *wartime* sunk cost dilemmas will be even higher than in the cases in this book. Contemporary adversaries are state actors with comparable or peer-plus capabilities in rapidly evolving domains or nuclear capabilities. They target the homeland, citizens, infrastructure, and institutions.[98] Since Vietnam, most US enemies have been nonstate actors. This was true in all these cases except for the Persian Gulf War. The Iraqi Army, though, was nothing compared to modern threats. In addition to Chinese and Russian nuclear and conventional strength, both are increasing their anti-access and area-denial capabilities, and asserting cyber, space, and influence operations across social media and other platforms. They have demonstrated the capability of integrating these and other activities to accomplish fait accompli operations in the

South China Sea, Crimea, and eastern Ukraine. Should an American president have to decide which way to adjust war policy against one of these countries or a formidable rogue state, the risks will outweigh those discussed in these cases, making implementation even more challenging.

For instance, a president may have to make a major sunk cost dilemma decision during a fight against North Korea, Iran, China, or Russia, while protecting the homeland and continuing at least an economy of force counterterrorism fight. Unlike much of the post-Vietnam history covered here, cutting losses in such a situation may not be the best approach. Asymmetric escalation in a place outside the combat theater or a hybrid solution that shows strength and provides an eventual off-ramp might be best.

Presidents and their advisers would be wise to ready themselves for such a fateful decision. The preferred learning method is from *others'* mistakes and *before* a crisis begins—not during it or after your own missteps. Unfortunately, that was not true in the sunk cost traps described in this book. There *was* a different outcome in the Gulf War *because* George H. W. Bush learned *ahead* of time and *applied* those lessons during his own sunk cost dilemma, eschewing the allure of going to Baghdad to remove the menace of Saddam Hussein because of the likely "barren outcome" that would ensue.[99]

Whether or not presidents have to make such a wartime decision, they will make decisions about whether and how to ramp up competitive activities with global and regional powers below the level of armed conflict. In some respects, America is already behind the power curve because of the jump start it ceded by its unnecessarily extended post-9/11 counterterrorism fixation. Although the context and solutions will differ, presidents and their administrations can also follow the principles herein to ramp up activities against the nation's primary competitors.

Sustained presidential engagement, regular policy reviews, ends-means alignment, creative and comprehensive policies, and effective strategic communication will matter in competition—just as in armed conflict. These will not be the same types of decisions about a potential surge or withdrawal. Instead, they will consider a host of other possibilities. Along with their civilian and military advisers, they will decide what levers to pull in pursuit of access, basing, and overflight agreements. They will determine the mix of forward-deployed troops versus those stationed at home. They will decide whether areas are better served by permanently stationed or regionally aligned, rotating forces. They can emphasize small, covert operations or large, overt exercises. They can prioritize trade deals, economic sanctions, or tariffs. They can create new opportunities by offering humanitarian aid and disaster relief to countries in need or choose to invest domestically. They can cede the information space or robustly engage in it with words *and* deeds. They can push the requisite authorities and incentives for interagency and whole-of-nation solutions down to those charged with these responsibilities or retain them. They will shape how space, cyberspace, information, and unconventional and emergent weapons are used, and which nation holds the advantages. They will determine budget levels and whether to fund new, multidomain units and the relative weight of resources applied.

These and other policy decisions will determine the military's preparedness, the impact of US alliances and partnerships, American success relative to other powers, and victory in war, should deterrence fail. Although different in the details, these decisions—like those in unadulterated conflict—must be about securing US influence, leverage, and advantage. In conflict and in competition, the artful application of the policy prescriptions herein will be absolutely critical to success. The skill with which presidents and their national security teams follow these policy prescriptions in competition and war will determine whether the United States retains or forfeits its preeminence.

Acknowledgments

While any mistakes are mine alone, to get a book published, it takes a great team.

Thanks to God for blessing me with just that.

To my family (who do not understand why I labored for more than a decade on this), thanks for supporting me, nonetheless. Richelle, you are my best friend, a strong and special gal with many gifts, and you are a wonderful mom to our kids. Nathan, Caleb, and Hope, you make me smile. I am very proud of you—for who you are and who you are becoming as God's kids. You follow Him and love others well.

Dad, you were the first to invest hours in helping me learn to write—with the special patience and grace that only you can offer. I am in your debt. A special thanks to my Duke dissertation committee of Peter Feaver, Bruce Jentleson, Hal Brands, and Bruce Kuniholm for later investing in me "as iron sharpens iron."

Many thanks to all those former senior civilian and military leaders who invested in me by taking the time to share their insights through interviews and emails. In addition to my dissertation committee, these include but are not limited to the following: Chairman of the Joint Chiefs of Staff (Persian Gulf War and Somalia) and Secretary of State (Iraq) Colin Powell; 24th Infantry Division commander (Gulf War), Joint Staff director of strategic plans and policy (Somalia) and later drug czar, General (Ret.) Barry McCaffrey; Combined Arms Center commander, commander of the wars in Iraq and Afghanistan, commander of Central Command, and later director of Central Intelligence, General (Ret.) David Petraeus (Iraq and Afghanistan); supreme Allied commander Europe, Admiral (Ret.) James Stavridis (Afghanistan); director of the Joint Staff, deputy national security adviser for Iraq and Afghanistan, and later ambassador to NATO, Lieutenant General (Ret.) Doug Lute (Iraq and Afghanistan); under President Barack Obama Undersecretary of Defense for Policy Michèle Flournoy (Afghanistan); Central Command commander and previously director of operations for the task force in Somalia, General (Ret.)

Anthony Zinni (Somalia); Attorney General Edwin Meese III (Lebanon); under President Ronald Reagan, National Security Adviser Robert "Bud" McFarlane (Lebanon); under President George H. W. Bush, national security adviser, Lieutenant General (Ret.) Brent Scowcroft (Persian Gulf); under President Bill Clinton, deputy national security adviser and special representative for Somalia, Admiral (Ret.) Jonathan Howe (Somalia); State and Defense Department officials, the Honorable Derek Chollet and Vikram Singh (Afghanistan). This book would not be what it is without your collective input.

Many thanks also to the Center for Presidential History at Southern Methodist University, which, at Dr. Peter Feaver's request, granted special early access to interviews for their book project *The Last Card: Inside George W. Bush's Decision to Surge in Iraq*. This included in-depth interviews with principal civilian policymakers and senior military leaders who influenced President Bush's Iraq surge decision-making. With titles reflecting their current position and status during the decision-making, the interviews included President George W. Bush; Vice President Richard (Dick) Cheney; Secretary of State Condoleezza Rice; Secretary of Defense Robert Gates; National Security Adviser Stephen Hadley; chairman of the Joint Chiefs of Staff, General (Ret.) Peter Pace; Central Command commander, General John Abizaid; White House Chief of Staff Joshua Bolten; Undersecretary of Defense for Intelligence Stephen Cambone; Deputy National Security Adviser J. D. Crouch; Undersecretary of Defense for Policy Eric Edelman; National Security Council Special Adviser for Strategic Planning and Institutional Reform Peter Feaver; National Security Adviser to the Vice President John Hannah; coordinator for Iraq and senior adviser to the Secretary of State, Ambassador James Jeffrey; American Enterprise Institute scholar Frederick Kagan; Georgetown University's Security Studies Program adjunct professor, Dr. Kimberly Kagan; Defense Policy Board member, General (Ret.) Jack Keane; US ambassador to Iraq Zalmay Khalilzad; director of the Joint Staff and then deputy national security adviser for Iraq and Afghanistan, Lieutenant General Douglas Lute; Joint Chiefs of Staff Strategic Dialogue Group, Colonel Peter Mansoor; deputy national security adviser for Iraq and Afghanistan, Dr. Meghan O'Sullivan; Senior Adviser to the President and White House Deputy Chief of Staff Karl Rove; Coordinator for Iraq and Senior Adviser to the Secretary of State David Satterfield; Joint Staff director of strategy and policy (J-5), Lieutenant General John Sattler; Executive Director of the Iraq Study Group Daniel Serwer; Representative Frank Wolf; and State Department counselor Dr. Philip Zelikow. I'm sure my readers will benefit from the insights of those who shaped, decided, or implemented this policy—just as I did.

To research assistants Danielle Fowler, Jennifer Ganapathy, Adrian Gariboldi, Jan Maceczek, Sujay Rao, Dana Raphael, Colleen Sharp, and Max Xu, I am thankful that during the early seasons of this project, you helped me move the ball down the field bit by bit. Thanks to the teams at the Ronald Reagan, George H. W. Bush, William (Bill) Clinton, and George W. Bush presidential libraries for their research support that helped me find key material. Kristen Moore, I appreciate your formatting help; you are a professional. Thanks to Ken Gleiman and Brian Drohan for believing in me and this project. Your support and advice opened doors.

Natalie O'Neal, Alice Brown, and Dane Ritter, thanks for being an outstanding Acquisitions team that enabled this project to gain momentum. Tara Dugan, Gayathri Umashankaran, Josephine Fabiola, Angel Daphnee, Margaret Whelan, Jackie Wilson, and the rest of the editing, production, and marketing teams, thanks for lending your expertise, for being advocates, and for working with me to get it right. I appreciate your recommendations and your willingness to compromise. You kept everything on track. To the entire University Press of Kentucky team, thanks for your academic excellence and for supporting our Army.

Finally—Panera, thanks for the Wi-Fi, as well as the (paid for) food and Mountain Dew that fueled my research, writing, and revisions.

Notes

1. WARTIME SUNK COST DILEMMAS IN VIETNAM'S SHADOW

The chapter 1 epigraphs are drawn from M. B. Young, "Two, Three, Many Vietnams," *Cold War History* 6, no. 4 (2006): 413; National Security Adviser McGeorge Bundy in VanDeMark, *Road to Disaster*, 261; President Johnson's Notes on Conversation with Henry Luce, February 21, 1966, in VanDeMark, *Road to Disaster*, 328; VanDeMark, *Road to Disaster*, 328.

1. Jessica Donati, "The Forgotten People: Fighting the Forever War," *Atlantic*, January 23, 2021, https://www.theatlantic.com/international/archive/2021/01/america-forever-war-afghanistan/617776/.

2. Kent Germany, "Lyndon B. Johnson: Foreign Affairs," Miller Center, University of Virginia, accessed February 19, 2019, https://millercenter.org/president/lbjohnson/foreign-affairs.

3. Elizabeth N. Saunders, "War and the Inner Circle: Democratic Elites and the Politics of Using Force," *Security Studies* 24, no. 3 (2015): 466–501; Fredrik Logevall, *Choosing War* (Berkeley: University of California Press, 1999); VanDeMark, *Road to Disaster*.

4. William (Bill) Clinton, *My Life* (New York: Random House, 2004), 100–104.

5. Andrew Priest, "From Saigon to Baghdad: The Vietnam Syndrome, the Iraq War and American Foreign Policy," *Intelligence and National Security* 24, no. 1 (2009): 171.

6. Ibid., 139–71.

7. VanDeMark, *Road to Disaster*, 113; Ken Burns and Lynn Novick, dirs., *The Vietnam War*, PBS, 2017.

8. Arnold R. Isaacs, *Vietnam Shadows: The War, Its Ghosts, and Its Legacy* (Baltimore: Johns Hopkins University Press, 2000).

9. Priest, "From Saigon to Baghdad," 142.

10. Richard Sobel, *The Impact of Public Opinion on US Foreign Policy since Vietnam* (Oxford: Oxford University Press, 2001), 5; Priest, "From Saigon to Baghdad," 150.

11. Kenneth H. Williams and George C. Herring, "The Issues Raised by Vietnam Go to the Very Heart of Who We Think We Are: An Interview with the University of Kentucky's George C. Herring," *Register of the Kentucky Historical Society* 102, no. 3 (2004): 287–355.

12. Ibid.

13. Arthur M. Schlesinger, *The Imperial Presidency* (Boston: Houghton Mifflin Harcourt, 2004).

14. Burns and Novick, *The Vietnam War*, 2017; George P. Shultz, *Turmoil and Triumph: My Years as Secretary of State* (New York: Charles Scribner's Sons, 1993), 294.

15. Isaacs, *Vietnam Shadows*, 67.

16. *Frontline*, season 3, episode 7, "Retreat from Beirut," aired February 26, 1985, on PBS.

17. Priest, "From Saigon to Baghdad," 148.

18. Brian VanDeMark, *Road to Disaster: A New History of America's Descent into Vietnam* (New York: HarperCollins, 2018), 328.

19. Herbert R. McMaster, *Dereliction of Duty: Lyndon Johnson, Robert McNamara, the Joint Chiefs of Staff, and the Lies That Led to Vietnam* (New York: HarperCollins, 1997).

20. George W. Ball, *The Past Has Another Pattern: Memoirs*, vol. 23 (New York: Norton, 1982), 366; Logevall, *Choosing War*, 2018; VanDeMark, *Road to Disaster*, 284–89.

21. VanDeMark, *Road to Disaster*, 215 (emphasis added).

22. Ibid., 274, 277; Robert A. Wicklund and Jack Williams Brehm, *Perspectives on Cognitive Dissonance* (Hillsdale, NJ: Lawrence Erlbaum, 1976); Hal R. Arkes and Catherine Blumer, "The Psychology of Sunk Cost," *Organizational Behavior and Human Decision Processes* 35, no. 1 (1985): 124; Barry M. Staw, "Knee-Deep in the Big Muddy: A Study of Escalating Commitment to a Chosen Course of Action," *Organizational Behavior and Human Performance* 16, no. 1 (1976): 27–44.

23. VanDeMark, *Road to Disaster*, 274.

24. John McNaughton, Department of State, Vietnam Negotiating Files: Lot 69 D 412, Project Mayflower, Top Secret [revealed in the Pentagon Papers leak]; Sensitive, March 10, 1965, at Historical Documents—Office of the Historian, www.state.gov.

25. Daniel Kahneman and Patrick Egan, *Thinking, Fast and Slow* (New York: Farrar, Straus and Giroux, 2011), 318–19.

26. VanDeMark, *Road to Disaster*, 297.

27. Williams and Herring, "The Issues Raised by Vietnam Go to the Very Heart of Who We Think We Are," 287–355.

28. Marvin Kalb and Deborah Kalb, *Haunting Legacy: Vietnam and the American Presidency from Ford to Obama* (Washington, DC: Brookings Institution Press, 2012).

29. VanDeMark, *Road to Disaster*, 234, 261; Logevall, *Choosing War*, 389–413; Leslie H. Gelb and Richard K. Betts, *The Irony of Vietnam: The System Worked* (Washington, DC: Brookings Institution, 2016); Herbert R. McMaster, *Dereliction of Duty: Lyndon Johnson, Robert McNamara, the Joint Chiefs of Staff, and the Lies That Led to Vietnam* (New York: HarperCollins, 1997); Memo from George Ball to Rusk, McNamara, both Bundys, McNaughton, and Unger, Part II Only, June 29, 1965, in the Pentagon Papers, Gravel ed., vol. 4 (Boston: Beacon, 1971), 609–10; Memorandum for the President from George Ball, "A Compromise Solution in South Vietnam," July 1, 1965, in the Pentagon Papers, Gravel ed., vol. 4 (Boston: Beacon, 1971), 615–19; Ball, *The Past Has Another Pattern*.

30. Irving M. Destler, Leslie H. Gelb, and Anthony Lake, *Our Own Worst Enemy: The Unmaking of American Foreign Policy* (New York: Touchstone, 1985), 17–19; Priest, "From Saigon to Baghdad," 139–71.

31. Gordon M. Goldstein, *Lessons in Disaster: McGeorge Bundy and the Path to War in Vietnam* (New York: Macmillan, 2008), 68.

32. VanDeMark, *Road to Disaster*, 234, 264, 295–378, 328.

33. James McAllister, "Who Lost Vietnam? Soldiers, Civilians, and US Military Strategy," *International Security* 35, no. 3 (2010): 95–123. Contrary to John Mueller in his famous 1973 book, *War, Presidents, and Public Opinion*, McAllister argues that public opinion was not a strong constraint on President Johnson during the Vietnam War. Further, the main

cause of democracies' challenge in winning counterinsurgencies is not a civilian aversion to casualties.

34. David Halberstam, *The Best and the Brightest* (New York: Modern Library, 2002); Joe P. Dunn, "In Search of Lessons: The Development of a Vietnam Historiography," *Parameters* 9, no. 4 (1979): 31.

35. VanDeMark, *Road to Disaster*, 2018.

36. Herbert Y. Schandler, *America in Vietnam: The War That Couldn't Be Won* (Washington, DC: Rowman & Littlefield, 2009).

37. Phillip E. Catton, "Refighting Vietnam in the History Books: The Historiography of the War," *OAH Magazine of History* 18, no. 5 (2004): 8.

38. Robert McNamara, *In Retrospect: The Tragedy and Lessons of Vietnam* (New York: Vintage, 2017), 322–24.

39. Michael Lind, *Vietnam: The Necessary War* (New York: Simon & Schuster, 2013).

40. Philip K. Jason, *Acts and Shadows: The Vietnam War in American Literary Culture* (Washington, DC: Rowman & Littlefield, 2000), 2–3; Fred Turner, *Echoes of Combat: The Vietnam War in American Memory* (New York: Anchor Books, 1996), 3–16, 185–95.

41. Catton, "Refighting Vietnam in the History Books," 8.

42. Thomas Kelly, "Sunk Costs, Rationality, and Acting for the Sake of the Past," *Noûs* 38, no. 1 (2004): 15.

43. Memo from George Ball to Rusk, 609–10; Memorandum for the President from George Ball, 615–19; Ball, *The Past Has Another Pattern*, 366.

44. Alastair Smith and Allan C. Stam, "Bargaining and the Nature of War," *Journal of Conflict Resolution* 48, no. 6 (2004): 783–813.

45. Eliot A. Cohen and John Gooch, *Military Misfortunes: The Anatomy of Failure in War* (New York: Free Press, 1990).

46. Gary Sheffield, "The Battle of the Atlantic: The U-Boat Peril," BBC, March 30, 2011, http://www.bbc.co.uk/history/worldwars/wwtwo/battle_atlantic_01.shtml.

47. Robert M. Gates, *Duty: Memoirs of a Secretary at War* (New York: Alfred A. Knopf, 2014).

48. Peter D. Feaver, "The Right to Be Right: Civil-Military Relations and the Iraq Surge Decision," *International Security* 35, no. 4 (2011): 108–11.

49. Peter D. Feaver, *Armed Servants: Agency, Oversight, and Civil-Military Relations* (Cambridge, MA: Harvard University Press, 2003); Saunders, "War and the Inner Circle," 466–501; Richard H. Kohn, "Building Trust: Civil-Military Behaviors for Effective National Security," in *American Civil-Military Relations: The Soldier and the State in a New Era*, ed. Suzanne C. Nielsen and Don M. Snider (Baltimore: Johns Hopkins University Press, 2009), 274–87.

50. Robert L. Helmbold, "Decision in Battle: Breakpoint Hypotheses and Engagement Termination Data," vol. 772, no. PR (Santa Monica, CA: RAND, 1971); Carrie Lee Lindsay, "The Politics of Military Operations," PhD diss., Stanford University, 2015.

2. HISTORICAL LESSONS DRIVE FEAR

The chapter 2 epigraphs are drawn from Andrew Priest, "From Saigon to Baghdad: The Vietnam Syndrome, the Iraq War and American Foreign Policy," *Intelligence and National Security* 24, no. 1 (2009): 166; James B. Steinberg, "History, Policymaking, and the Balkans: Lessons Imported and Lessons Learned," in *The Power of the Past: History and Statecraft*, ed.

Hal Brands and Jeremi Suri (Washington, DC: Brookings Institution, 2015), 248; H. R. McMaster, video telephone conference with the Advanced Strategic Policy and Planning Program's PhD fellows, speaking about his time as national security adviser to President Trump, November 13, 2020; Priest, "From Saigon to Baghdad," 166.

1. Philip Zelikow, "The Nature of History's Lessons," in Brands and Suri, *The Power of the Past*, 290.

2. Hal Brands and Jeremi Suri, eds., *The Power of the Past: History and Statecraft* (Washington, DC: Brookings Institution, 2015), 14–16. Margaret MacMillan, *The Uses and Abuses of History* (London: Profile Books, 2010).

3. James B. Steinberg, "History, Policymaking, and the Balkans: Lessons Imported and Lessons Learned," in *The Power of the Past: History and Statecraft*, ed. Hal Brands and Jeremi Suri (Washington, DC: Brookings Institution, 2015), 242.

4. Steinberg, "History, Policymaking, and the Balkans," 248. Robert Jervis, *Perception and Misperception in International Politics* (Princeton, NJ: Princeton University Press, 1976), 215.

5. Scott MacDonald, "Hitler's Shadow: Historical Analogies and Iraqi Invasion of Kuwait," *Diplomacy and Statecraft* 13, no. 4 (2002), referenced by Priest, "From Saigon to Baghdad," 139.

6. Steinberg, "History, Policymaking, and the Balkans," 245.

7. Ibid., 247–48.

8. Ernest R. May, *"Lessons" of the Past: The Use and Misuse of History in American Foreign Policy*, vol. 429 (Oxford: Oxford University Press, 1973).

9. Jeffrey Record, *Perils of Reasoning by Historical Analogy* (Montgomery: Air War College Press, 1998), 1.

10. Yuen Foong Khong, *Analogies at War: Korea, Munich, Dien Bien Phu, and the Vietnam Decisions of 1965* (Princeton, NJ: Princeton University Press, 1992).

11. Zelikow, "The Nature of History's Lessons," 286.

12. Steinberg, "History, Policymaking, and the Balkans," 248.

13. May, *"Lessons" of the Past*; Richard E. Neustadt and R. Ernest May, "Thinking in Time," in Brands and Suri, *The Power of the Past*; Priest, "From Saigon to Baghdad," 139–71; Record, *Perils of Reasoning by Historical Analogy*, 23.

14. MacMillan, *The Uses and Abuses of History*; May, *"Lessons" of the Past*, ix–xii; Neustadt and May, "Thinking in Time"; Khong, *Analogies at War*; Record, *Perils of Reasoning by Historical Analogy*.

15. Khong, *Analogies at War*, 262.

16. Ibid., 11, 66–67, 99–122, 262.

17. Ibid., 117.

18. MacDonald, "Hitler's Shadow," referenced by Priest, "From Saigon to Baghdad," 139.

19. MacMillan, *The Uses and Abuses of History*; May, *"Lessons" of the Past*, xii, 18.

20. May, *Lessons of the Past*, 51.

21. Neustadt and May, "Thinking in Time"; Khong, *Analogies at War*; Brands and Suri, *The Power of the Past*.

22. George Packer, "What Obama and the Generals Are Reading," *New Yorker*, October 8, 2009, http://www.newyorker.com/news/george-packer/what-obama-and-the-generals-are-reading; MacMillan, *The Uses and Abuses of History*.

23. MacDonald, "Hitler's Shadow," referenced by Priest, "From Saigon to Baghdad," 139–71.

24. Lyndon Baines Johnson, *The Vantage Point: Perspectives of the Presidency, 1963–1969* (New York: Holt, Rinehart and Winston, 1971), 151, paraphrased in Khong, *Analogies at War*, 255.

25. Barry M. Staw, "Knee-Deep in the Big Muddy: A Study of Escalating Commitment to a Chosen Course of Action," *Organizational Behavior and Human Performance* 16, no. 1 (1976): 27–44.

26. Hal R. Arkes and Catherine Blumer, "The Psychology of Sunk Cost," *Organizational Behavior and Human Decision Processes* 35, no. 1 (1985): 124–40; Howard Garland, "Throwing Good Money after Bad: The Effect of Sunk Costs on the Decision to Escalate Commitment to an Ongoing Project," *Journal of Applied Psychology* 75, no. 6 (1990): 728.

27. Donald E. Conlon and Howard Garland, "The Role of Project Completion Information in Resource Allocation Decisions," *Academy of Management Journal* 36, no. 2 (1993): 402–13.

28. Howard Garland and Donald E. Conlon, "Too Close to Quit: The Role of Project Completion in Maintaining Commitment," *Journal of Applied Social Psychology* 28, no. 22 (1998): 2025–48.

29. Marcel Zeelenberg and Eric Van Dijk, "A Reverse Sunk Cost Effect in Risky Decision-Making: Sometimes We Have Too Much Invested to Gamble," *Journal of Economic Psychology* 18, no. 6 (1997): 682.

30. Kin Fai Ellick Wong and Jessica Y. Y. Kwong, "The Role of Anticipated Regret in Escalation of Commitment," *Journal of Applied Psychology* 92, no. 2 (2007): 545–54; Gillian Ku, "Learning to De-escalate: The Effects of Regret in Escalation of Commitment," *Organizational Behavior and Human Decision Processes* 105, no. 2 (2008): 221–32.

31. Wong and Kwong, "The Role of Fear in Escalation of Commitment," *Journal of Applied Psychology* 92, no. 2 (2007): 545–54.

32. Ku, "Learning to De-Escalate," 230. Italics added.

33. Ibid.

34. George W. Bush, "State of the Union Address to the 107th Congress, January 29, 2002, Selected Speeches of President George W. Bush: 2001–2009," 107, accessed May 6, 2018, https://www.google.com/url?sa=t&rct=j&q=&esrc=s&source=web&cd=1&cad=rja&uact=8&ved=0ahUKEwjdpJSs3PLaAhUK24MKHSSyDb8QFggpMAA&url=https%3A%2F%2Fgeorgewbush-whitehouse.archives.gov%2Finfocus%2Fbushrecord%2Fdocuments%2FSelected_Speeches_George_W_Bush.pdf&usg=AOvVaw3d_uOOlUhBHYUSD2u6pUwk.

35. Zelikow, "The Nature of History's Lessons," 290.

36. Zeelenberg and Dijk, "A Reverse Sunk Cost Effect in Risky Decision Making," 680; Daniel Kahneman and Amos Tversky, "Prospect Theory: An Analysis of Decision under Risk," *Econometrica: Journal of the Econometric Society* 12 (1979): 286.

37. Ibid., 682.

38. John E. Mueller, *War, Presidents, and Public Opinion* (Hoboken, NJ: John Wiley & Sons, 1973); Bruce W. Jentleson, "The Pretty Prudent Public: Post Post-Vietnam American Opinion on the Use of Military Force," *International Studies Quarterly* 36 (1992): 49–73; Christopher Gelpi, Peter D. Feaver, and Jason Reifler, "Success Matters: Casualty Sensitivity and the War in Iraq," *International Security* 30, no. 3 (2006): 7–46.

39. This methodological approach follows political science convention laid out in Alexander L. George and Andrew Bennett, *Case Studies and Theory Development in the Social Sciences* (Cambridge, MA: MIT Press, 2005); Alexander L. George and Richard Smoke, *Deterrence in American Foreign Policy: Theory and Practice* (New York: Columbia University Press, 1974).

40. Khong, *Analogies at War*, 64.

41. Dustin J. Sleesman, Donald Conlon, Gerry McNamara, and Jonathan Miles, "Cleaning Up the Big Muddy: A Meta-Analytic Review of the Determinants of Escalation of Commitment," *Academy of Management Journal* 55, no. 3 (2012): 541–62.

42. Gregory B. Northcraft and Margaret A. Neale, "Opportunity Costs and the Framing of Resource Allocation Decisions," *Organizational Behavior and Human Decision Processes* 37, no. 3 (1986): 349.

43. Dominic D. P. Johnson and Dominic Tierney, *Failing to Win* (Cambridge, MA: Harvard University Press, 2006), 289–98; David C. Brooks, "Cutting Losses: Ending Limited Interventions," *Parameters* 43, no. 3 (2013): 99; Dominic Tierney, *The Right Way to Lose a War: America in an Age of Unwinnable Conflicts* (Cambridge, MA: Harvard University Press, 2015).

44. "Statement on the Situation in Lebanon," February 7, 1984, Online by Gerhard Peters and John T. Woolley, "The American Presidency Project," accessed April 30, 2016, https://www.presidency.ucsb.edu/documents/statement-the-situation-lebanon.

45. Peter D. Feaver, "The Right to Be Right: Civil-Military Relations and the Iraq Surge Decision," *International Security* 35, no. 4 (2011): 87, 99.

3. REAGAN IN LEBANON

The chapter 3 epigraphs are drawn from Sam Nunn, "U.S. Marines," September 17, 1983; Sen. Nancy Landon Kassebaum (R-KS), in T. R. Reid, "Senate Panel Votes to Extend Marines' Duty by 18 Months," *Washington Post*, September 24, 1983, https://www.washingtonpost.com/archive/politics/1983/09/24/senate-panel-votes-to-extend-marines-duty-by-18-months/045c7183-c510-4e19-ab44-8df465161a51/?noredirect=on&utm_term=.9684efa5a800; Robert McFarlane with Zofia Smardz, *Special Trust* (London: Cadell and Davies, 1994), 272; Anthony Lewis, "Quagmire, Here We Come," *New York Times*, September 22, 1983, http://www.nytimes.com/1983/09/22/opinion/abroad-at-home-quagmire-here-we-come.html; P. V. Narasimha Rao, "The Future of India: The Bangalore Enlightenment," *Economist*, March 19, 2009, http://www.economist.com/node/13315599; Lou Cannon, *President Reagan: The Role of a Lifetime* (New York: Simon & Schuster, 1991), 405; George P. Shultz, *Turmoil and Triumph: My Years as Secretary of State* (New York: Charles Scribner's Sons, 1993), 646, 649–51; Chinese proverb; Caspar Weinberger, "The Uses of Military Power," Remarks Prepared for Delivery by the Hon. Caspar Weinberger, Secretary of Defense, to the National Press Club, Washington, DC, November 28, 1984, http://www.pbs.org/wgbh/pages/frontline/shows/military/force/weinberger.html.

1. Ronald Reagan, *An American Life: The Autobiography* (New York: Simon & Schuster, 1990), 465; Cannon, *President Reagan*, 445.

2. Reagan, *An American Life*, 466.

3. Memo, "MNF Options for the President," January/February 1984 [No specific date], Lebanon–MNF (Multinational Force) 1984 (2) folder, box 91136, Near East and South Asia Affairs Directorate: Records, Reagan Library; Itamar Rabinovich, *The War for Lebanon, 1970–1985* (Ithaca, NY: Cornell University Press, 1985), 185–86; Cannon, *President Reagan*, 445.

4. "1982: Israeli Ambassador Shot in London," BBC, June 3, 1982, http://news.bbc.co.uk/onthisday/hi/dates/stories/june/3/newsid_2496000/2496109.stm; Rabinovich, *The War for Lebanon*, 132–43; Ze'ev Schiff and Ehud Ya'Ari, *Israel's Lebanon War* (New York: Simon & Schuster, 1985), 59–60; John Boykin, *Cursed Is the Peacemaker: The American Diplomat*

versus the Israeli General, Beirut 1982 (Bridgewater, NJ: Applegate, 2002), 226–27, 231, 234, 313–15, 322–23.

5. Boykin, *Cursed Is the Peacemaker*, 258–63; DOD "Mickey's" Secret Database of War Costs, unclassified material, Joint History Office, OCJCS, accessed May 10, 2010; *Frontline*, season 3, episode 6, "Retreat from Beirut," aired February 26, 1985, on PBS.

6. President Ronald Reagan, "Address to the Nation on United States Policy for Peace in the Middle East," September 1, 1982, https://www.reaganlibrary.gov/archives/speech/address-nation-united-states-policy-peace-middle-east.

7. Boykin, *Cursed Is the Peacemaker*, 271.

8. Thomas L. Friedman, *From Beirut to Jerusalem* (New York: Macmillan, 1989).

9. Seth Anziska, "A Preventable Massacre," *New York Times*, September 16, 2012, http://www.nytimes.com/2012/09/17/opinion/a-preventable-massacre.html.

10. Friedman, *From Beirut to Jerusalem*; Institute for Middle East Understanding (IMEU), "Sabra and Shatila Massacres," IMEU, September 17, 2012, http://imeu.org/article/the-sabra-shatila-massacre.

11. President Ronald Reagan, "Address to the Nation on Events in Lebanon and Grenada," October 27, 1983, https://reaganlibrary.archives.gov/archives/speeches/1983/102783b.htm.

12. *Frontline*, season 3, episode 6, "Retreat from Beirut"; Brands, *Making the Unipolar Moment*, 245; Richard Haass, *Intervention: The Use of American Military Force in the Post-Cold War World* (Washington, DC: Carnegie Endowment for International Peace, 1999), 24.

13. Ronald Reagan, *NSDD 64: Next Steps in Lebanon* (Washington, DC: NSC, October 28, 1982).

14. Robert ("Bud") McFarlane, phone interview, April 4, 2016; Dept. of State, "Papers for Interagency Steering Group on Lebanon," October 6, 1982.

15. John H. Kelly, "Lebanon: 1982–1984," in *U.S. and Russian Policymaking with Respect to the Use of Force*, ed. Jeremy R. Azrael and Emil A. Payin (Santa Monica, CA: RAND Corporation, 1996), http://www.rand.org/pubs/conf_proceedings/CF129/CF-129-chapter6.html; Nunn, "U.S. Marines," September 17, 1983.

16. "Document 382: Statement by President Reagan, American Foreign Policy Current Documents" (Washington, DC: Dept. of State, October 24, 1983), 791; "Document 383: Statement by Secretary of State Shultz to Congress, American Foreign Policy Current Documents" (Washington, DC: Dept. of State, October 24, 1983), 791–94; Memo, "Progress on Peace in the Middle East," Summer or Fall 1983 [No specific date], [Progress on Peace for the Middle East—Undated Paper] folder, box 2, John Poindexter, Files, Ronald Reagan Library, 1; Reagan, "Address to the Nation on Events in Lebanon and Grenada."

17. Reagan, *An American Life*, 430, 432; Cable, Donald Rumsfeld to George Shultz, January 29, 1984 (1631Z), Rumsfeld Middle East Mission (January 1984–February 1984) (1)–(5) folder, box 46, Executive Secretariat, NSC: Records: Country File, Reagan Library: 3; Memo, "Progress on Peace in the Middle East"; Shultz, *Turmoil and Triumph*, 232.

18. Colin Powell, phone interview, August 8, 2016; Charles Hill, Secretary George P. Shultz's executive secretary, phone interview, April 15, 2016; Caspar W. Weinberger, *Fighting for Peace: Seven Critical Years in the Pentagon* (New York: Warner Books, 1990), 151–52.

19. Hill, phone interview.

20. Caspar Weinberger, interview, *Frontline*, PBS, late September 2001, http://www.pbs.org/wgbh/pages/frontline/shows/target/interviews/weinberger.html.

21. McFarlane, phone interview; Cannon, *President Reagan*, 439–50.

22. Tim Naftali, *Blind Spot: The Secret History of American Counterterrorism* (New York: Basic Books, 2009), 135; Weinberger, *Fighting for Peace*, 154; Peter Jennings, "ABC Nightly News," April 18, 1983, https://abcnews.go.com/Archives/video/april-18-1983-us-embassy-bombed-beirut-9808367.

23. "Memorandum of Agreement between the Governments of the United States of America and Israel," pursuant to the "Israel-Lebanon Agreement," May 16, 1983, Lebanon: President Amin Gemayel (8390635) folder, box 22, Executive Secretariat, NSC: Records: Head of State File, Ronald Reagan Library, 2; Schiff and Ya'Ari, *Israel's Lebanon War*, 112, 299.

24. Charles Winslow, *Lebanon: War and Politics in a Fragmented Society* (New York: Routledge, 1996), 241.

25. David C. Martin and John L. Walcott, *Best Laid Plans: The Inside Story of America's War against Terrorism* (New York: Harper & Row, 1988), 115.

26. "Multinational Force in Lebanon Resolution," October 12, 1983 [S. J. Res. 159]; Sen. Nancy Landon Kassebaum (R-KS) in Reid, "Senate Panel Votes to Extend Marines' Duty by 18 Months."

27. Public Law 98–119, signed into law by Reagan on October 12, 1983, came from S. J. Res. 159, S. J. Res. 159, accessed October 29, 2018, https://www.congress.gov/bill/98th-congress/senate-joint-resolution/159/actions.

28. Naftali, *Blind Spot*.

29. McFarlane with Smardz, *Special Trust*, 270; Douglas Brinkley, *The Reagan Diaries* (New York: HarperCollins, 2007), 190.

30. McFarlane, phone interview; Brands, *Making the Unipolar Moment*, 246–47.

31. Powell, phone interview.

32. Brands, *Making the Unipolar Moment*, 246–47.

33. Brinkley, *The Reagan Diaries*, 197–98.

34. Robert C. McFarlane with Zofia Smardz, *Special Trust*, 271.

35. Miller Center, "Interview with Caspar Weinberger," University of Virginia, November 19, 2002, 16, http://millercenter.org/oralhistory/interview/caspar-weinberger.

36. Weinberger, *Fighting for Peace*, 161–67.

37. James R. Locher III, *Victory on the Potomac: The Goldwater-Nichols Act Unifies the Pentagon* (College Station: Texas A&M University Press, 2002), 143. (Locher cites the following sources in this passage: Andrew J. Bacevich, "Discord Still: Clinton and the Military," *Washington Post*, January 3, 1999, C01; Bernard W. Rogers, James R. Locher III, interview, December 10, 1998; Michael Getler, "Diplomats Are Bold, Pentagon Wary," *Washington Post*, March 4, 1984, I; McFarlane with Smardz, *Special Trust*, 211.)

38. Ronald Smothers, "Syria Frees Flier, Attributing Step to Jackson's Trip," *New York Times*, January 4, 1984, http://www.nytimes.com/1984/01/04/world/syria-frees-flier-attributing-step-to-jackson-s-trip.html.

39. Brinkley, *The Reagan Diaries*, 199; Naftali, *Blind Spot*, 135; Weinberger, *Fighting for Peace*, 145.

40. McFarlane with Smardz, *Special Trust*, 271.

41. Smothers, "Syria Frees Flier."

42. Cannon, *President Reagan*, 390; Cable, Theros and Stanton to Rumsfeld and Bartholomew, January 30, 1984, CPPG [Crisis Pre-Planning Group] (Lebanon)-01/31/1984 folder, box 91834, William Burns Files, Ronald Reagan Library.

43. Cannon, *President Reagan*, 445.

44. John Mueller, "American Public Opinion and Military Ventures Abroad: Attention, Evaluation, Involvement, Politics, and the Wars of the Bushes," Annual Meeting of the American Political Science Association, Philadelphia, August 2003, 47.

45. Sam Hall, "Congressional Debate about the Marine Barracks Bombing" Cong. Record, 98th Congress, 1st Session, House of Representatives, vol. 129, part 21, October 24, 1983, 29030.

46. Cable, McFarlane to Rumsfeld, "Information Support Cable for January 27, 1984," January 28, 1984, Lebanon Documents (01/26/1984) (Rumsfeld Support) (2) folder, RAC box 8, Crisis Management Center (CMC), NSC: Records, Reagan Library, 3.

47. Powell, phone interview; Richard A. Clarke, phone interview, July 5, 2016; Hill, phone interview; Bob Woodward, interview, *Frontline*, PBS, late September 2001, http://www.pbs.org/wgbh/pages/frontline/shows/target/interviews/woodward.html.4.

48. McFarlane with Smardz, *Special Trust*, 268.

49. Hal Brands, *From Berlin to Baghdad* (Lexington: University Press of Kentucky, 2008), 270.

50. Anthony Lake, *6 Nightmares: Real Threats in a Dangerous World and How America Can Meet Them* (Boston: Little, Brown, 2000), 129; Memo, "MNF Options" January/February 1984 Lebanon–MNF, Reagan Library; Notes, Rumsfeld and Pierce to DOS/White House, "Proposed Edits to Draft Resolution," February 1, 1984, CPPG [Crisis Pre-Planning Group] (Lebanon)-02/03/1984 folder, box 91834, William Burns files, Reagan Library, Meeting Agenda, Crisis Pre-Planning Group (CPPG), February 3, 1984 (5–6 PM), CPPG [Crisis Pre-Planning Group] (Lebanon)-02/03/1984 folder, box 91834, William Burns files, Ronald Reagan Library; Naftali, *Blind Spot*.

51. Richard A. Clarke, *Against All Enemies: Inside America's War on Terror* (New York: Free Press, 2004), 88.

52. Report of the DOD Commission on Beirut International Airport Terrorist Act, October 23, 1983 ("Long Commission"), December 23, 1983, 11–20.

53. Clarke, phone interview; McFarlane with Smardz, *Special Trust*, 272–73.

54. Ronald Reagan, "NSDD 123: Next Steps in Lebanon" (Washington, DC: NSC, February 1, 1984); Draft, "NSDD 123: Next Steps in Lebanon," January 1984 [No specific date], CPPG [Crisis Pre-Planning Group] (Lebanon)-01/31/1984 folder, box 91834, William Burns files, Ronald Reagan Library.

55. Meeting Agenda, CPPG, February 3, 1984, CPPG (Lebanon)-02/03/1984 folder, box 91834, William Burns files, Ronald Reagan Library.

56. "Lebanese Cabinet Resigns to Ease Conflict," *Los Angeles Times* reported in the *Stanford Daily*, February 6, 1984, 2.

57. "Document 393: Statement by President Reagan in Interview, American Foreign Policy Current Documents" (Washington, DC: Dept. of State, December 14, 1983), 808–809; "Document 394: Clarification of the U.S. Withdrawal Policy at a Press Conference, American Foreign Policy Current Documents" (Washington, DC: Dept. of State, December 20, 1983), 809–11; Ronald Reagan, "Remarks and a Question-and-Answer Session with Reporters on the Pentagon Report on the Security of United States Marines in Lebanon," December 27, 1983, online by Gerhard Peters and John T. Woolley, *The American Presidency Project*, accessed April 14, 2016, http://www.presidency.ucsb.edu/ws/?pid=40899; Notes, "Strategy for US Actions in Lebanon," January 4, 1984, Lebanon Documents (01/04/1984) (Rumsfeld

Cables) II (1)-(9) folder, RAC box 8, Crisis Management Center (CMC), NSC: Records, Reagan Library, 1.

58. "Lebanese Cabinet Resigns to Ease Conflict," 2; David B. Crist, "The Joint Chiefs of Staff and Limits to the Use of Military Power in Lebanon, 1982–1984," Special Historical Study 8, Top Secret Report—Unclassified Portion, Joint History Office, OCJCS, Washington, DC, 2015, 67–68; Cable, Theros and Stanton to Rumsfeld and Bartholomew, 4; EUCOM Command History, 1984, 114–15 in Crist, "The Joint Chiefs of Staff," 68; Joint Staff, J-5, Memo to CJCS, "Increasing Pressure on Muslim Officers to Leave the Ranks of the LAF," March 1, 1984.

59. "Statement on the Situation in Lebanon," February 7, 1984; Naftali, *Blind Spot*, 139.

60. Hal Brands, *Making the Unipolar Moment: U.S. Foreign Policy and the Rise of the Post-Cold War Order* (Ithaca, NY: Cornell University Press, 2016), 247.

61. Cable, Rumsfeld to Shultz, January 29, 1984 (1631Z), Rumsfeld Middle East Mission (January 1984–February 1984) (1)–(5) folder, box 46, Executive Secretariat, NSC: Records: Country File, Reagan Library, 3.

62. McFarlane with Smardz, *Special Trust*, 272–73.

63. Ibid., 272–73; Memo, "MNF Options."

64. McFarlane with Smardz, *Special Trust*, 272.

65. Cable, Rumsfeld to Shultz, January 29, 1984 (1631Z), Ronald Reagan Library, 34.

66. Cable, Rumsfeld to Shultz, January 31, 1984 (2305Z), Rumsfeld Middle East Mission (January 1984–February 1984) (1)–(5) folder, box 46, Executive Secretariat, NSC: Records: Country File, Ronald Reagan Library.

67. Shultz, *Turmoil and Triumph*, 62–85; Reagan, "Address to the Nation on United States Policy for Peace in the Middle East."

68. Reagan, "Address to the Nation on United States Policy for Peace in the Middle East"; Reagan, "Address to the Nation on Events in Lebanon and Grenada"; Ronald Reagan, "Address Before a Joint Session of the Congress on the State of the Union," January 25, 1984, online by Gerhard Peters and John T. Woolley, *The American Presidency Project*, accessed June 7, 2016, http://www.presidency.ucsb.edu/ws/?pid=40205.

69. Timothy J. Geraghty, *Peacekeepers at War: Beirut 1983—The Marine Commander Tells His Story* (Dulles, VA: Potomac Books, 2011), xv; Brands, *Making the Unipolar Moment*, 246.

70. Ronald Reagan, "Letter to the Speaker of the House and the President Pro Tempore of the Senate on the Termination of United States Participation in the Multinational Force in Lebanon," March 30, 1984, online by Gerhard Peters and John T. Woolley, *American Presidency Project*, accessed January 25, 2016, http://www.presidency.ucsb.edu/ws/?pid=39709.

71. Memo, "Progress on Peace in the Middle East"; Seth Anziska, "Reagan's Cold War in the Middle East: Israel, the Palestinians, and the Limits of Lebanon, 1981–1984," manuscript, Cold War Essay Contest, Columbia University, 2014; President Ronald Reagan, "Address to the Nation on United States Policy for Peace in the Middle East"; Reagan, "Address to the Nation on Events in Lebanon and Grenada"; Benjamin Jones, "The Vietnam Analogy and Lebanon: History's Inability to Compete with Preconceptions," *Pi Sigma Alpha Undergraduate Journal of Politics* 6 (Spring 2006): 77–78, 82–83.

72. John Lewis Gaddis, *The Cold War* (New York: Penguin, 2005), 222.

73. President Ronald Reagan, "Address to the British Parliament," June 8, 1982, http://millercenter.org/president/speeches/speech-3408.

74. Ronald Reagan, "Address to the National Association of Evangelicals," *Voices of Democracy*, March 8, 1983, http://voicesofdemocracy.umd.edu/reagan-evil-empire-speech-text/.

75. Reagan, "Address to the Nation on Events in Lebanon and Grenada."

76. Brinkley, *The Reagan Diaries*, 178–79.

77. Ibid., 177.

78. "Document 393"; "Document 394"; Ronald Reagan, "Remarks and a Question-and-Answer Session with Reporters on the Pentagon Report on the Security of U.S. Marines in Lebanon," December 27, 1983, online by Gerhard Peters and John T. Woolley, *The American Presidency Project*, accessed April 14, 2016, http://www.presidency.ucsb.edu/ws/?pid=40899; Brinkley, *The Reagan Diaries*, 177–229.

79. Powell, phone interview; Clarke, phone interview; Hill, phone interview; Woodward, interview, *Frontline*; Memo, "MNF Options"; McFarlane with Smardz, *Special Trust*, 272–73; Elizabeth Drew, *Campaign Journal: The Political Events of 1983–1984* (New York: Macmillan, 1985), 150–52; Cannon, *President Reagan*, 445, 454–56; Weinberger, *Fighting for Peace*, 167, 180–81, 361; Shultz, *Turmoil and Triumph*, 646–50; Rabinovich, *The War for Lebanon*, 185–86.

80. Drew, *Campaign Journal*, 215.

81. Cannon, *President Reagan*, 445.

82. Brinkley, *The Reagan Diaries*, 215.

83. Reagan, *An American Life*, 461–67.

84. Shultz, *Turmoil and Triumph*, 646.

85. "Document 245: Testimony of Deputy Secretary of State Dam to Senate Foreign Relations Committee, American Foreign Policy Current Documents" (Washington, DC: Dept. of State, January 11, 1984), 547–53; "Document 249: Interview with Secretary of State Shultz, American Foreign Policy Current Documents" (Washington, DC: Dept. of State, January 22, 1984), 557–58.

86. Memo, "MNF Options," 3.

87. Reagan, "Address to the Nation on Events in Lebanon and Grenada."

88. "Document 383."

89. William Clinton, "Address to the Nation on Somalia," October 7, 1993; William Clinton, "Letter to Congress," October 13, 1993; Hans J. Morgenthau, "To Intervene or Not to Intervene," *Foreign Affairs* 45, no. 3 (1967): 425–36.

90. McFarlane with Smardz, *Special Trust*, 273.

91. Reagan, *An American Life*, 465.

92. Memo, "Lebanon Report: Feb. 13, 1984," Records, Reagan Library, 8.

93. Reagan, *An American Life*, 465; McFarlane with Smardz, *Special Trust*, 272–73.

94. Admiral Small message to Admiral Watkins, November 4, 1983, in Crist, "The Joint Chiefs of Staff," 80.

95. Ronald Reagan, "Question-and-Answer Session with Reporters on Domestic and Foreign Policy Issues," December 14, 1983, online by Gerhard Peters and John T. Woolley, *The American Presidency Project*, accessed February 13, 2016, http://www.presidency.ucsb.edu/ws/?pid=40863.

96. Cable, Rumsfeld to Shultz, January 31, 1984 (2305Z), Ronald Reagan Library, 3.

97. "Lebanese Cabinet Resigns to Ease Conflict," 2.

98. Memo, "MNF Options."

99. Ibid.

100. Ibid., 1–4.

101. A variant of this option was to leave only one company of marines, approximately 120 to 150 men, since only a small force was required to serve the "presence" and "trip wire" functions; Memo, "MNF Options," 3–4.

102. Memo, "MNF Options," 5–6.

103. White paper, "Lebanon: A 90-Day Withdrawal Scenario," January 4, 1984, International Public Policy Research Council, Lebanon Documents (01/04/1984) (Rumsfeld Cables) II (1)-(9), RAC box 8, Crisis Management Center (CMC), NSC: Records, Ronald Reagan Library.

104. Memo, "MNF Options," 5–6.

105. Meeting notes, "Lebanon Group," January 16, 1984, Lebanon Documents (01/04/1984) (Rumsfeld Cables) II (6) folder, RAC box 8, Crisis Management Center (CMC), NSC: Records, Ronald Reagan Library, 1.

106. Memo, "MNF Options," 1, 6.

107. White paper, "Lebanon: A 90-Day Withdrawal Scenario," 1.

108. Weinberger, interview, *Frontline*.

109. Cannon, *President Reagan*, 456.

110. Shultz's travel schedule, accessed May 28, 2016, https://history.state.gov/departmenthistory/travels/secretary/shultz-george-pratt.

111. McFarlane, phone interview.

112. Cannon, *President Reagan*, 455–56.

113. Ibid., 456.

114. Memo, "MNF Options."

115. Cannon, *President Reagan*, 455–56.

116. Memo, "MNF Options."

117. Ibid., 5.

118. Dan Quayle, "Proceedings and Debates of the 98th Congress, 1st Session," August 4, 1983, vol. 129, part 17, Senate, Cong. Record, Rec. 22775, 23107.

119. Ronald Reagan, "Peace: Restoring the Margin of Safety," August 18, 1980, Veterans of Foreign Wars Convention, Chicago, IL, accessed June 2, 2016, https://reaganlibrary.archives.gov/archives/reference/8.18.80.html; Les Janka, deputy White House press secretary in 1983, in *Frontline*, season 3, episode 6, "Retreat from Beirut."

120. Memo, "MNF Options," 3; Isaacs, *Vietnam Shadows*, 73–74; Drew, *Campaign Journal*, 149.

121. Shultz, *Turmoil and Triumph*, 646, 649–51; Hill, phone interview; McFarlane with Smardz, *Special Trust*, 272–73.

122. Colin Powell, interview, February 23, 1989, in Cannon, *President Reagan*, 405.

123. Weinberger, *Fighting for Peace*, 154, 157, 162, 165, 167.

124. David B. Crist, "The Joint Chiefs of Staff and Limits to the Use of Military Power in Lebanon, 1982–1984," Special Historical Study 8, Top Secret Report, Unclassified Portion, Joint History Office, OCJCS, Washington, DC, 2015, 78; Isaacs, *Vietnam Shadows*, 68–69.

125. Weinberger, *Fighting for Peace*, 154, 157, 162, 165, 167; Cannon, *President Reagan*, 404.

126. *Department of State Bulletin* (Washington, DC: Office of Public Communication, Bureau of Public Affairs, 1983), 43–44, https://ia802205.us.archive.org/9/items/departmentofstatd1982unit/departmentofstatd1982unit_bw.pdf.

127. Shultz, *Turmoil and Triumph*, 646.

128. Jones, "The Vietnam Analogy and Lebanon," 81; Cannon, *President Reagan*, 405; Jeffrey Record, *Making War, Thinking History: Munich, Vietnam, and Presidential Uses of Force from Korea to Kosovo* (Annapolis, MD: Naval Institute Press, 2002), 86.

129. Alex Brummer, "Spectre of Vietnam Haunts America," *Guardian Weekly*, October 10, 1982, A6; David Shribman, "Foreign Policy Costing Reagan Public Support," *New York*

Times, September 30, 1983, http://www.nytimes.com/1983/09/30/world/foreign-policy-costing-reagan-public-support.html?pagewanted=all.

130. John M. Goshko, "Reagan Condemns Bombing; Vows to Pursue Peace," *Washington Post*, April 19, 1983, A17.

131. James Florio, Debate on House Jt. Resolution 364, "Extending Authorization for the Marines Deployment in Lebanon," Cong. Record, 98th Cong., 1st Session. House of Representatives, vol. 129, part 19, September 28, 1983, 26172.

132. Sam Gibbons, "Congressional Debate about the Marine Barracks Bombing" Cong. Record, 98th Congress, 1st Session, House of Representatives, vol. 129, part 21, October 24, 1983, 29030.

133. Steven V. Roberts, "Some Democrats Want Marines Out," *New York Times*, October 25, 1983, http://www.nytimes.com/1983/10/25/world/some-democrats-want-marines-out.html?pagewanted=print.

134. Michael Bilirakis, Debate on House Jt. Resoln 364, "Extending Authorization for the Marines Deployment in Lebanon," Cong. Record, 98th Congress, 1st Session, House of Representatives, vol. 129, part 19, September 28, 1983, 26174.

135. Shribman, "Foreign Policy Costing Reagan Public Support."

136. Gallup Organization, Gallup Poll and producers, October 7–10, 1983 (based on 1,513 interviews of American adults), USGALLUP.102483.R2 (Ithaca, NY: Cornell University, Roper Center for Public Opinion Research), iPOLL (distributor), accessed March 28, 2016, https://ropercenter.cornell.edu/CFIDE/cf/action/ipoll/questionDetail.cfm?keyword=lebanon%20AND%20%20vietnam&keywordoptions=1&exclude=&excludeOptions=1&topic=Any&organization=Any&label=&fromdate=1/1/1983&toDate=12/31/1984&stitle=&sponsor=&studydate=01-JAN-34&sample=1513&qstn_list=&qstnid=140912&qa_list=&qstn_id4=140912&study_list=&lastSearchId=317671050947&archno=&keywordDisplay=.

137. Time/Yankelovich, Skelly, and White Poll and producers, December 6–8, 1983 (based on one thousand interviews of registered voters); USYANK.835652.R25G, Dataset Archive Number: USYANK1983–5652 (Ithaca, NY: Cornell University, Roper Center for Public Opinion Research), iPOLL (distributor), accessed March 28, 2016, https://ropercenter.cornell.edu/CFIDE/cf/action/ipoll/ipollResult.cfm?keyword=lebanon+vietnam&exclude=&topic=Any&organization=Any&fromDate=1983&toDate=1984&questionViewId=&label=&studyId=&sortBy=BEG_DATE_DESC&search=submit.

138. Record, *Making War, Thinking History*, 86.

139. Reagan, *An American Life*, 466; Weinberger, "The Uses of Military Power."

140. Reagan, *An American Life*, 465.

141. "Statement on the Situation in Lebanon."

142. Naftali, *Blind Spot*, 139.

143. Memo, "Lebanon Report: Feb. 13, 1984," 1.

144. "Statement on the Situation in Lebanon."

145. Memo, "MNF Options," 4–5.

146. "Statement on the Situation in Lebanon."

147. Ibid.

148. Brinkley, *The Reagan Diaries*, 215; Memo, "Comments of Lebanon's Ambassador Bouhabib on President Gemayel's Request for Redeployment of the MNF," January 21, 1984, Lebanon—MNF (Multinational Force) 1984 (2) folder, box 91136, Near East and South Asia Affairs Directorate: Records, Reagan Library.

149. Reagan, NSDD 123, February 1, 1984, 2.

150. "Statement on the Situation in Lebanon."

151. Background briefing by senior administration official on the situation in Lebanon, Point Mugu NAS, California, Office of the Press Secretary, February 7, 1984, in Cannon, *President Reagan*, 457.

152. Notes, "Strategy for US Actions in Lebanon," January 4, 1984, 1.

153. Cannon, *President Reagan*, 456.

154. Memo, "MNF Options"; "Statement on the Situation in Lebanon."

155. "Statement on the Situation in Lebanon."

156. Memo, "MNF Options," 4–5.

157. "Statement on the Situation in Lebanon."

158. McFarlane with Smardz, *Special Trust*, 273.

159. "Documents 256 and 258: Announcements Regarding the Redeployment of Marines to Ships off the Coast of Lebanon, American Foreign Policy Current Documents" (Washington, DC: Dept. of State, February 7, 1984).

160. Lewis, "Quagmire, Here We Come."

161. Weinberger, "The Uses of Military Power"; Weinberger, *Fighting for Peace*, 180–81, 361.

162. Yuen Foong Khong, *Analogies at War: Korea, Munich, Dien Bien Phu, and the Vietnam Decisions of 1965* (Princeton, NJ: Princeton University Press, 1992), 64.

163. Shultz, *Turmoil and Triumph*, 646, 649–51; Weinberger, "The Uses of Military Power"; House Jt. Resolution 364, "Congressional Debate about Extending Authorization for the President's Deployment of Marines in Lebanon," Congressional Record, 98th Congress, 1st Session, House of Representatives, vol. 129, part 19, September 28–29, 1983; CQ Almanac, "A Reluctant Congress Adopts Lebanon Policy," accessed March 12, 2016, https://library.cqpress.com/cqalmanac/document.php?id=cqal83-1198422; Statutory Authorization under the War Powers Resolution—Lebanon: Hearing and Markup Before the Committee on Foreign Affairs, House of Representatives, Ninety-Eighth Congress, First Session (Washington, DC, 1983).

164. McFarlane, phone interview; Hill, phone interview; Reagan, *An American Life*, 465–66; Shultz, *Turmoil and Triumph*, 646, 649–51; Weinberger, *Fighting for Peace*, 180–81, 361.

165. Memo, "MNF Options."

166. Shultz, *Turmoil and Triumph*, 646, 649–51.

167. Weinberger, "The Uses of Military Power."

168. Ibid.

169. Ibid.

170. Reagan, *An American Life*, 465–67.

171. Ibid., 466.

172. Ibid.

4. BLACK HAWK DOWN

The chapter 4 epigraphs are drawn from Arnold R. Isaacs, *Vietnam Shadows: The War, Its Ghosts, and Its Legacy* (Baltimore: Johns Hopkins University Press, 1997), 86–87; David Halberstam, *War in a Time of Peace: Bush, Clinton, and the Generals*, vol. 34 (New York: Simon & Schuster, 2001), 254; Isaacs, *Vietnam Shadows*, 86; William (Bill) Clinton, *My Life* (New York: Random House, 2004), 104; Halberstam, *War in a Time of Peace*, 264–65.

1. Clinton, *My Life*, 554.

2. Ibid., 100–104.

3. Ibid., 103–104.

4. Ibid., 103; Elizabeth Drew, *On the Edge: The Clinton Presidency* (New York: Simon & Schuster, 1994), 328.

5. Yuen Foong Khong, *Analogies at War: Korea, Munich, Dien Bien Phu, and the Vietnam Decisions of 1965* (Princeton, NJ: Princeton University Press, 1992), 64; Drew, *On the Edge*, 328; Halberstam, *War in a Time of Peace*, 261, 263–64; Hal Brands, *From Berlin to Baghdad: America's Search for Purpose in the Post-Cold War World* (Lexington: University of Kentucky Press, 2008), 133–34.

6. George Stephanopoulos, *All Too Human: A Political Education* (New York: Back Bay Books, 2008), 217; Drew, *On the Edge*, 326; Curtis Wilkie, "Beirut Revisited: Somalia Is Being Compared to the 'Quagmire' in Vietnam, but Lebanon Is the More Precise Analogy," *Boston Globe*, October 10, 1993, https://www.highbeam.com/doc/1P2-8248947.html; Richard A. Clarke, *Against All Enemies: Inside America's War on Terror* (New York: Free Press, 2004), 88.

7. National Security Council, Office of Press and Communications, and Philip "PJ" Crowley, "Somalia [1]," OA/ID 2011-0516-S, box 13, Clinton Digital Library, accessed May 26, 2016, http://clinton.presidentiallibraries.us/items/show/48603, 2–7; Halberstam, *War in a Time of Peace*, 248.

8. Brands, *From Berlin to Baghdad*, 131–36.

9. Richard A. Clarke, phone interview, July 5, 2016.

10. Leon Panetta and Jim Newton, *Worthy Fights: A Memoir of Leadership in War and Peace* (London: Penguin, 2014).

11. Halberstam, *War in a Time of Peace*, 256, 258–59.

12. Brands, *From Berlin to Baghdad*, 133; Halberstam, *War in a Time of Peace*, 260.

13. John L. Hirsch and Robert B. Oakley, *Somalia and Operation Restore Hope* (Washington, DC: United States Institute of Peace Press, 1995), 49–176.

14. Dale Shrader and Shanna Shrader, and Steve Fowler, interviews, January 31, 2017, and December 7, 2017, respectively.

15. Clarke, phone interview.

16. Peter D. Feaver, *Armed Servants: Agency, Oversight, and Civil-Military Relations* (Cambridge, MA: Harvard University Press, 2003).

17. Peter Feaver and Richard H. Kohn, *Soldiers and Civilians: The Civil-Military Gap and American National Security* (Cambridge: MIT Press, 2001), 93–94; Halberstam, *War in a Time of Peace*, 265.

18. Feaver, *Armed Servants*, 239.

19. Clarke, phone interview; Shawn Thomas Cochran, "Civil-Military Balance of Resolve: The Domestic Politics of Withdrawal from Protracted Small War" (PhD diss., University of Chicago, 2012).

20. Sarah E. Croco, *Peace at What Price?* (Cambridge: Cambridge University Press, 2015).

21. John E. Mueller, *War, Presidents, and Public Opinion* (New York: Wiley, 1973).

22. Drew, *On the Edge*, 325–29.

23. Madeleine Korbel Albright, Bill Woodward, and Lisbeth Warburg, *Madam Secretary* (New York: Miramax Books, 2003), 145; Clinton, *My Life*, 552–53.

24. Hirsch and Oakley, *Somalia and Operation Restore Hope*, 42.

25. Feaver, *Armed Servants*, 256–72.

26. Hirsch and Oakley, *Somalia and Operation Restore Hope*, 145.

27. Ibid., 63–93.

28. Ambassador Robert Oakley, interview, "Ambush in Mogadishu," *Frontline*, PBS, 1995, http://www.pbs.org/wgbh/pages/frontline/shows/ambush/interviews/oakley.html; Hirsch and Oakley, *Somalia and Operation Restore Hope*.

29. Anthony Zinni, UNITAF director of operations, phone interview, July 28, 2016.

30. Robert B. Oakley, "An Envoy's Perspective," *Joint Forces Quarterly* 2 (1993): 52; Hirsch and Oakley, *Somalia and Operation Restore Hope*, 63–95.

31. Hirsch and Oakley, *Somalia and Operation Restore Hope*, 63–145.

32. Addis Ababa General Agreement, January 8, 1993, and Agreement to establish the Ad Hoc Committee on National Reconciliation, January 15, 1993; Hirsch and Oakley, *Somalia and Operation Restore Hope*, 93–99.

33. Zinni, phone interview; Hirsch and Oakley, *Somalia and Operation Restore Hope*, 49–99.

34. "Resolution 814" (S/RES/814), Official Record, UN Security Council, March 26, 1993, 48th year.

35. Walter S. Clarke, "Testing the World's Resolve in Somalia," *Parameters* 23, no. 4 (1993): 52–54.

36. "Resolution 837" (S/RES/837), Official Record, UN Security Council, June 6, 1993, 48th year.

37. Halberstam, *War in a Time of Peace*, 254, 256, 258–60; Bruce Jentleson, interview, February 25, 2016.

38. Anthony Lake, *6 Nightmares: Real Threats in a Dangerous World and How America Can Meet Them* (Boston: Little, Brown, 2000), 174.

39. Barry McCaffrey, phone interview, July 22, 2016; Helen Dewar and Kevin Merida, "From Congress, More Questions," *Washington Post*, October 5, 1993, http://www.washingtonpost.com/archive/politics/1993/10/05/from-congress-more-questions/ce194c11-1cc1-4fe7-a6fc-d9d0ef95ecee/; Walter S. Poole, "The Effort to Save Somalia: August 1992 to March 1994," Office of the Chairman of the Joint Chiefs of Staff, Joint History Office, 2005.

40. Drew, *On the Edge*, 331; John R. Bolton, "Wrong Turn in Somalia," *Foreign Affairs* 73 (1994): 64; Feaver, *Armed Servants*, 239–48; Brands, *From Berlin to Baghdad*, 129–35.

41. Halberstam, *War in a Time of Peace*, 254, 256, 258–60; Michael Gordon, "U.S. Officers Were Divided on Somali Raid," *New York Times*, May 12, 1994, http://www.nytimes.com/1994/05/13/world/us-officers-were-divided-on-somali-raid.html; Thomas Montgomery, *Frontline*, PBS, accessed September 16, 2015, http://www.pbs.org/wgbh/pages/frontline/shows/ambush/interviews/montgomery.html#tanks.

42. Jonathan Howe, phone interview, July 27, 2016.

43. Richard Bernstein, "The World; Against New Odds, The U.N. Insists on Helping in Somalia," *New York Times*, July 18, 1993, http://www.nytimes.com/1993/07/18/weekinreview/the-world-against-new-odds-the-un-insists-on-helping-in-somalia.html.

44. Bolton, "Wrong Turn in Somalia," 63.

45. Drew, *On the Edge*, 331.

46. "Resolution 865" (S/RES/865), Official Record, UN Security Council, September 22, 1993, 48th year.

47. Halberstam, *War in a Time of Peace*, 254, 260; Barton Gellman, "U.S. Rhetoric Changed, but Hunt Persisted," *Washington Post*, October 7, 1993, http://www.washingtonpost.com/archive/politics/1993/10/07/us-rhetoric-changed-but-hunt-persisted/4e068083-6442-4674-a83b-8fdfce67109c/.

48. Halberstam, *War in a Time of Peace*, 260.

49. Ibid.; Peter Feaver, interview, November 5, 2015; Drew, *On the Edge*, 331.

50. Anthony Lake, "From Containment to Enlargement," Johns Hopkins University, September 21, 1993, https://clinton.presidentiallibraries.us/items/show/9013.

51. Leslie Aspin Jr., "U.N. Intervention in Somalia," speech to Center for Strategic and International Studies, August 27, 1993, C-SPAN video, 23:05, http://www.c-span.org/video/?49523-1/un-intervention-somalia.

52. Aspin, "U.N. Intervention in Somalia"; Zinni, phone interview.

53. William J. Clinton, "Remarks to the 48th Session of the United Nations General Assembly in New York City," September 27, 1993, online by Gerhard Peters and John T. Woolley, *The American Presidency Project*, http://www.presidency.ucsb.edu/ws/?pid=47119.

54. Halberstam, *War in a Time of Peace*, 260.

55. Colin Powell, phone interview, August 8, 2016; Shrader and Shrader, and Fowler, interviews.

56. Poole, "The Effort to Save Somalia."

57. Powell, phone interview.

58. Halberstam, *War in a Time of Peace*, 260–61.

59. Powell, phone interview.

60. Feaver, interviews, March 1 and 8, 2016.

61. Halberstam, *War in a Time of Peace*, 254, 260; Drew, *On the Edge*, 325–29.

62. Powell, phone interview.

63. Clarke, phone interview.

64. Zinni, phone interview.

65. Howe, phone interview.

66. Powell, phone interview; Halberstam, *War in a Time of Peace*, 259; Howe, phone interview.

67. Powell, phone interview.

68. Poole, "The Effort to Save Somalia," 46.

69. Ibid., 53; Anthony Zinni, interview, "Ambush in Mogadishu," *Frontline*, PBS, 1995, http://www.pbs.org/wgbh/pages/frontline/shows/ambush/interviews/zinni.html.

70. Poole, "The Effort to Save Somalia," 58.

71. Clarke, phone interview; Feaver, interview, March 1 and 8, 2016; Drew, *On the Edge*, 325–26.

72. Poole, "The Effort to Save Somalia," 57–58.

73. Hirsch and Oakley, *Somalia and Operation Restore Hope*, 115.

74. Task Force Ranger participant, presentation, Fort Bragg, NC, October 3, 2016.

75. Shrader and Shrader, and Fowler, interviews.

76. Clinton, *My Life*, 552–53.

77. Ibid., 551; National Security Council, Office of Press and Communications, and Philip "PJ" Crowley, "Somalia [1]," 2–7; Drew, *On the Edge*, 325–26.

78. Lake, "From Containment to Enlargement," https://clinton.presidentiallibraries.us/items/show/9013; Madeleine Albright, *Dispatch Magazine*, US Department of State, June 28, 1993; William Clinton, "Address to the UN General Assembly," September 27, 1993.

79. Halberstam, *War in a Time of Peace*, 263.

80. Kenneth Menkhaus and Louis Ortmayer, *Key Decisions in the Somalia Intervention* (Washington, DC: Georgetown University, School of Foreign Service, Institute for the Study of Diplomacy, 1995), 19.

81. Powell, phone interview; Shrader and Shrader, and Fowler, interviews.

82. Clinton, *My Life*, 552–53.

83. Drew, *On the Edge*, 325–26.

84. Clinton, "Remarks to the 48th Session of the United Nations General Assembly in New York City."

85. Carolyn Logan, "US Public Opinion and the Intervention in Somalia: Lessons for the Future of Military-Humanitarian Interventions," *Fletcher Forum of World Affairs* 20, no. 2 (1996): 156, 166–67; Louis J. Klarevas, "Trends: The United States Peace Operation in Somalia," *Public Opinion Quarterly* 64, no. 4 (2000): 523–40.

86. Logan, "US Public Opinion and the Intervention in Somalia," 156, 166–67.

87. John G. Sommer, "Hope Restored? Humanitarian Aid in Somalia 1990–1994," RPG Refugee Policy Group, Center for Policy Analysis and Research on Refugee Issues, 1994, C-4–C-5.

88. Logan, "US Public Opinion and the Intervention in Somalia," 156, 166–67; Bruce W. Jentleson and Rebecca L. Britton, "Still Pretty Prudent Post-Cold War American Public Opinion on the Use of Military Force," *Journal of Conflict Resolution* 42, no. 4 (1998): 395–417.

89. Drew, *On the Edge*, 326; Halberstam, *War in a Time of Peace*, 254, 256, 258–60.

90. Halberstam, *War in a Time of Peace*, 256.

91. Feaver, *Armed Servants*, 239.

92. Gallup Presidential Approval Ratings (Bill Clinton), 1993, https://news.gallup.com/poll/116584/presidential-approval-ratings-bill-clinton.aspx.

93. Ibid.

94. Ibid.

95. Ibid.

96. Feaver, *Armed Servants*, 239.

97. Halberstam, *War in a Time of Peace*, 248; Clinton, *My Life*, 552–58.

98. Brands, *From Berlin to Baghdad*, 270.

99. Osama bin Laden, "Declaration of Jihad against the Americans Occupying the Land of the Two Holiest Sites," Combatting Terrorism Center, August 23, 1996, https://ctc.usma.edu/harmony-program/declaration-of-jihad-against-the-americans-occupying-the-land-of-the-two-holiest-sites-original-language-2/; Brands, *From Berlin to Baghdad*, 270; Clarke, *Against All Enemies*, 88.

100. Clarke, *Against All Enemies*, 87–88.

101. Hans J. Morgenthau, "To Intervene or not to Intervene," *Foreign Affairs* 45, no. 3 (1967): 425–36.

102. Halberstam, *War in a Time of Peace*, 264.

103. William Clinton, "Address to the Nation on Somalia," October 7, 1993.

104. William Clinton, "Letter to Congress," October 13, 1993.

105. Halberstam, *War in a Time of Peace*, 264; Drew, *On the Edge*, 326–31.

106. Clarke, *Against All Enemies*, 87; Drew, *On the Edge*, 326–31; Feaver, interview, March 1, 2016; Halberstam, *War in a Time of Peace*, 248–66.

107. Feaver, interview, March 1, 2016.

108. Clarke, *Against All Enemies*, 87.

109. Ibid., 87–88; Mueller, *War, Presidents, and Public Opinion*; Feaver, *Armed Servants*, 239–50; Drew, *On the Edge*, 325–29.

110. Mueller, *War, Presidents, and Public Opinion*.

111. Halberstam, *War in a Time of Peace*, 248–60; Drew, *On the Edge*, 325–30.

112. Gallup Presidential Approval Ratings (Bill Clinton).

113. Feaver, interview, March 1, 2016.

114. Clarke, *Against All Enemies*, 87.

115. Ibid., 87–88; Halberstam, *War in a Time of Peace*, 248–66; Drew, *On the Edge*, 325–30.

116. Senate Committee on Foreign Relations, US Policy in Somalia: Hearing before the Committee on Foreign Relations, United States Senate, One Hundred Third Congress, First Session, July 29, 1993, S Hrg., US GPO, Washington, DC.

117. Dewar and Merida, "From Congress, More Questions"; James Burk, "Public Support for Peacekeeping in Lebanon and Somalia: Assessing the Casualties Hypothesis," *Political Science Quarterly* 114, no. 1 (1999): 53–78.

118. Clinton, *My Life*, 552–53.

119. Albright, Woodward, and Warburg, *Madam Secretary*, 145.

120. Lake, *6 Nightmares*, 131, 135.

121. Clifford Krauss, "The Somalia Mission: White House Tries to Calm Congress," *New York Times*, October 6, 1993, http://www.nytimes.com/1993/10/06/world/the-somalia-mission-white-house-tries-to-calm-congress.html.

122. https://ropercenter.cornell.edu/CFIDE/cf/action/ipoll/ipollResult.cfm?keyword=somalia&exclude=&topic=Any&organization=Any&fromDate=1992&toDate=1994&questionViewId=&label=&studyId=&sortBy=BEG_DATE_DESC&search.x=52&search.y=12.

123. Clinton, *My Life*, 552–53; Drew, *On the Edge*, 325–26; Stephanopoulos, *All Too Human*, 214–17.

124. Feaver, interviews, November 5, 2015, March 1 and 8, 2016.

125. Stephanopoulos, *All Too Human*, 214.

126. Clarke, *Against All Enemies*, 86–87.

127. Halberstam, *War in a Time of Peace*, 264.

128. Clarke, phone interview.

129. Menkhaus and Ortmayer, *Key Decisions in the Somalia Intervention*, 21–22.

130. Dewar and Merida, "From Congress, More Questions."

131. Menkhaus and Ortmayer, *Key Decisions in the Somalia Intervention*, 21–22.

132. Halberstam, *War in a Time of Peace*, 264; Stephanopoulos, *All Too Human*, 214; Drew, *On the Edge*, 326–28.

133. Aspin, "U.N. Intervention in Somalia."

134. Stephanopoulos, *All Too Human*, 214; Drew, *On the Edge*, 326.

135. Drew, *On the Edge*, 328.

136. Ibid., 326.

137. Halberstam, *War in a Time of Peace*, 264.

138. Brands, *From Berlin to Baghdad*, 134.

139. CNN, USA Today, and Gallup survey, October 5, 1993, Dataset: USAIPOCNUS1993-422016, accessed October 5, 2015, https://ropercenter.cornell.edu/CFIDE/cf/action/ipoll/ipollResult.cfm?keyword=somalia&exclude=&topic=Any&organization=Any&fromDate=1992&toDate=1994&questionViewId=&label=&studyId=&sortBy=BEG_DATE_DESC&search.x=52&search.y=12.

140. Clinton, "Letter to Congress."

141. Survey, Roper iPoll, accessed October 5, 2015, https://ropercenter.cornell.edu/CFIDE/cf/action/ipoll/ipollResult.cfm?keyword=somalia&exclude=&topic=Any&organization=Any&fromDate=1992&toDate=1994&questionViewId=&label=&studyId=&sort

By=BEG_DATE_DESC&search.x=52&search.y=12 (see Graph 4.3; note that "(a) 'W'" stands for *Washington Post* data).

142. Time/CNN/Yankelovich Partners survey, Roper iPoll, October 7, 1993, Dataset: USAIPOCNUS1993-422016, accessed October 5, 2015, https://ropercenter.cornell.edu/CFIDE/cf/action/ipoll/ipollResult.cfm?keyword=somalia&exclude=&topic=Any&organization=Any&fromDate=1992&toDate=1994&questionViewId=&label=&studyId=&sortBy=BEG_DATE_DESC&search.x=52&search.y=12. In the same poll, 35 percent also indicated that "no goal is worth the death of one more U.S. soldier." Although not a majority, the totality of this data paints a complicated picture.

143. CNN, *USA Today*, and Gallup survey, Roper iPoll, October 5, 1993, https://ropercenter.cornell.edu/CFIDE/cf/action/ipoll/ipollResult.cfm?keyword=somalia&exclude=&topic=Any&organization=Any&fromDate=1992&toDate=1994&questionViewId=&label=&studyId=&sortBy=BEG_DATE_DESC&search.x=52&search.y=12.

144. Feaver, *Armed Servants*, 247; Peter D. Feaver and Christopher Gelpi, *Choosing Your Battles: American Civil-Military Relations and the Use of Force* (Princeton, NJ: Princeton University Press, 2004), 136, 148.

145. Feaver, *Armed Servants*, 247.

146. Christopher Aspin and Adm. David Jeremiah, press briefing, October 7, 1993, http://clinton6.nara.gov/1993/10/1993-10-07-briefing-on-somalia.html; Menkhaus and Ortmayer, *Key Decisions in the Somalia Intervention*, 22; Poole, "The Effort to Save Somalia," 59.

147. Drew, *On the Edge*, 329.

148. Hirsch and Oakley, *Somalia and Operation Restore Hope*, 115; Peter Feaver, comments to author, spring 2016.

149. Aspin and Jeremiah, press briefing.

150. Clarke, *Against All Enemies*, 87; Poole, "The Effort to Save Somalia," 60–61.

151. CNN, *USA Today*, and Gallup survey.

152. Clinton, "Address to the Nation on Somalia"; Drew, *On the Edge*, 329–30.

153. Clinton, "Address to the Nation on Somalia."

154. Mark Bowden, *Black Hawk Down: A Story of Modern War* (New York: Grove Press, 2010); Howe, phone interview; Trusten Frank Crigler, "Go Back to Peacekeeping in the Somali Quagmire: Letters to the Editor," *New York Times*, June 18, 1993, http://www.nytimes.com/1993/06/18/opinion/18iht-edlet_70.html; Wilkie, "Beirut Revisited"; Jentleson, phone interview.

155. Drew, *On the Edge*, 328–29.

156. Clinton, *My Life*, 100–104; Krauss, "The Somalia Mission."

157. Clinton, *My Life*, 103–104; J. William Fulbright, "Fatal Arrogance of Power," *New York Times Magazine*, 1966, 28–29; J. William Fulbright, "The Arrogance of Power," *New York Times Magazine*, 1967.

158. Clinton, *My Life*, 104; Halberstam, *War in a Time of Peace*, 262–65; Drew, *On the Edge*, 328.

159. Ronald Reagan, "Address to the Nation on United States Policy for Peace in the Middle East," September 1, 1982, https://reaganlibrary.archives.gov/archives/speeches/1982/90182d.htm.

160. Drew, *On the Edge*, 326; National Security Council, Office of Press and Communications, and Philip "PJ" Crowley, "Somalia [1]," 1–4; Feaver, interview, November 5, 2015; Feaver, *Armed Servants*, 247; Feaver and Gelpi, *Choosing Your Battles*.

161. Clinton, *My Life*, 103–104.

162. Stephanopoulos, *All Too Human*, 217.

163. Ibid.; Drew, *On the Edge*, 326; Clarke, *Against All Enemies*, 88.

164. Clinton, "Letter to Congress"; Clinton, "Address to the Nation on Somalia."

165. William A. Boettcher and Michael D. Cobb, "'Don't Let Them Die in Vain' Casualty Frames and Public Tolerance for Escalating Commitment in Iraq," *Journal of Conflict Resolution* 53, no. 5 (2009): 677; Croco, *Peace at What Price?*; Donna J. Nincic and Miroslav Nincic, "Commitment to Military Intervention: The Democratic Government as Economic Investor," *Journal of Peace Research* 32, no. 4 (1995): 413–26; George W. Downs and David M. Rocke, "Conflict, Agency, and Gambling for Resurrection: The Principal-Agent Problem Goes to War," *American Journal of Political Science* 38 (1994): 362–80; Giacomo Chiozza and Hein Erich Goemans, *Leaders and International Conflict* (Cambridge: Cambridge University Press, 2011).

166. Clinton, "Address to the Nation on Somalia."

167. Ibid.; Feaver, *Armed Servants*, 246.

168. Hirsch and Oakley, *Somalia and Operation Restore Hope*, 132.

169. Clinton, "Address to the Nation."

170. Halberstam, *War in a Time of Peace*, 264.

171. Clinton, "Address to the Nation on Somalia."

172. Clinton, "Letter to Congress"; Brands, *From Berlin to Baghdad*, 270.

173. Clarke, *Against All Enemies*, 87; Drew, *On the Edge*, 329.

174. Poole, "The Effort to Save Somalia."

175. Clinton, "Address to the Nation on Somalia."

176. Halberstam, *War in a Time of Peace*, 264; Feaver, *Armed Servants*, 247.

177. Drew, *On the Edge*, 326–29.

178. Clinton, "Address to the Nation on Somalia"; Clinton, "Letter to Congress."

179. Hirsch and Oakley, *Somalia and Operation Restore Hope*, 137.

180. Bowden, *Black Hawk Down*, 311–12.

181. Brands, *From Berlin to Baghdad*, 135.

182. Feaver, *Armed Servants*, 247.

183. Poole, "The Effort to Save Somalia," 60–61.

184. Osama bin Laden's Declaration of Jihad against Americans, http://webcache.googleusercontent.com/search?q=cache:DMa6U5xmBUwJ:salempress.com/store/pdfs/bin_laden.pdf+&cd=2&hl=en&ct=clnk&gl=us; Brands, *From Berlin to Baghdad*, 270; Clarke, *Against All Enemies*, 88.

185. Halberstam, *War in a Time of Peace*, 265; Caspar Weinberger, "The Uses of Military Power," Remarks Prepared for Delivery by the Hon. Caspar Weinberger, Secretary of Defense, to the National Press Club, Washington, DC, November 28, 1984, http://www.pbs.org/wgbh/pages/frontline/shows/military/force/weinberger.html; Cori Dauber, "Implications of the Weinberger Doctrine for American Military Intervention in a Post-Desert Storm Age," *Contemporary Security Policy* 22, no. 3 (2001): 66–90; Kenneth J. Campbell, "Once Burned, Twice Cautious: Explaining the Powell-Weinberger Doctrine," *Armed Forces and Society* 24, no. 3 (1998): 357–74; *Presidential Decision Directive 25 (PDD-25): Reforming Multilateral Peace Operations*, May 3, 1994; Andrew Priest, "From Saigon to Baghdad: The Vietnam Syndrome, the Iraq War and American Foreign Policy," *Intelligence and National Security* 24, no. 1 (2009): 164–65.

186. Powell, phone interview.

187. Feaver, interviews, November 5, 2015, and March 1 and 8, 2016.

188. Crigler, "Go Back to Peacekeeping in the Somali Quagmire."

189. National Security Council, Office of Press and Communications, and Philip "PJ" Crowley, "Somalia [1]."

190. Powell, phone interview; Clarke, phone interview; Shrader and Shrader, and Fowler interviews.

191. Clinton, *My Life*, 101–104.

192. Stephanopoulos, *All Too Human*, 217.

193. Richard Lugar, interview, "Ambush in Mogadishu," *Frontline*, PBS, 1995, http://www.pbs.org/wgbh/pages/frontline/shows/ambush/interviews/lugar.html; Colonel (Retired) Kenneth Allard, interview, "Ambush in Mogadishu," *Frontline*, PBS, October 26, 2001, http://www.pbs.org/wgbh/pages/frontline/shows/ambush/interviews/allard.html.

194. Clinton, *My Life*, 101–104.

195. CNN, *USA Today*, and Gallup survey; Gallup Presidential Approval Ratings (Clinton); Drew, *On the Edge*, 325–26.

196. David Howell Petraeus, *The American Military and the Lessons of Vietnam: A Study of Military Influence and the Use of Force in the Post-Vietnam Era* (Princeton, NJ: Princeton University Press, 1987), 133.

197. Weinberger, "The Uses of Military Power."

198. *Presidential Decision Directive 25 (PDD-25).*

199. Andrew Bacevich, "The Forgotten Lessons of Black Hawk Down: The Disaster in Somalia Offered America a Glimpse of the Future of Warfare. No One Listened," *New York Times*, October 3, 2018, https://www.nytimes.com/2018/10/03/opinion/the-forgotten-lessons-of-black-hawk-down.html.

200. Ibid.

5. THE IRAQ SURGE

The chapter 5 epigraphs are drawn from Christopher Dandeker, "What 'Success' Means in Afghanistan, Iraq, and Libya," in *How 9/11 Changed Our Ways of War*, ed. James Burk (Stanford, CA: Stanford University Press, 2013), 123; Matthew Duss and Lawrence Korb, "Hagel Should Stand by Iraq Opposition," *Politico*, January 31, 2013, http://www.politico.com/stry/2013/01/chuck-hagel-should-stand-by-iraq-opposition-086931;. Fred Kaplan, *The Insurgents: David Petraeus and the Plot to Change the American Way of War*, (New York: Simon and Schuster, 2013), 211 (emphasis in original); George W. Bush, "Remarks at the Veterans of Foreign Wars National Convention in Kansas City, Missouri," Public Papers of the Presidents, Book 2, August 22, 2007, 1105; George W. Bush, "The Fifth Anniversary of September 11, 2001," September 11, 2006, http://2001-2009.state.gov/p/nea/rls/72057.htm; Eliot Cohen, "Analyzing Past Military Strategies to Interpret the Wars in Afghanistan and Iraq," West Point Center for Oral History, Transcript: 10, July 29, 2011, http://www.westpointcoh.org/interviews/analyzing-past-military-strategies-to-interpret-the-wars-in-iraq-and-afghanistan; Robert Gates, *Duty: Memoirs of a Secretary at War* (New York: Random House, 2014), 212; Condoleezza Rice, interview, Southern Methodist University Center for Presidential History (hereafter SMU-CPH), July 20, 2015, https://vimeo.com/134265433; Doug Lute, interview, SMU-CPH, May 28, 2015, https://vimeo.com/131253237; Pete Mansoor, interview, SMU-CPH, June 12, 2015, https://vimeo.com/131169447.

1. Andrew F. Krepinevich Jr., "How to Win in Iraq," *Foreign Affairs* 84 (September/October 2005): 87–104; Andrew F. Krepinevich Jr., *The Army and Vietnam* (Baltimore: Johns Hopkins University Press, 1986).

2. John P. Abizaid, "Preparing for War after 9/11," West Point Center for Oral History, Transcript: 23, April 9, 2013, http://www.westpointcoh.org/interviews/preparing-for-war-after-9-11.

3. Douglas J. Feith, *War and Decision: Inside the Pentagon at the Dawn of the War on Terrorism* (New York: HarperCollins, 2008), 425–55.

4. Peter Baker, "George W. Bush: The Decider and Delegator," in *Triumphs and Tragedies of the Modern Presidency*, ed. Maxmillian Angerholzer III, James Kitfield, Norman Ornstein, and Stephen Skowronek, Center for the Study of the Presidency and Congress (Santa Barbara, CA: Praeger, 2001), 307.

5. Michael R. Gordon and Bernard E. Trainor, *Cobra II: The Inside Story of the Invasion and Occupation of Iraq*. (New York: Vintage, 2006), 688–92; Frank Wolf, interview, Southern Methodist University, Center for Presidential History, January 10, 2016, https://vimeo.com/album/3353422/video/152513103; Michael R. Gordon and Bernard E. Trainor, *The Endgame: The Inside Story of the Struggle for Iraq, from George W. Bush to Barack Obama* (New York: Pantheon, 2012), 136, 270; Richard Haass, "Revisiting the Iraq War," Project Syndicate, July 8, 2016, https://www.project-syndicate.org/commentary/chilcot-report-iraq-war-lessons-by-richard-n--haass-2016-07.

6. Karl Rove, *Courage and Consequence: My Life as a Conservative in the Fight* (New York: Simon & Schuster, 2010), 300–301; Jack Mitchell, "20 Years Ago, the U.S. Warned of Iraq's Alleged 'Weapons of Mass Destruction,'" NPR, February 3, 2023, https://www.npr.org/2023/02/03/1151160567/colin-powell-iraq-un-weapons-mass-destruction; William C. Martel, "2003 Invasion of Iraq," in *Victory in War: Foundations of Modern Military Policy* (Cambridge: Cambridge University Press, 2006), 243–64, https://www.cambridge.org/core/books/abs/victory-in-war/2003-invasion-of-iraq/7D5BA68572D9EE0AF537DF72C6CF607A.

7. George W. Bush, "Second Inaugural Address," C-SPAN, January 20, 2005, https://www.c-span.org/video/?185043-6/presidential-inaugural-address; Jim Jeffrey, interview, SMU-CPH, August 17, 2015, https://vimeo.com/137794310; Joseph Collins and Nicholas Rostow, "An Interview with Stephen Hadley," *Prism* 5, no. 3 (July 2014): 150.

8. Tom Raum, "Bush's Rationale for War Shifting," *Deseret News*, October 15, 2006, A20, http://webcache.googleusercontent.com/search?q=cache:onypKOCr9AgJ:glitterhelm.com/article/650198804/Bushs-rationale-for-war-shifting.html+&cd=1&hl=en&ct=clnk&gl=us.

9. Condoleezza Rice, "Iraq and U.S. Policy," Congressional testimony before the Senate Committee on Foreign Relations, October 19, 2005, https://www.c-span.org/video/?189410-1/iraq-us-foreign-policy; Rice, Condoleezza, interview, SMU-CPH; Lewis Sorley, *A Better War: The Unexamined Victories and Final Tragedy of America's Last Years in Vietnam* (New York: Harcourt Brace, 1999); Rove, *Courage and Consequence*, 475; George W. Bush, "President Bush Delivers Remarks on the War on Terrorism," *Washington Post*, November 11, 2005, http://www.washingtonpost.com/wp-dyn/content/article/2005/11/11/AR2005111100987.html; George W. Bush, "Transcript of Bush Speech," CNN, December 12, 2005, http://www.cnn.com/2005/POLITICS/12/12/bush.transcript.philly.speech/.

10. Peter Feaver, interview, SMU-CPH, April 27, 2015, https://vimeo.com/131688470; Meghan O'Sullivan, interview, SMU-CPH, May 12, 2016, https://vimeo.com/album/3353422/video/166466344; Thomas E. Ricks, *The Gamble: General David Petraeus and the American Military Adventure in Iraq, 2006–2008* (Penguin, 2009), 42–45.

11. Feaver, interview, SMU-CPH; Ricks, *The Gamble*, 42–45; Krepinevich Jr., *The Army and Vietnam*.

12. O'Sullivan, interview, SMU-CPH; Feaver, interview, SMU-CPH.

13. Joshua Bolten, interview, SMU-CPH, May 15, 2015, https://vimeo.com/128817283.

14. O'Sullivan, interview, SMU-CPH; Karl Rove, interview, SMU-CPH, February 2, 2016, https://vimeo.com/album/3353422/video/153930806; Stephen Hadley, Meghan O'Sullivan, and Peter Feaver, "How 'the Surge' Came to Be," SMU-CPH, Ten Year Anniversary Manuscript Draft (pt. 2, chap. 1), January 2017, 375–78, 421–24, 431.

15. J. D. Crouch, interview, SMU-CPH, June 25, 2015, https://vimeo.com/132171275.

16. Feaver, interview, SMU-CPH; Bolten, interview, SMU-CPH; Crouch, interview, SMU-CPH.

17. Crouch, interview, SMU-CPH. In retrospect, then lieutenant general Doug Lute believed that the ends should have been the starting point; Lute, interview, SMU-CPH.

18. Bob Woodward, *The War Within: A Secret White House History 2006–2008* (New York: Simon & Schuster, 2008), 207–208.

19. Peter Baker, *Days of Fire: Bush and Cheney in the White House* (New York: Anchor, 2014), 510–13.

20. Rice, interview, SMU-CPH; David Satterfield, interview, SMU-CPH, January 14, 2016, https://vimeo.com/album/3353422/video/151922310; Peter Pace, interview, SMU-CPH, January 20, 2016, https://vimeo.com/album/3353422/video/152509838.

21. Donald Rumsfeld, *Known and Unknown: A Memoir* (New York: Penguin, 2011), 482–83.

22. Baker, *Days of Fire*, 490.

23. Crouch, interview, SMU-CPH.

24. James A. Baker III and Lee H. Hamilton, Co-Chairs, with Lawrence S. Eagleburger, Vernon E. Jordan Jr., Edwin Meese III, Sandra Day O'Connor, Leon Panetta, William J. Perry, Charles S. Robb, and Alan K. Simpson, *The Iraq Study Group Report: The Way Forward—A New Approach*, authorized ed. (New York: Vintage Books, 2006), http://bakerinstitute.org/research/the-iraq-study-group-report/.

25. Baker et al., *Iraq Study Group Report*, 73. Bush saw most recommendations as a withdrawal rationale, so he discounted them because he wanted options that could salvage the situation; Robert Gates, interview, SMU-CPH, October 12, 2015, https://vimeo.com/album/3353422/video/149181345; Michael Gordon, "Endgame Interview," *Frontline*, PBS, January 11, 2007, http://www.pbs.org/wgbh/pages/frontline/endgame/interviews/gordon.html. Ed Meese's perspective, however, was that the overall report was supportive of a surge; Edwin Meese, Iraq Study Group Signatory, phone interview, November 2, 2018.

26. Woodward, *The War Within*, 131–32.

27. Peter Mansoor and David Petraeus, *Surge: My Journey with General David Petraeus and the Remaking of the Iraq War* (New Haven, CT: Yale University Press, 2013), 52.

28. Bolten, interview, SMU-CPH; Woodward, *The War Within*, 170; Baker, *Days of Fire*, 517; Feaver, interview, SMU-CPH; Eliot A. Cohen, *Supreme Command: Soldiers, Statesmen and Leadership in Wartime* (New York: Simon & Schuster, 2012); Ricks, *The Gamble*, 98–101.

29. Jack Keane, interview, SMU-CPH, August 18, 2015, https://vimeo.com/137792537.

30. Steve Hadley, speaking engagement, Duke University, December 2, 2014.

31. Peter D. Feaver, "The Right to be Right: Civil-Military Relations and the Iraq Surge Decision," *International Security* 35, no. 4 (2011): 108; Feaver, interview, SMU-CPH.

32. John Hannah, interview, SMU-CPH, April 27, 2015, https://vimeo.com/131666291; O'Sullivan, interview, SMU-CPH.

33. Kaplan, *The Insurgents*, 232, 230, 202–3; "Weekly Attacks in Iraq, January 2004–May 2010" and "Civilian Deaths, January 2006–May 2010" charts in Gordon and Trainor, *The Endgame*, xv–xvi; Rumsfeld, *Known and Unknown*, 679; O'Sullivan, interview, SMU-CPH; Ricks, *The Gamble*, 55.

34. John P. Abizaid, Senate Hearing 109–885, US Government Printing Office, S. Hrg. 109–885, "Iraq, Afghanistan, and the Global War on Terrorism," testimony before the Senate Armed Services Committee, August 3, 2006, https://www.gpo.gov/fdsys/pkg/CHRG-109shrg35223/html/CHRG-109shrg35223.htm; John P. Abizaid, interview, SMU-CPH, April 13, 2016, https://vimeo.com/album/3353422/video/162773252.

35. William Douglas, "Bush Rejects Notion Iraq Has Fallen into Civil War," *Miami Herald*, November 29, 2006, 20A, http://infoweb.newsbank.com/resources/doc/nb/news/115C55E6E5CC3D30?p=NewsBank.

36. Gordon and Trainor, *The Endgame*, 295.

37. Mansoor and Petraeus, *Surge*, 45.

38. Joseph Stiglitz and Linda Bilmes, *The Three Trillion Dollar War: The True Cost of the Iraq Conflict* (London: Allen Lane, 2008), 251.

39. Bob Woodward, *State of Denial* (New York: Simon & Schuster, 2006), 472.

40. Richard D. Hooker Jr. and Joseph J. Collins, *Lessons Encountered: Learning from the Long War* (Fort McNair, DC: National Defense University Press, 2015), 402; Iraq Body Count database, accessed April 15, 2016, https://www.iraqbodycount.org/database/.

41. Hooker Jr. and Collins, *Lessons Encountered*, 432.

42. Stiglitz and Bilmes, *The Three Trillion Dollar War*, 31.

43. George W. Bush, *Decision Points* (New York: Broadway Books, 2011), 262.

44. Job Approval, George W. Bush, *The American Presidency Project*, Gallup Poll data, compiled by Gerhard Peters, accessed July 7, 2016, http://www.presidency.ucsb.edu/data/popularity.php?pres=43&sort=pop&direct=DESC&Submit=DISPLAY.

45. Rove, interview, SMU-CPH.

46. Peter D. Feaver, "Anatomy of the Surge," Commentary, *New York-American Jewish Committee* 125, no. 4 (2008): 28.

47. Eric Schmitt, "Fast Withdrawal of G.I.'s Is Urged by Key Democrat," *New York Times*, November 18, 2005, https://www.nytimes.com/2005/11/18/politics/fast-withdrawal-of-gis-is-urged-by-key-democrat.html.

48. Joseph R. Biden Jr. and Leslie H. Gelb, "Unity Through Autonomy in Iraq," *New York Times*, May 1, 2006, http://www.nytimes.com/2006/05/01/opinion/01biden.html?_r=0.

49. Adam Nagourney, "Democrats Turned War into Ally," *New York Times*, November 9, 2006, http://www.nytimes.com/2006/11/09/us/politics/09recon.html?ref=politics&_r=0.

50. Baker, *Days of Fire*, 466–67.

51. Ibid., 404.

52. Ibid., 482.

53. Stephen Cambone, interview, SMU-CPH, May 15, 2015, https://vimeo.com/128817215.

54. Baker, *Days of Fire*, 482.

55. Philip Zelikow, interview, SMU-CPH, March 24, 2015, https://vimeo.com/125156284.

56. Jeffrey, interview, SMU-CPH.

57. Condoleezza Rice, *No Higher Honor: A Memoir of My Years in Washington* (New York: Crown, 2011), 506.

58. Ricks, *The Gamble*, 13.

59. Woodward, *State of Denial*, 480.
60. Rove, interview, SMU-CPH.
61. Hadley et al., "How 'the Surge' Came to Be," 375–78, 421–24, 431.
62. Rice, interview, SMU-CPH.
63. Hadley et al., "How 'the Surge' Came to Be."
64. Peter Feaver, email, January 2017.
65. Emma Sky, *The Unraveling: High Hopes and Missed Opportunities in Iraq* (New York: PublicAffairs Books, 2015), 169; Woodward, *The War Within*, 203–204; Feaver, email, January 2017.
66. Woodward, *The War Within*, 190–92.
67. Ibid.; Zalmay Khalilzad, *The Envoy* (New York: St. Martin's, 2016), 278.
68. Woodward, *The War Within*, 170.
69. Baker, *Days of Fire*, 516.
70. Feaver, interview, SMU-CPH.
71. Rice, interview, SMU-CPH; Baker, *Days of Fire*, 515.
72. Baker et al., *Iraq Study Group Report*; Mansoor and Petraeus, *Surge*, 50.
73. O'Sullivan, interview, SMU-CPH.
74. Baker, "George W. Bush," 308; Bush, *Decision Points*, 363–64; Feaver, "The Right to Be Right," 101–103, 111; Ali Allawi, *The Occupation of Iraq: Winning the War, Losing the Peace* (New Haven, CT: Yale University Press, 2008).
75. O'Sullivan, interview, SMU-CPH.
76. Bush, *Decision Points*, 268; Frederick Kagan, interview, SMU-CPH, May 7, 2015, https://vimeo.com/128816876; Eric Edelman, interview, SMU-CPH, March 24, 2015, https://vimeo.com/125160432; Rove, interview, SMU-CPH; Richard Cheney, interview, SMU-CPH, August 6, 2015, https://www.dropbox.com/s/9vsz4e3qj9u2eqa/Dick%20Cheney%20-%20The%20Surge%20%28edited%20audio%2C%20compressed%29.mp3?dl=0.
77. Baker, *Days of Fire*, 518; Rice, interview, SMU-CPH; O'Sullivan, interview, SMU-CPH; Crouch, interview, SMU-CPH.
78. Woodward, *The War Within*, 188.
79. Zalmay Khalilzad, interview, SMU-CPH, June 25, 2015, https://vimeo.com/132171274.; Khalilzad, *The Envoy*, 281–83.
80. Khalilzad, *The Envoy*, 281; Baker, *Days of Fire*, 513.
81. Bush, *Decision Points*, 377.
82. Feaver, interview, SMU-CPH.
83. Crouch, interview, SMU-CPH.
84. Dandeker, "What 'Success' Means in Afghanistan, Iraq, and Libya," 118.
85. Stephen Biddle and Peter Feaver, "Assessing Strategic Choices in the War on Terror," in Burk, *How 9/11 Changed Our Ways of War*, 29; James B. Steinberg, "History, Policymaking, and the Balkans," in *The Power of the Past: History and Statecraft*, ed. Hal Brands and Jeremi Suri (Washington, DC: Brookings Institution, 2015), 248–49; Rove, *Courage and Consequence*, 299; Rice, *No Higher Honor*, 504; David Howell Petraeus, *The American Military and the Lessons of Vietnam: A Study of Military Influence and the Use of Force in the Post-Vietnam Era* (Princeton, NJ: Princeton University Press, 1987), 31–32.
86. Bruce W. Jentleson, *American Foreign Policy: The Dynamics of Choice in the 21st Century*, 5th ed. (New York: W. W. Norton, 2014), 459–66, 467–80; Brian Michael Jenkins, Bruce Hoffman, and Martha Crenshaw, "How Much Really Changed about Terrorism on 9/11?,"

Panel Discussion, *Atlantic Monthly*, September 11, 2016, http://www.theatlantic.com/international/archive/2016/09/jenkins-hoffman-crenshaw-september-11-al-qaeda/499334/.

87. George W. Bush, "West Point Graduation Speech," June 1, 2002, https://georgewbush-whitehouse.archives.gov/news/releases/2002/06/20020601-3.html.

88. George W. Bush, "Address to the Nation on Military Operations in Iraq," Public Papers of the Presidents: 2007, Book 1, January 10, 2007, 16.

89. George W. Bush, "President's News Conference," Public Papers of the Presidents: 2007, Book 1, February 14, 2007, 130.

90. George W. Bush, "President's News Conference," Public Papers of the Presidents: 2007, Book 1, May 24, 2007, 618.

91. Bush, *Decision Points*, 375.

92. George W. Bush, "Remarks to the American Legislative Exchange Council in Philadelphia, Pennsylvania," Public Papers of the Presidents: 2007, Book 2, July 26, 2007, 1017.

93. George W. Bush, "Address to the Nation on Military Operations in Iraq," Public Papers of the Presidents: 2007, Book 2, September 13, 2007, 1194–99, https://www.gpo.gov/fdsys/pkg/PPP-2007-book2/html/PPP-2007-book2-doc-pg1194-2.htm.

94. Dick Cheney and Liz Cheney, *In My Time: A Personal and Political Memoir* (New York: Simon & Schuster, 2012), 438.

95. Jeffrey, interview, SMU-CPH.

96. Feaver, "The Right to Be Right," 107–109.

97. Bush, *Decision Points*, 229 (emphasis added).

98. Rove, *Courage and Consequence*, 299.

99. Feaver, "The Right to be Right," 120.

100. Feaver, email, January 2017.

101. Kaplan, *The Insurgents*, 240; Ricks, *The Gamble*, 337–41, 343–71; Emma Sky, email, August 22, 2016.

102. Feaver, email, August 11, 2016.

103. Rove, *Courage and Consequence*, 475.

104. Petraeus, *The American Military and the Lessons of Vietnam*; David Petraeus, phone interview, August 25, 2016.

105. David Petraeus, email exchange, August 28, 2016.

106. Petraeus, phone interview; David Petraeus, "Engine of Change: Road to Deployment," PowerPoint presentation, updated version June 6, 2012, Fort Leavenworth, KS.

107. Conrad Crane, lead author of FM 3-24, email exchange, July 21, 2016; *Field Manual (FM) 3-24 Counterinsurgency* (Fort Leavenworth, KS, December 2006); Conrad Crane, *Cassandra in Oz: Counterinsurgency and Future War* (Annapolis, MD: Naval Institute Press, 2016).; Krepinevich Jr., *The Army and Vietnam*.

108. Sarah Sewall, *FM 3-24 Counterinsurgency* (2006), ix–x.

109. Daniel Serwer, interview, SMU-CPH, June 11, 2015, https://vimeo.com/131166159.

110. David Petraeus, phone interview and email exchange, August 25 and 28, 2016, respectively; Petraeus, *Engine of Change*.

111. Keane, interview, SMU-CPH; Nagl, *Knife Fights*, 212–13.

112. Cheney, interview, SMU-CPH; O'Sullivan, interview, SMU-CPH; Cheney and Cheney, *In My Time*, 441.

113. Kagan, interview, SMU-CPH; Stanley McChrystal, *My Share of the Task: A Memoir* (New York: Penguin, 2013), 240.

114. Edelman, interview, SMU-CPH.

115. Gordon and Trainor, *The Endgame*, 178–79.

116. McChrystal, *My Share of the Task*, 240–42.

117. Feaver, email, August 11, 2016.

118. Herbert R. McMaster, *Dereliction of Duty: Johnson, McNamara, the Joint Chiefs of Staff, and the Lies That Led to Vietnam* (New York: Perennial, 1998).

119. Mansoor, interview, SMU-CPH.

120. The counterinsurgency field manual draft and the lessons learned along the way were fed into the NSC, mostly by back channel through the Petraeus-O'Sullivan connection; Feaver, email, January 2017.

121. H. R. McMaster, email, September 13, 2016; Petraeus, phone interview.

122. John A. Nagl, *Knife Fights: A Memoir of Modern War in Theory and Practice* (New York: Penguin, 2015), 214.

123. Donald Rumsfeld, Senate Hearing 109–885, US Government Printing Office, S. Hrg. 109–85, "Iraq, Afghanistan, and the Global War on Terrorism."

124. Kaplan, *The Insurgents*, 225.

125. Keane, interview, SMU-CPH; Woodward, *The War Within*, 133–34.

126. Jeffrey, interview, SMU-CPH.

127. George Packer, "The Lesson of Tal Afar: Is It Too Late for the Administration to Correct Its Course in Iraq?," *New Yorker*, April 10, 2006, http://www.newyorker.com/magazine/2006/04/10/the-lesson-of-tal-afar.

128. Bush, "Remarks at the Veterans of Foreign Wars."

129. Henry Kissinger, memorandum to President Nixon, "Our Present Course on Vietnam," September 10, 1969, 2, https://www.docsteach.org/documents/document/salted-peanuts-memo-kissinger-nixon.

130. Feaver, email, January 2017.

131. Mark Atwood Lawrence, "Policymaking and the Uses of the Vietnam War," in Brands and Suri, *The Power of the Past*, 50.

132. Ibid.

133. Feaver, "The Right to be Right," 108.

134. Bush, *Decision Points*, 367.

135. Ibid.

136. Sorley, *A Better War*, 1999.

137. Keane, interview, SMU-CPH.

138. Jeffrey, interview, SMU-CPH.

139. Rove, *Courage and Consequence*, 475.

140. Rove, interview, SMU-CPH.

141. Crouch, interview, SMU-CPH.

142. Harry G. Summers, *On Strategy: A Critical Analysis of the Vietnam War* (New York: Random House Digital, 1995), 1.

143. Woodward, *State of Denial*, 482–83; Abizaid, interview, SMU-CPH.

144. O'Sullivan, interview, SMU-CPH.

145. Feaver, email, August 11, 2016.

146. Cohen, *Supreme Command*; Bolten, interview, SMU-CPH; Woodward, *The War Within*, 170; Baker, *Days of Fire*, 517; Feaver, interview, SMU-CPH; Kaplan, *The Insurgents*; Ricks, *The Gamble*, 98–101; Kagan, interview, SMU-CPH.

147. Bush, "Remarks at the Veterans of Foreign Wars"; Rove, *Courage and Consequence*, 475; Jeffrey, interview, SMU-CPH; Keane, interview, SMU-CPH; Lute, interview, SMU-CPH; Petraeus, *The American Military and the Lessons of Vietnam*, 32.

148. McMaster, email; Keane, interview, SMU-CPH; Jeffrey, interview, SMU-CPH.

149. Petraeus, *The American Military and the Lessons of Vietnam*, 133.

150. Yuen Foong Khong, *Analogies at War: Korea, Munich, Dien Bien Phu, and the Vietnam Decisions of 1965* (Princeton, NJ: Princeton University Press, 1992), 64.

151. Ibid., 64–65; Feaver, email, August 11, 2016.

152. Ricks, *The Gamble*, 54–55.

153. Rove, interview, SMU-CPH.

154. George W. Bush, "The President's Radio Address," March 18, 2006, online by Gerhard Peters and John T. Woolley, *The American Presidency Project*, accessed July 7, 2016, http://www.presidency.ucsb.edu/ws/?pid=65416.

155. Baker, *Days of Fire*, 452.

156. George W. Bush, "Remarks on the Nomination of Robert J. Portman to Be Director of the Office of Management and Budget and Susan C. Schwab to Be United States Trade Representative and an Exchange with Reporters," Public Papers of the Presidents: 2006, Book 1, April 18, 2006, 736; Bolten, interview, SMU-CPH; Rove, interview, SMU-CPH; Baker, *Days of Fire*, 452–53.

157. Ricks, *The Gamble*, 54–55.

158. Peter Baker, "U.S. Not Winning in Iraq, Bush Says for 1st Time," *Washington Post*, December 20, 2006, http://www.washingtonpost.com/wp-dyn/content/article/2006/12/19/AR2006121900880.html.

159. Cheney, interview, SMU-CPH.

160. Woodward, *The War Within*, 294.

161. Woodward, *State of Denial*, 456.

162. Woodward, *The War Within*, 193.

163. Woodward, *State of Denial*, 490–91.

164. Feaver, multiple conversations with the author, 2013–2019.

165. George W. Bush, "Remarks on the Resignation of Secretary of Defense Donald H. Rumsfeld and the Nomination of Robert M. Gates to be Secretary of Defense," Public Papers of the Presidents: Book II, November 8, 2006, 2064–66; Woodward, *The War Within*, 193.

166. Ricks, *The Gamble*, 123.

167. Crouch, interview, SMU-CPH; Stephen Hadley, interview, SMU-CPH, June 2, 2015, https://vimeo.com/131167565; Feaver, interview, SMU-CPH.

168. Baker, *Days of Fire*, 524.

169. Cambone, interview, SMU-CPH.

170. Bush, "Address to the Nation on Military Operations in Iraq," January 10, 2007, 16; George W. Bush, "Remarks to the American Enterprise Institute for Public Policy Research," Public Papers of the Presidents: 2007, Book 1, February 15, 2007, 146; Bush, "Remarks at the Veterans of Foreign Wars"; Bush, "Address to the Nation on Military Operations in Iraq," September 13, 2007; Rice, interview, SMU-CPH; Rice, *No Higher Honor*, 546; Bolten, interview, SMU-CPH; Rove, *Courage and Consequence*, 299, 341, 475; Jeffrey, interview, SMU-CPH; Feaver, email, August 11, 2006; Woodward, *The War Within*, 124; Rumsfeld, *Known and Unknown*, 666–68, 670, 695–96, 700.

171. Feaver, email, August 11, 2016.

172. Hooker Jr. and Collins, *Lessons Encountered*, 432; "Weekly Attacks in Iraq, January 2004–May 2010" and "Civilian Deaths, January 2006–May 2010" charts in Gordon and Trainor, *The Endgame*, xv–xvi; Bush, "Remarks to the American Enterprise Institute for Public Policy Research"; Bush, "Address to the Nation on Military Operations in Iraq."

173. Hal Brands and Jeremi Suri, eds., *The Power of the Past: History and Statecraft* (Washington, DC: Brookings Institution, 2015), 5.

174. Feaver, email, August 11, 2016; Meese, phone interview.

175. The State Department thought that America would lose leverage in the region and every other problem would become more difficult if the nation pulled out of Iraq. This rebuts traditional sunk costs logic and is an example of why policymakers rarely behave as classic economists recommend; Feaver, email, January 2017.

176. Ibid.

177. Feaver, "The Right to be Right," 108; Crouch, interview, SMU-CPH.

178. Hadley, interview, SMU-CPH.

179. Rice, interview, SMU-CPH.

180. Hadley et al., "How 'the Surge' Came to Be," 375–78, 421–32.

181. Bush, *Decision Points*, 268.

182. Bush, "Address to the Nation on Military Operations in Iraq," January 10, 2007, 16–20; Bush, *Decision Points*, 375; Bush, "President's News Conference," May 24, 2007, 618.

183. Steven Metz, *Decision Making in Operation Iraqi Freedom: The Strategic Shift of 2007* (Carlisle, PA: Strategic Studies Institute, 2010), https://press.armywarcollege.edu/monographs/597/; Osama bin Laden, "Osama Bin Laden's Declaration of Jihad Against Americans," July 5, 1996, https://safe.menlosecurity.com/doc/docview/viewer/docNA582E7E3E6870b64ad807cc7adc8c2e1399a11a57f2bdfe6d813274236799c0f17604140e347; Osama bin Laden, "Osama Bin Laden's 1998 Fatwa" February 23, 1998, http://www.mideastweb.org/osamabinladen2.htm; Peter Feaver, interview, November 5, 2015.

6. AFGHANISTAN

The chapter 6 epigraphs are drawn from Hal Brands and Jeremi Suri, eds. *The Power of the Past: History and Statecraft* (Washington, DC: Brookings Institution, 2015), 5; Denis McDonough, talk, Duke University, April 15, 2016; Thomas Donilon, talk, Duke University, November 19, 2015; Michèle Flournoy, phone interview, August 22, 2016; Stanley McChrystal, "International Security Assistance Force Commander's Classified Assessment," in Coll, *Directorate S* (November 2008), 369; Vikram Singh, phone interview, September 10, 2016; Stanley McChrystal, "COMISAF Initial Assessment (Unclassified)," *Washington Post*, September 21, 2009, http://www.washingtonpost.com/wp-dyn/content/article/2009/09/21/AR2009092100110.html; Joseph Collins, Frank Hoffman, and Nathan White, Stanley McChrystal interview, April 2, 2015, 22; Peter Bergen, "The General's Victory," *New Republic*, December 16, 2010, https://newrepublic.com/article/80045/the-generals-victory-obamas-wars-woodward; Obama in Peter Baker, "How Obama Came to Plan for 'Surge' in Afghanistan," http://www.nytimes.com/2009/12/06/world/asia/06reconstruct.html?pagewanted=all&_r=0Baker; Longtime White House correspondent Helen Thomas said this to General David Petraeus in Bob Woodward, *Obama's Wars* (New York: Simon & Schuster, 2011), 112; Barack Obama, "Way Forward in Afghanistan and Pakistan," speech, West Point, NY, December 1, 2009, https://obamawhitehouse.archives.gov/blog/2009/12/01/new-way-forward-presidents-address; David Petraeus, phone interview, August 25, 2016; Nick Patton Walsh, "Trump's Strategy Is Failing, and the Taliban Is Winning," CNN, August

16, 2018, https://www.cnn.com/2018/08/16/asia/afghan-analysis-npw-intl/index.html; Brands and Suri, *The Power of the Past*, 5; Elliot Ackerman, "What Did Our Generation Learn in Iraq and Afghanistan?," *Daily Beast*, May 27, 2018, https://www.thedailybeast.com/what-did-our-generation-learn-in-iraq-and-afghanistan?via=rss.

1. Obama, "Way Forward in Afghanistan and Pakistan"; Kin Fai Ellick Wong and Jessica Y. Y. Kwong, "The Role of Anticipated Regret in Escalation of Commitment," *Journal of Applied Psychology* 92, no. 2 (2007): 545–54; Gillian Ku, "Learning to De-escalate: The Effects of Regret in Escalation of Commitment," *Organizational Behavior and Human Decision Processes* 105, no. 2 (2008): 221–32.

2. Barack Obama, *The Audacity of Hope: Thoughts on Reclaiming the American Dream* (Edinburgh: Canongate Books, 2007), 289–93; Barack Obama, "Speech on Iraq," Council on Foreign Relations, March 19, 2008, http://www.cfr.org/elections/obamas-speech-iraq-march-2008/p15761; Barack Obama, "Remarks on Iraq and Afghanistan," *New York Times*, July 15, 2008, http://www.nytimes.com/2008/07/15/us/politics/15text-obama.html.

3. Woodward, *Obama's Wars*, 324–28. That lesson reinforced his wariness of state building gleaned from the Iraq War. Karl Eikenberry, email, August 23, 2016.

4. Obama, "Speech on Iraq"; Obama, "Remarks on Iraq and Afghanistan"; Obama, *The Audacity of Hope*, 289–93; Leon Panetta and Jim Newton, *Worthy Fights: A Memoir of Leadership in War and Peace* (London: Penguin, 2014), 290.

5. Barbara Starr, "Obama Approves Afghanistan Troop Increase," CNN, February 18, 2009, http://www.cnn.com/2009/POLITICS/02/17/obama.troops/; Robert Gates, *Duty: Memoirs of a Secretary at War* (New York: Random House, 2014); Singh, phone interview.

6. Gates, *Duty*.

7. Singh, phone interview; Jonathan Alter, *The Promise* (New York: Simon & Schuster, 2010).

8. Alter, *The Promise*; Flournoy, phone interview.

9. Woodward, *Obama's Wars*.

10. Steve Coll, *Directorate S: The CIA and America's Secret Wars in Afghanistan and Pakistan, 2001–2016* (London: Penguin, 2018), 409.

11. Obama, "Speech on Iraq"; Obama, "Remarks on Iraq and Afghanistan"; Obama, *The Audacity of Hope*, 289–93; Panetta and Newton, *Worthy Fights*, 290.

12. Stanley McChrystal, *My Share of the Task: A Memoir* (New York: Portfolio, 2013).

13. Singh, interview.

14. Gates, *Duty*.

15. Seth G. Jones, *In the Graveyard of Empires: America's War in Afghanistan* (New York: W. W. Norton, 2010), 338.

16. "Afghanistan's Elections," *Washington Post*, accessed January 3, 2019, http://www.washingtonpost.com/wp-srv/special/world/afghanistan-election/.

17. Ewen MacAskill, "US Liberals Express Anger over Obama's Decision to Raise Troop Levels: Deployment of 30,000 More Troops to Afghanistan Causes Most Ardent Supporters to Become Disillusioned," *Guardian*, December 2, 2009, https://www.theguardian.com/world/2009/dec/02/obama-afghanistan-liberal-backlash; Kevin Marsh, "Obama's Surge: A Bureaucratic Politics Analysis of the Decision to Order a Troop Surge in the Afghanistan War," *Foreign Policy Analysis*, July 1, 2014, https://academic.oup.com/fpa/article-abstract/10/3/265/1788667?redirectedFrom=fulltext.

18. Scott Wilson and Jon Cohen, "Support for Afghan War Rises, Poll Shows," *Washington Post*, June 6, 2011, https://www.washingtonpost.com/national/national-security/support-for-afghan-war-rises-poll-shows/2011/06/06/AGRokYKH_story.html; Matthew Dickinson,

"A Lawyer in the White House and the Surge in Afghanistan: Why They Are Linked," *Middlebury*, December 7, 2009, https://sites.middlebury.edu/presidentialpower/2009/12/07/a-laywer-in-the-white-house-and-the-surge-in-afghanistan-why-they-are-linked/.

19. Donilon, talk, Duke University; McDonough, talk, Duke University. Both Obama officials mentioned these two objectives as what the president wanted to accomplish. Woodward, *Obama's Wars*, 328; Coll, *Directorate S*, 406.

20. Panetta and Newton, *Worthy Fights*, 290.

21. Patrick Howell, General McChrystal's lead military planner for the 2009 surge planning options, phone interview, August 18, 2016.

22. John Barry, "Could Afghanistan Be Obama's Vietnam?," *Newsweek*, January 30, 2009, http://www.newsweek.com/could-afghanistan-be-obamas-vietnam-77749.

23. McChrystal, "COMISAF Initial Assessment (Unclassified)."

24. Thomas Nagorski, "Editor's Notebook: Afghan War Now Country's Longest," ABC News, June 7, 2010, http://abcnews.go.com/Politics/afghan-war-now-longest-war-us-history/story?id=10849303.

25. This figure comes from the "by year" and "by country" casualties figures listed on iCasualties, "Operation Enduring Freedom," accessed July 17, 2015, http://icasualties.org/OEF/index.aspx.

26. Barack Obama, "Remarks by the President on a New Strategy for Afghanistan and Pakistan," the White House, Washington, DC, March 27, 2009.

27. Joseph J. Collins and Richard D. Hooker, *Lessons Encountered: Learning from the Long War* (Washington, DC: National Defense University Press, 2015), 127.

28. Ann S. Tyson, "Rising U.S. Toll in Afghanistan Stirs Unease on Hill, among Families," *Washington Post*, September 23, 2009, http://www.washingtonpost.com/wp-dyn/content/article/2009/09/22/AR2009092204296.html?hpid=topnews.

29. Tyson, "Rising U.S. Toll in Afghanistan Stirs Unease on Hill."

30. That is the amount spent through fiscal year 2009. Anthony Cordesman, "The US Cost of the Afghan War: FY2002-FY2013," Center for Strategic and International Studies (CSIS), 2012, 4–7.

31. Christopher Dandeker, "What 'Success' Means in Afghanistan, Iraq, and Libya," in *How 9/11 Changed Our Ways of War*, ed. James Burk (Stanford, CA: Stanford University Press, 2013), 116–48.

32. John Arquilla and Hy Rothstein, *Afghan Endgames: Strategy and Policy Choices for America's Longest War* (Washington, DC: Georgetown University Press, 2012), 145.

33. Luke Hartig, "Can Trump and His Generals Avoid Another Black Hawk Down?," *Newsweek*, September 4, 2017, https://www.newsweek.com/can-trump-and-his-generals-avoid-another-black-hawk-down-658716.

34. Donilon, talk, Duke University.

35. Singh, phone interview; Woodward, *Obama's Wars*.

36. Stanley McChrystal, "Remarks during a Question-and-Answer Session with Reporters," International Institute for Security Studies (IISS), October 1, 2009; Max Hastings, "The Runaway General," *Rolling Stone*, June 22, 2010, http://www.rollingstone.com/politics/news/the-runaway-general-20100622?page=2.

37. Woodward, *Obama's Wars*; Alter, *The Promise*.

38. Woodward, *Obama's Wars*.

39. Carl Von Clausewitz, *On War*, ed. and trans. Michael Howard and Peter Paret (Princeton, NJ: Princeton University Press, 1976), 92. Clausewitz wrote, "Once the expenditure of effort exceeds the value of the political object, the object must be renounced and peace must follow."

40. Woodward, *Obama's Wars*, loc. 6523, Kindle.

41. Doug Lute, phone interview, August 19, 2016.

42. Near-universal assessment of the intelligence community, top commanders, and chief US diplomat in Afghanistan late July–August 2009 as expressed firsthand to author.

43. Richard Hooker and Joseph Collins, interview with Douglas Lute, April 10, 2015, 6.

44. Adam Entous and Andrew Gray, "Scenarios: Obama's Options in Afghan War," Reuters, October 5, 2009, http://www.reuters.com/article/us-afghanistan-usa-obama-options-sb-idUSTRE5944AB20091005.

45. These options and their corresponding risk assessments come from an August 18, 2016, phone interview with Colonel (Ret.) Patrick Howell, General McChrystal's lead military planner for the 2009 surge.

46. Jeffrey Goldberg, "The Obama Doctrine," *Atlantic*, April 2016, http://www.theatlantic.com/magazine/archive/2016/04/the-obama-doctrine/471525/.

47. Vali Nasr explained that Holbrooke's understanding of the military's proclivities in providing options came from historical lessons. Holbrooke had seen military leaders present options to civilian leaders in the same way during the Vietnam War. Vali Nasr, *The Dispensable Nation* (New York: Anchor Books, 2013), 25, 33–34.

48. Woodward, *Obama's Wars*; Tyson, "Rising U.S. Toll in Afghanistan Stirs Unease on Hill."

49. Tyson, "Rising U.S. Toll in Afghanistan Stirs Unease on Hill."

50. Eric Schmitt, "U.S. Envoy's Cables Show Worries on Afghan Plans," January 25, 2010, http://www.nytimes.com/2010/01/26/world/asia/26strategy.html?pagewanted=all&_r=0.

51. This is what civilian and military analysts General McChrystal and Ambassador Eikenberry and their staffs indicated to the author and the Combating Terrorism Center team of which he was a part during a July–August 2009 visit of key locations in Afghanistan.

52. Schmitt, "U.S. Envoy's Cables Show Worries on Afghan Plans."

53. Obama, "Way Forward in Afghanistan and Pakistan"; Gates, *Duty*.

54. Woodward, *Obama's Wars*, 324–45.

55. Miles Amoore and Christina Lamb, "Get Set for Surge in Bloody Battles," *Sunday Times*, December 6, 2009, http://search.proquest.com/docview/316523209?accountid=10598.

56. Obama in Baker, "How Obama Came to Plan for Surge."

57. Woodward, *Obama's Wars*, 357.

58. Admiral (Ret.) James Stavridis, phone interview, September 1, 2016.

59. Frederick Kagan, interview, SMU-CPH, May 7, 2015, https://vimeo.com/128816876; McChrystal, *My Share of the Task*, 240.

60. Panetta and Newton, *Worthy Fights*, 290; Woodward, *Obama's Wars*, 328.

61. Eikenberry, email.

62. Woodward, *Obama's Wars*, 324–28.

63. Obama, "Speech on Iraq"; Obama, "Remarks on Iraq and Afghanistan"; Richard D. Hooker Jr. and Joseph J. Collins, *Lessons Encountered: Learning from the Long War* (Fort McNair, DC: National Defense University Press, 2015), 113.

64. Hartig, "Can Trump and His Generals Avoid Another Black Hawk Down?"

65. "The U.S. War in Afghanistan, 1999–2018: The Taliban Insurgency Remains Resilient Seventeen Years after U.S.-Led Forces Toppled Its Regime in What Led to the United States' Longest War," Council on Foreign Relations, accessed December 23, 2018, https://www.cfr.org/timeline/us-war-afghanistan.

66. Obama, "Speech on Iraq"; Obama, "Remarks on Iraq and Afghanistan"; Panetta and Newton, *Worthy Fights*, 241–69, 289–90, 463; Hooker Jr. and Collins, *Lessons Encountered*, 113.

67. Lute, phone interview, August 19, 2016. Panetta and Newton, *Worthy Fights*, 241–69, 289–90, 463.

68. Woodward, *Obama's Wars*, 328.

69. Obama, "Remarks on Iraq and Afghanistan."

70. McDonough, talk, Duke University.

71. Flournoy phone interview.

72. Panetta and Newton, *Worthy Fights*, 290.

73. McChrystal, "COMISAF Initial Assessment (Unclassified)."

74. Obama, "Remarks on Iraq and Afghanistan."

75. David Petraeus, talk, Duke University, September 11, 2013. Petraeus mentioned that he and others recognized that Iraq did not equal Afghanistan and that adjustments would have to be made. Yet a former member of the International Security Assistance Force staff indicated that he regularly made comments to the effect that "this is how we did it in Iraq." Also: David Petraeus, Joseph Collins, and Nathan White, "Reflections by General David Petraeus, USA (ret.) on the Wars in Afghanistan and Iraq," *PRISM* 7, no. 1 (2017): 150–67.

76. David Caldwell, *Vortex of Conflict: U.S. Policy toward Afghanistan, Pakistan and Iraq* (Stanford, CA: Stanford University Press, 2011), 242.

77. Flournoy, phone interview; Dandeker, "What 'Success' Means in Afghanistan, Iraq, and Libya," 121.

78. Petraeus, *The American Military and the Lessons of Vietnam*, 31–32.

79. Flournoy, phone interview; Amos Tversky and Daniel Kahneman, "Judgment under Uncertainty: Heuristics and Biases," in *Utility, Probability, and Human Decision Making* (Dordrecht: Springer Netherlands, 1975), 1127–28.

80. Caldwell, *Vortex of Conflict*, 242; Woodward, *Obama's Wars*; Collins, Hoffman, and White, Stanley McChrystal interview, 22.

81. Flournoy, phone interview.

82. Eikenberry, email.

83. Nasr, *The Dispensable Nation*, 25, 33–34.

84. Singh, phone interview.

85. Woodward, *Obama's Wars*, 327.

86. Lute, phone interview, August 19, 2016.

87. Flournoy, phone interview; Stavridis, phone interview; Woodward, *Obama's Wars*.

88. "Weekly Attacks in Iraq, January 2004–May 2010" and "Civilian Deaths, January 2006–May 2010," xv–xvi.

89. Panetta and Newton, *Worthy Fights*, 415.

90. Hastings, "The Runaway General."

91. Flournoy, phone interview.

92. Bergen, "The General's Victory."

93. Goldberg, "The Obama Doctrine."

94. Obama, *The Audacity of Hope*, 295.

95. Woodward, *Obama's Wars*, 324; Bob Woodward interview in Ted Koppel and Neal Conan, "Clashes with Pentagon Shaped 'Obama's Wars,'" NPR, December 13, 2010, http://www.npr.org/2010/12/13/132030072/clashes-with-pentagon-shaped-obama-s-wars.

96. Barry, "Could Afghanistan Be Obama's Vietnam?"

97. Alter, *The Promise*.

98. Woodward, *Obama's Wars*; Alter, *The Promise*.

99. Flournoy, phone interview; Obama in Baker, "How Obama Came to Plan for Surge"; Woodward, *Obama's Wars*, 324–28.

100. Marvin Kalb, "The Vietnam War and the Presidency," C-SPAN, August 7, 2011, http://www.c-span.org/video/?300948-5/vietnam-war-presidency.

101. Flournoy, phone interview.

102. Panetta and Newton, *Worthy Fights*, 290.

103. Woodward, *Obama's Wars*, 324.

104. Woodward interview.

105. Woodward, *Obama's Wars*, 324.

106. Ibid., 324–28.

107. Ibid.

108. Woodward interview.

109. Woodward, *Obama's Wars*, 324, loc. 6438–23, Kindle.

110. Yuen Foong Khong, *Analogies at War: Korea, Munich, Dien Bien Phu, and the Vietnam Decisions of 1965* (Princeton, NJ: Princeton University Press, 1992), 64–65.

111. John A. Nagl, *Knife Fights: A Memoir of Modern War in Theory and Practice* (London: Penguin, 2014), 217; Woodward, *Obama's Wars*.

112. Obama, "Way Forward in Afghanistan and Pakistan."

113. These similarities come from Gordon Goldstein, "Book Discussion: Lessons in Disaster," C-SPAN, October 6, 2009, http://www.c-span.org/video/?289314-4/book-discussion-lessons-disaster (starting at 19 minutes). The similarities Goldstein saw paralleled those drawn by Special Envoy to Afghanistan and Pakistan, Ambassador Richard Holbrooke. Derek Chollet and Samantha Power, *The Unquiet American: Richard Holbrooke in the World* (New York: Public Affairs, 2011), 95. Chollet and Power wrote that Holbrooke "had privately explained to a handful of people he was close to that the three common dynamics shared by the conflicts in Vietnam and Afghanistan that troubled him the most were the existence of an indefensible border harboring enemy sanctuaries; American reliance on a corrupt partner government; and, most critically, the embrace of counterinsurgency doctrine, which he had learned through painful experience was an exceedingly difficult military and civilian strategy to execute." Andrew F. Krepinevich Jr., *The Army and Vietnam* (Baltimore: Johns Hopkins University Press, 1986).

114. Daniel Byman and Steven Simon, "Trump's Surge in Afghanistan: Why We Can't Seem to End the War," *Foreign Affairs*, September 18, 2017, https://www.foreignaffairs.com/articles/afghanistan/2017-09-18/trumps-surge-afghanistan?cid=int-rec&pgtype=art.

115. Obama in Baker, "How Obama Came to Plan for 'Surge' in Afghanistan"; Woodward, *Obama's Wars*, 324–28.

116. This saying was how soldiers and the administration referred to options that were not perfect but would be better than the status quo and would allow America to count efforts in Afghanistan as a win and transition out of Afghanistan.

117. Nagl, *Knife Fights*, 217.

118. Brands and Suri, *The Power of the Past*, 5.

119. Obama, "Speech on Iraq"; Obama, "Remarks on Iraq and Afghanistan."

120. Woodward, *Obama's Wars*, 324–28.

121. Lute, phone interview, August 19, 2016; Eikenberry, email.

122. Goldberg, "The Obama Doctrine."

123. Flournoy, phone interview; Petraeus, phone interview.

124. Obama, "Way Forward in Afghanistan and Pakistan."

125. Flournoy, phone interview; Hillary Rodham Clinton, *Hard Choices* (New York: Simon & Schuster, 2014); Gates, *Duty*; Woodward, *Obama's Wars*.

126. Obama, "Way Forward in Afghanistan and Pakistan."

127. Woodward, *Obama's Wars*, 324–28.

128. Obama, "Way Forward in Afghanistan and Pakistan"; Goldberg, "The Obama Doctrine"; Eikenberry, email.

129. Obama, "Way Forward in Afghanistan and Pakistan."

130. Woodward, *Obama's Wars*, 324–28.

131. Obama, "Way Forward in Afghanistan and Pakistan."

132. Obama, *The Audacity of Hope*, 289–93; Obama, "Speech on Iraq"; Obama, "Remarks on Iraq and Afghanistan"; Obama, "Way Forward in Afghanistan and Pakistan."

133. Obama, "Way Forward in Afghanistan and Pakistan"; Nagl, *Knife Fights*, 216.

134. Woodward interview.

135. Woodward, *Obama's Wars*, 324–28.

136. Ibid., 328; Donilon, talk, Duke University; McDonough, talk, Duke University.

137. Peter Bergen et al., "America's Counterterrorism Wars—Drone Strikes: Pakistan," New America Foundation, accessed May 26, 2017, https://www.newamerica.org/in-depth/americas-counterterrorism-wars/pakistan/; Jessica Purkiss and Jack Serle, "Obama's Covert Drone War in Numbers: Ten Times More Strikes Than Bush," Bureau of Investigative Journalism, January 17, 2017, https://www.thebureauinvestigates.com/stories/2017-01-17/obamas-covert-drone-war-in-numbers-ten-times-more-strikes-than-bush.

138. Peter Bergen, "Drones Are Obama's Weapon of Choice," CNN, September 6, 2012, http://peterbergen.com/drone-is-obamas-weapon-of-choice/.

139. Obama, "Way Forward in Afghanistan and Pakistan."

140. Obama, *The Audacity of Hope*, 289–93; Obama, "Speech on Iraq"; Obama, "Remarks on Iraq and Afghanistan"; Nagl, *Knife Fights*, 216; Panetta and Newton, *Worthy Fights*, 290; Flournoy, phone interview.

141. Woodward, *Obama's Wars*, 324–28; Eikenberry, email.

142. Flournoy, phone interview; McDonough, talk, Duke University.

143. Woodward, *Obama's Wars*, 324–28.

144. Ackerman, "What Did Our Generation Learn in Iraq and Afghanistan?"; Walsh, "Trump's Strategy Is Failing, and the Taliban Is Winning."

145. Walsh, "Trump's Strategy Is Failing, and the Taliban Is Winning."

146. George Ball, "Memorandum for the President from George Ball: A Compromise Solution in South Vietnam," In *1 July 1965, The Pentagon Papers*, Gravel Edition, vol. 4, (Boston: Beacon Press, 1971), 615–619. George W. Ball, *The Past Has Another Pattern: Memoirs*, vol. 23 (New York: W. W. Norton, 1982), 336; George W. Ball and Douglas B. Ball, *The Passionate Attachment: America's Involvement with Israel, 1947 to the Present* (New York:

W. W. Norton, 1992); Brian VanDeMark, *Road to Disaster: A New History of America's Descent into Vietnam* (New York: HarperCollins, 2019); Woodward, *Obama's Wars.*

147. VanDeMark, *Road to Disaster*; Fredrik Logevall, *Choosing War: The Lost Chance for Peace and the Escalation of War in Vietnam* (Oakland: University of California Press, 2001); Woodward, *Obama's Wars*; Daniel Kahneman and Patrick Egan, *Thinking, Fast and Slow*, vol. 1 (New York: Farrar, Straus and Giroux), 2011.

148. Alter, *The Promise.*

149. Bryan Groves, "Principal-Agent Problems: Why War Strategy Doesn't Always Match Policy Aims," *International Journal of Political Science and Development* 3, no. 2 (February 7, 2015): 63–78.

150. Petraeus, talk, Duke University; Petraeus, Collins, and White, "Reflections by General David Petraeus," 150–67; Clinton, *Hard Choices*; Gates, *Duty*; Woodward, *Obama's Wars*. Flournoy, phone interview.

151. Flournoy, phone interview; International Security Assistance Force staff member, phone interview, August 22, 2016.

152. Walsh, "Trump's Strategy Is Failing, and the Taliban Is Winning."

153. Karl W. Eikenberry, "The Limits of Counterinsurgency Doctrine in Afghanistan: The Other Side of the COIN," *Foreign Affairs* 92 (2013): 59.

154. Petraeus, phone interview and email exchange, August 25, 2016, and September 8, 2016; Byman and Simon, "Trump's Surge in Afghanistan"; "The U.S. War in Afghanistan: 1999–2018," https://www.cfr.org/timeline/us-war-afghanistan.

155. Marvin Kalb and Deborah Kalb, *Haunting Legacy: Vietnam and the American Presidency from Ford to Obama* (Washington, DC: Brookings Institution, 2012).

156. Harry G. Summers, *On Strategy: A Critical Analysis of the Vietnam War* (Novato, CA: Presidio, 1982); Arnold R. Isaacs, *Vietnam Shadows: The War, Its Ghosts, and Its Legacy* (Baltimore: Johns Hopkins University Press, 2000), 67; Ackerman, "What Did Our Generation Learn in Iraq and Afghanistan?"; Philip K. Jason, *Acts and Shadows: The Vietnam War in American Literary Culture* (Washington, DC: Rowman & Littlefield, 2000), 2–3; Fred Turner, *Echoes of Combat: The Vietnam War in American Memory* (New York: Anchor Books, 1996), 3–16, 185–95; Leslie H. Gelb and Richard K. Betts, *The Irony of Vietnam: The System Worked* (Washington, DC: Brookings Institution, 1979), 347–69; Caspar Weinberger, "The Uses of Military Power," Remarks Prepared for Delivery by the Hon. Caspar Weinberger, Secretary of Defense, to the National Press Club, Washington, DC, November 28, 1984, http://www.pbs.org/wgbh/pages/frontline/shows/military/force/weinberger.html; Robert S. McNamara and Brian VanDeMark, *In Retrospect: The Tragedy and Lessons of Vietnam* (Vancouver, WA: Vintage, 1996); John Norton Moore and Robert F. Turner, eds., *The Real Lessons of the Vietnam War: Reflections Twenty-Five Years after the Fall of Saigon* (Durham, NC: Carolina Academic Press, 2002); Robert S. McNamara et al., "Argument without End: In Search of Answers to the Vietnam Tragedy," (New York: PublicAffairs,2007): 373–98; Goldstein, *Lessons in Disaster.*

7. GULF WAR ENDGAME

The chapter 7 epigraphs are drawn from Harry G. Summers, *On Strategy II: A Critical Analysis of the Gulf War*, vol. 2 (New York: Dell, 1992), 1; President George H. W. Bush, Inaugural Address, January 20, 1989, http://www.presidency.ucsb.edu/ws/?pid=16610;

George H. W. Bush in Jon Meacham, *Destiny and Power: The American Odyssey of George Herbert Walker Bush* (New York: Random House, 2015), 462; James A. Baker, *The Politics of Diplomacy* (New York: Putnam Adult, 1995), 437; George H. W. Bush, "Meetings with World Leaders," September–October 1990 folder, George Bush Presidential Library; George H. W. Bush, "Presidential Radio Address to Troops in the Gulf," DRAFT 2 on February 28, 1991, for March 1 delivery, White House Office of Speechwriting, Speech File Draft Files, Chronological Files: 1989–93, OA/ID box 13557, George Bush Presidential Library; Arnold R. Isaacs, *Vietnam Shadows: The War, Its Ghosts and Its Legacy* (Baltimore: Johns Hopkins University Press, 2000), 76; Baker, *The Politics of Diplomacy*, 331.

1. George H. W. Bush and Brent Scowcroft, *A World Transformed*, 1st ed (New York: Knopf, 1998), 454–86.

2. Jon Meacham, answer to author's question during a book tour event at the George Bush Presidential Library, attended by President George H. W. and Mrs. Barbara Bush, November 9, 2015.

3. Bush in Meacham, *Destiny and Power*, 462, 465.

4. Ibid., 462, 465.

5. Bush and Scowcroft, *A World Transformed*, 482–83; Michael R. Gordon and Bernard E. Trainor, "Powell Wanted an Early End to Gulf War," *Plain Dealer*, October 23, 1994.

6. Colin L. Powell and Joseph E. Persico, *My American Journey* (New York: Random House, 1995), 518–21.

7. Caspar Weinberger, "The Uses of Military Power," Remarks Prepared for Delivery by the Secretary of Defense to the National Press Club, Washington, DC, November 28, 1984, http://www.pbs.org/wgbh/pages/frontline/shows/military/force/weinberger.html.

8. Bush and Scowcroft, *A World Transformed*, 488–89.

9. Richard Haass, *War of Necessity, War of Choice: A Memoir of Two Iraq Wars* (New York: Simon & Schuster, 2009); Richard B. Cheney and Liz Cheney, *In My Time: A Personal and Political Memoir* (New York: Simon & Schuster, 2011), 228; "Daily Press Releases," February 22, 1991, box 17, White House Press Office, George Bush Presidential Library; "Statement by Press Secretary Fitzwater on Incremental Costs for Operation Desert Shield," Public Papers of the Presidents of the United States: George H. W. Bush, US Government Printing Office, Book 1, January 11, 1991, 31, http://www.gpo.gov/fdsys/pkg/PPP-1991-book1/html/PPP-1991-book1-doc-pg31.htm; Stephen Daggett, "Costs of Major U.S. Wars, Congressional Research Service (CRS)" (current year figures), 2010, 2, http://cironline.org/sites/default/files/legacy/files/June2010CRScostofuswars.pdf.

10. Bush and Scowcroft, *A World Transformed*, 482–89; Bob Woodward, *The Commanders* (New York: Simon & Schuster, 1991).

11. Rick Atkinson, *Crusade: The Untold Story of the Persian Gulf War* (Boston: Houghton Mifflin, 1993).

12. Norman Schwarzkopf with Peter Petre, *It Doesn't Take a Hero* (New York: Bantam Books, 1992); Michael R. Gordon and Bernard E. Trainor, *The Generals' War: The Inside Story of the Conflict in the Gulf*, vol. 144 (Boston: Little, Brown, 1995).

13. Bush and Scowcroft, *A World Transformed*, 482–83; Weinberger, "The Uses of Military Power."

14. Bush and Scowcroft, *A World Transformed*, 482–89.

15. This is not to say that the United States had the right to invade the sovereignty of another country. That was not to be taken for granted but was another complicating factor.

16. Carl Von Clausewitz, *On War*, ed. and trans. Michael Howard and Peter Paret (Princeton, NJ: Princeton University Press, 1976), 92.

17. "Transcript of Meeting between U.S. Ambassador April Glaspie and Iraqi President Saddam Hussein," ed. State, Collection: Iraq-Gate (Digital National Security Archive, July 25, 1990); "Excerpts from Iraqi Document on Meeting with U.S. Envoy," *New York Times International*, 1990, http://msuweb.montclair.edu/~furrg/glaspie.html.

18. Hal Brands and David Palkki, "Conspiring Bastards: Saddam Hussein's Strategic View of the United States," *Diplomatic History* 36, no. 3 (2012): 625–59.

19. Interview of Tariq Aziz by Milton Viorst, "Report from Baghdad," *New Yorker*, June 24, 1991, 55–73, especially 66–67, in Janice Gross Stein, "Deterrence and Compellence in the Gulf, 1990–91: A Failed or Impossible Task?," *International Security* 2 (1992): 154.

20. Secretary of Defense Richard (Dick) Cheney, NSC meeting minutes, August 3, 1990, 3–4.

21. Stein, "Deterrence and Compellence in the Gulf," 168–69.

22. George H. W. Bush, "National Security Directive 54: Responding to Iraqi Aggression in the Gulf" (Washington, DC: the White House, January 15, 1991).

23. UNSCRs 660, August 2, 1990, 661–62, 664–67, 669–70, 674, 677, and 678, November 29, 1990. America also implemented a naval blockade of Iraqi oil-exporting capacity to support the sanctions.

24. Hal Brands, *From Berlin to Baghdad: America's Search for Purpose in the Post-Cold War World* (Lexington: University Press of Kentucky, 2008), 55.

25. Before these additional troops arrived in the theater between November and January, there were 230,000 US forces deployed to the region. These consisted of 165,000 ground and air forces, with 65,000 seaborne personnel, plus 25,000 international forces. Thomas R. Dubois, "The Weinberger Doctrine and the Liberation of Kuwait Air War College," *US Army War College Quarterly: Parameters* 21, no. 1 (1991): 31.

26. Remark by former deputy national security adviser and later secretary of defense Robert (Bob) Gates during a twenty-year anniversary panel celebrating the end of the Cold War and the successful conclusion of the Persian Gulf War, January 20, 2011.

27. Gordon and Trainor, *The Generals' War*, 152–58.

28. Robert (Bob) Gates, remarks, "Persian Gulf War Twenty Year Anniversary Panel," Texas A&M University, February 23, 2011.

29. Brands, *From Berlin to Baghdad*, 53.

30. Baker, *The Politics of Diplomacy*, 355–63; Brands, *From Berlin to Baghdad*, 59; President Bush letter to Iraqi president Saddam Hussein, January 1991 in Woodward, *The Commanders*, 354.

31. Baker, *The Politics of Diplomacy*, 363; James A. Baker III, *Work Hard, Study . . . and Keep Out of Politics! Adventures and Lessons from an Unexpected Public Life* (New York: G.P. Putnam's Sons, 2006), 297–98.

32. Bush and Scowcroft, *A World Transformed*, 421–22, 444–46.

33. Woodward, *The Commanders*, 354–55, 358.

34. Pell in Senate Foreign Relations Committee, U.S. Policy in the Persian Gulf, January 8, 1991, 1, in Brands, *From Berlin to Baghdad*, 58; Congressional Record, 102nd Cong., 1st sess., vol. 137, 1:S11; ibid., 5:H101; Gordon S. Black, *USA Today* poll, USGBU-SA.903227. R007, iPoll Database, December 2, 1990; Congressional Joint Resolution, Public Law No. 102–1, 102nd Congress, January 14, 1991.

35. Brands, *From Berlin to Baghdad*, 59.

36. Ibid., 57.

37. Bush in Meacham, *Destiny and Power*, 459, 461.

38. National Security Directive (NSD)-45, August 20, 1990, and NSD-54, January 15, 1991. NSD 54 reiterated support for the four interests outlined in NSD 45 (p. 2). George H. W. Bush would not end military operations until he determined that all of these had been accomplished. The document then specified the ways in which the military should advance those interests. First, the military should defend Saudi Arabia and other Gulf Cooperation Council states from attack. Second, coalition and American forces should prevent Iraqi ballistic missile launches against neighboring states. Third, the destruction of Iraq's weapons of mass destruction was a specific goal, as was destroying its command, control, and communications infrastructure and rendering the Republican Guard an ineffective fighting force. Fourth, the military should design its operations "to drive Iraqi forces from Kuwait," break their will, encourage defection, "and weaken Iraqi popular support for the current government."

39. Bush, "National Security Directive 54," 2–3.

40. Conflict Records Research Center, "A Revolutionary Command Council Meeting about Coalition Operations against Iraq, January 18, 1991" (Washington, DC: Conflict Records Research Center, 1991), 8.

41. Ibid., 11–12.

42. Powell and Persico, *My American Journey*, 511; Conflict Records Research Center, "A Revolutionary Command Council Meeting about Coalition Operations against Iraq, January 18, 1991," 11–12.

43. Saddam Hussein interview with an FBI special agent, session 11, March 3, 2004, 3.

44. Phone conversation with USSR president Mikhail Gorbachev, #1331, February 21, 1991, 6:45–7:20 p.m. EST, Bush Presidential Records, transcript; phone conversation with USSR president Mikhail Gorbachev, #1326, February 22, 1991, 11:31 a.m.–12:43 p.m. EST, Bush Presidential Records, transcript; phone conversation with USSR president Mikhail Gorbachev, #1338, February 23, 1991, 11:15–11:43 a.m. EST, Bush Presidential Records, transcript.

45. Public Papers of the Presidents of the United States: George H. W. Bush, 1991, Book 1, February 22, 1991, 165–66, 168–70, from the US Government Printing Office, accessed August 7, 2015, http://www.gpo.gov/fdsys/pkg/PPP-1991-book1/html/PPP-1991-book1-doc-pg165.htm.

46. Brands, *From Berlin to Baghdad*, 62–63.

47. Dubois, "The Weinberger Doctrine and the Liberation of Kuwait," 30.

48. John Mueller, *War, Presidents, and Public Opinion* (New York: Wiley, 1973), 267.

49. "George H. W. Bush's Job Approval Ratings Trend," accessed January 13, 2025, http://www.gallup.com/poll/116677/presidential-approval-ratings-gallup-historical-statistics-trends.aspx.

50. Ibid.; Bruce W. Jentleson, "The Pretty Prudent Public: Post Post-Vietnam American Opinion on the Use of Military Force," *International Studies Quarterly* 36, no. 1 (1992): 49–73; Dubois, "The Weinberger Doctrine and the Liberation of Kuwait," 33.

51. Phone conversation with President Mubarak of Egypt on February 26, 1991, #1458, Document No. 10, Restriction (b)(1), Class C, February 26, 1991, 3:02–3:05 p.m., Bush Presidential Records, Presidential Telephone Calls—Memorandum of Conversations 2/22/91–3/6/91, transcript.

52. Phone conversation with President Turgut Ozal of Turkey, #1586, February 28, 1991, 8:05–8:17 a.m. EST, Bush Presidential Records, transcript, 3; Powell and Persico, *My American Journey*, 519.

53. Baker III, *Work Hard, Study . . . and Keep Out of Politics!*, 303.

54. Cheney and Cheney, *In My Time*, 222–23.

55. Ibid., 220.

56. Powell and Persico, *My American Journey*, 521–22.

57. Phone conversation with President Mubarak of Egypt on February 26, 1991, #1458, Document No. 10; phone conversation with Turgut Ozal, president of Turkey on February 26, 1991, #1444, February 26, 1991, 2:37–2:49 p.m. EST, Bush Presidential Records, transcript; phone conversation with King Fahd of Saudi Arabia on February 28, 1991, #1501, Document No. 19, Restriction (b)(1), Class C, February 28, 1991, 6:58–7:19 p.m. EST, Bush Presidential Records, Presidential Telephone Calls—Memorandum of Conversations 2/22/91–3/6/91, transcript.

58. Bush, answer to a question from the press, February 15, 1991. Bush said, "There's another way (other than by coalition military action) for the bloodshed to stop, and that is for the Iraqi military and the Iraqi people to take matters into their own hands—to force Saddam Hussein, the dictator, to step aside"; Public Papers of the Presidents of the United States: George H. W. Bush, 1991, Book 1, February 15, 1991, 145.

59. Bush and Scowcroft, *A World Transformed*, 481.

60. Ibid., 481–82.

61. "Statement by Press Secretary Fitzwater on the Persian Gulf Conflict," Public Papers of the Presidents of the United States: George H. W. Bush, 1991, Book 1, February 25, 1991, 175, http://www.gpo.gov/fdsys/pkg/PPP-1991-book1/html/PPP-1991-book1-doc-pg175-2.htm.

62. Powell and Persico, *My American Journey*, 520.

63. Brands, *From Berlin to Baghdad*, 63–64.

64. Powell and Persico, *My American Journey*, 518–21.

65. Atkinson, *Crusade*; Powell and Persico, *My American Journey*, 518–21; Schwarzkopf with Petre, *It Doesn't Take a Hero*; Gordon and Trainor, *The Generals' War*; Woodward, *The Commanders*; Bush and Scowcroft, *A World Transformed*, 486.

66. Bush and Scowcroft, *A World Transformed*, 485.

67. Ibid., 485; Schwarzkopf with Petre, *It Doesn't Take a Hero*.

68. Bush and Scowcroft, *A World Transformed*, 485; Powell and Persico, *My American Journey*.

69. Bush and Scowcroft, *A World Transformed*, 485, 86; Powell and Persico, *My American Journey*; Atkinson, *Crusade*; Gordon and Trainor, *The Generals' War*.

70. President Bush address to the nation, February 27, 1991.

71. National Security Directive (NSD)-45, August 20, 1990, and NSD-54, January 15, 1991.

72. Yuen Foong Khong, *Analogies at War: Korea, Munich, Dien Bien Phu, and the Vietnam Decisions of 1965* (Princeton, NJ: Princeton University Press, 1992), 261–62.

73. Baker, *The Politics of Diplomacy*, 303.

74. Powell and Persico, *My American Journey*, 147–49.

75. Arnold R. Isaacs, *Vietnam Shadows: The War, Its Ghosts and Its Legacy* (Baltimore: Johns Hopkins University Press, 2000), 76; Brent Scowcroft, email correspondence, September 13, 2016; Scowcroft recalled that "during the air campaign before our ground forces moved in, there was pressure to ease off. We did not give in to the pressure, in no small

part because President Bush remembered the bombing pauses that Johnson and Nixon were pressured into calling in Vietnam, and how they gave the enemy a chance to regroup."

76. Les Janka, White House Press Secretary, in *Frontline*, season 3, episode 6, "Retreat from Beirut," aired February 26, 1985, on PBS.

77. National Security Directive (NSD)-45, August 20, 1990, and NSD-54, January 15, 1991. These documents outline a "no-more-Vietnams" policy approach with limited objectives as well as the importance of the coalition and decisive force from the start. Dubois, "The Weinberger Doctrine and the Liberation of Kuwait," 33; Bush and Scowcroft, *A World Transformed*, 489.

78. Scowcroft, email; Bush and Scowcroft, *A World Transformed*, 489.

79. Bush, Inaugural Address.

80. Gregory Daddis, *Westmoreland's War: Reassessing American Strategy in Vietnam* (Oxford: Oxford University Press, 2013); Gregory A. Daddis, "The Problem of Metrics: Assessing Progress and Effectiveness in the Vietnam War," *War in History* 19, no. 1 (2012): 73–98; Fredrik Logevall, *Choosing War: The Lost Chance for Peace and the Escalation of War in Vietnam* (Oakland: University of California Press, 2001); Herbert R. McMaster, *Dereliction of Duty: Johnson, McNamara, the Joint Chiefs of Staff, and the Lies That Led to Vietnam* (New York: HarperCollins, 1998).

81. Cheney and Cheney, *In My Time*, 185; Scowcroft, email; Bush and Scowcroft, *A World Transformed*, 489.

82. Robert S. McNamara and Brian VanDeMark, *In Retrospect: The Tragedy and Lessons of Vietnam* (New York: Vintage, 1996), 322–24; Logevall, *Choosing War*.

83. Cheney and Cheney, *In My Time*, 185.

84. Isaacs, *Vietnam Shadows*, 76.

85. Ibid., 76.

86. Ibid., 85.

87. Bush and Scowcroft, *A World Transformed*, 489.

88. Weinberger, "The Uses of Military Power."

89. George H. W. Bush, "The President's News Conference" (Washington, DC: the White House, January 12, 1991).

90. Eric Schmitt, "How to Fight Iraq: Four Outlines, All Are Disputed," *New York Times*, November 19, 1990, in Dubois, "The Weinberger Doctrine and the Liberation of Kuwait," 29.

91. Dubois, "The Weinberger Doctrine and the Liberation of Kuwait," 33.

92. Khong, *Analogies at War*, 261–62.

93. Bush and Scowcroft, *A World Transformed*, 489. Regarding the decision not to topple Saddam, Bush and Scowcroft wrote, "Apprehending him [Hussein] was probably impossible. We [initially] had been unable to find Noriega in Panama, which we knew intimately. We would have been forced to occupy Baghdad and, in effect, rule Iraq. . . . Furthermore, we had been self-consciously trying to set a pattern for handling aggression in the post-Cold War world. Going in and occupying Iraq, thus unilaterally exceeding the United Nations' mandate, would have destroyed the precedent of international response to aggression that we hoped to establish. Had we gone the invasion route, the United States could conceivably still be an occupying power in a bitterly hostile land. It would have been a dramatically different—and perhaps barren—outcome."

94. Ibid., 489.

95. Ibid., 488–89.

96. Scowcroft, email; Meacham, answer to author's question during a book tour event.

97. Colin Powell, phone interview, August 8, 2016.

98. Scowcroft, email.

99. Isaacs, *Vietnam Shadows*, 76.

100. Weinberger, "The Uses of Military Power."

101. Jeffrey Record, *Hollow Victory: A Contrary View of the Gulf War* (Upperville, VA: Potomac Books, 1993), 155–60; Christopher Layne, "Why the Gulf War Was Not in the National Interest," *Atlantic Monthly*, July 1991, 68.

102. Jim Hoagland, "Desert Storm Ticktock," *Washington Post*, January 26, 1992.

103. Mary Ann Tétreault, "Kuwait: The Morning After," *Current History* 91, no. 561 (January 1992): 7; Record, *Hollow Victory*, 155–60.

104. Saddam Hussein, for instance, invaded Iran in 1980 and gassed his own people.

105. William Nester, *Haunted Victory: The American Crusade to Destroy Saddam and Impose Democracy on Iraq* (Upperville, VA: Potomac Books), 2012.

106. George H. W. Bush, Public Papers of the Presidents: Bush, 1991, 1:145 in David F. Schmitz, *Brent Scowcroft: Internationalism and Post-Vietnam War American Foreign Policy* (Lanham, MD: Rowman & Littlefield, 2011), 158.

107. Schmitz, *Brent Scowcroft*, 161; Bush and Scowcroft, *A World Transformed*, 488–89.

108. Phone conversation with President Mubarak of Egypt.

109. Scowcroft, email.

110. Bush and Scowcroft, *A World Transformed*, 484–85.

111. Panel discussion, Gulf War Twenty-Year Anniversary, Texas A&M University, January 20, 2011; Bush and Scowcroft, *A World Transformed*, 485.

112. Gordon and Trainor, *The Generals' War*, 400–32; Woodward, *The Commanders*.

113. Powell and Persico, *My American Journey*; Schwarzkopf with Petre, *It Doesn't Take a Hero*; Bush and Scowcroft, *A World Transformed*, 484–85; Atkinson, *Crusade*.

114. Bush and Scowcroft, *A World Transformed*, 485–86.

115. Public Papers of the Presidents: Bush, 1991, 1, 187–88; Bush and Scowcroft, *A World Transformed*, 486.

116. Bush and Scowcroft, *A World Transformed*, 489; Dubois, "The Weinberger Doctrine and the Liberation of Kuwait," 31.

117. Scowcroft, email; Colin Powell, phone interview; Bush, "Presidential Radio Address to Troops in the Gulf"; Bush, "Meetings with World Leaders"; Meacham, answer to author's question during a book tour event; Khong, *Analogies at War*, 261–62; Dubois, "The Weinberger Doctrine and the Liberation of Kuwait," 33; Isaacs, *Vietnam Shadows*, 76.

118. Gordon and Trainor, *The Generals' War*, 465.

119. Schmitz, *Brent Scowcroft*, 162–63.

8. Winning the Next (versus the Last) War

The chapter 8 epigraphs are drawn from General Martin Dempsey in Richard D. Hooker Jr. and Joseph J. Collins, *Lessons Encountered: Learning from the Long War* (Fort McNair, DC: National Defense University, 2015), 257; John Lewis Gaddis, "The History That Made the World Today: A Conversation with John Lewis Gaddis and Margaret MacMillan," Council on Foreign Relations, September 1, 2022, https://www.foreignaffairs.com/podcasts/gaddis-macmillan/history-made-world-today; Caspar Weinberger, "The Uses of Military Power,"

Remarks Prepared for Delivery by the Secretary of Defense to the National Press Club, Washington, DC, November 28, 1984, http://www.pbs.org/wgbh/pages/frontline/shows/military/force/weinberger.html; David Petraeus, phone interview, August 25, 2016, and email exchange, September 8, 2016; David Frum in Peter Baker, "George W. Bush: The Decider and Delegator," in *Triumphs and Tragedies of the Modern Presidency*, ed. Maxmillian Angerholzer III, James Kitfield, Norman Ornstein, and Stephen Skowronek, Center for the Study of the Presidency and Congress (Santa Barbara, CA: Praeger, 2001), 309; Colin S. Gray, "What Should the U.S. Army Learn from History?," 40; Michael Howard in Thomas E. Ricks, *The Gamble: General David Petraeus and the American Military Adventure in Iraq, 2006–2008* (London: Penguin, 2009), 100; 274; Henry Kissinger, *Crisis: The Anatomy of Two Major Foreign Policy Crises* (New York: Simon & Schuster, 2003), 37; Ash Carter, *Inside the Five-Sided Box: Lessons from a Lifetime of Leadership in the Pentagon* (London: Penguin, 2020), 427; Ash Carter, *Inside the Five-Sided Box: Lessons from a Lifetime of Leadership in the Pentagon* (London: Penguin, 2020), 426; Leon Panetta and Jim Newton, *Worthy Fights: A Memoir of Leadership in War and Peace* (London: Penguin, 2014), 290, 415.

1. George H. W. Bush and Brent Scowcroft, *A World Transformed*, 1st ed (New York: Knopf, 1998), 488–89.

2. John Mueller, *War, Presidents, and Public Opinion* (New York: Wiley, 1973), 273; John Mueller, "American Public Opinion and Military Ventures Abroad: Attention, Evaluation, Involvement, Politics, and the Wars of the Bushes," Annual Meeting of the American Political Science Association, Philadelphia, August 2003, 47.

3. Donna J. Nincic and Miroslav Nincic, "Commitment to Military Intervention: The Democratic Government as Economic Investor," *Journal of Peace Research* 32, no. 4 (1995): 413–26.

4. Kin Fai Ellick and Jessica Y. Y. Kwong, "The Role of Anticipated Regret in Escalation of Commitment," *Journal of Applied Psychology* 92, no. 2 (2007): 545–54; Gillian Ku, "Learning to De-escalate: The Effects of Regret in Escalation of Commitment," *Organizational Behavior and Human Decision Processes* 105, no. 2 (2008): 221–32.

5. George W. Downs and David M. Rocke, "Conflict, Agency, and Gambling for Resurrection: The Principal-Agent Problem Goes to War," *American Journal of Political Science* 38, no. 2 (1994): 362–80.

6. Marcel Zeelenberg and Eric Van Dijk, "A Reverse Sunk Cost Effect in Risky Decision Making: Sometimes We Have Too Much Invested to Gamble," *Journal of Economic Psychology* 18, no. 6 (1997): 679–89; Daniel Kahneman and Amos Tversky, "Prospect Theory: An Analysis of Decision under Risk," *Econometrica: Journal of the Econometric Society* 23 (1979): 263–91.

7. Zeelenberg and Van Dijk, "A Reverse Sunk Cost Effect in Risky Decision Making," 679–89; Kahneman and Tversky, "Prospect Theory," 263–91.

8. Peter D. Feaver, "The Right to Be Right: Civil-Military Relations and the Iraq Surge Decision," *International Security* 35, no. 4 (2011): 108; Peter Feaver, interview, November 5, 2015; Peter Feaver, interview, Southern Methodist University, Center for Presidential History (hereafter SMU-CPH), April 27, 2015, https://vimeo.com/131688470.

9. Bob Woodward, *Obama's Wars* (New York: Simon & Schuster, 2011), 324–28.

10. Andrew Payne, "Presidents, Politics, and Military Strategy: Electoral Constraints during the Iraq War," *International Security* 44, no. 3 (2019): 202.

11. Dick Cheney, interview, SMU-CPH, August 6, 2015, https://www.dropbox.com/s/9vsz4e3qj9u2eqa/; Feaver, interview, SMU-CPH; Steve Hadley, speaking engagement,

Duke University, December 2, 2014; Meghan O'Sullivan, interview, SMU-CPH, May 12, 2016, https://vimeo.com/album/3353422/video/166466344.

12. CNN Wire Staff, "Obama Announces Afghanistan Troop Withdrawal Plan," CNN, June 23, 2011, http://www.cnn.com/2011/POLITICS/06/22/afghanistan.troops.drawdown/index.html.

13. Kelly McHugh, "A Tale of Two Surges: Comparing the Politics of the 2007 Iraq Surge and the 2009 Afghanistan Surge," *Sage Open* 5, no. 4 (2015): 215.

14. Woodward, *Obama's Wars*, 324–28.

15. Kissinger, *Crisis*, 37; David Howell Petraeus, *The American Military and the Lessons of Vietnam: A Study of Military Influence and the Use of Force in the Post-Vietnam Era* (Princeton, NJ: Princeton University Press, 1987); Yuen Foong Khong, *Analogies at War: Korea, Munich, Dien Bien Phu, and the Vietnam Decisions of 1965* (Princeton, NJ: Princeton University Press, 1992), 10, 63–64.

16. Frank G. Hoffman, "One Decade Later: Debacle in Somalia," *Proceedings* 130, no. 1 (2004): 66–71.

17. Weinberger, "The Uses of Military Power."

18. William Clinton, *My Life* (New York: Random House, 2004); Feaver, interview.

19. Presidential Decision Directive-25: US Policy on Reforming Multilateral Peace Operations, May 3, 1994.

20. Madeleine Korbel Albright and William Woodward, *Madam Secretary* (New York: Miramax Books, 2003), 147.

21. Petraeus, phone interview and email exchange.

22. H. R. McMaster and Quassim Cassam, *Battlegrounds: The Fight to Defend the Free World* (New York: HarperCollins, 2020), 4–19; Christian Brose, *The Kill Chain: Defending America in the Future of High-Tech Warfare* (London: Hachette 2020), 1–20; Qiao Liang and Wang Xiangsui, *Unrestricted Warfare* (Beijing: PLA Literature and Art Publishing House, 1999).

23. Andrew J. Bacevich, *The Limits of Power: The End of American Exceptionalism* (New York: Metropolitan Books), 2008.

24. Clinton, *My Life*, 103–104.

25. Carl Von Clausewitz, *On War*, ed. and trans. Michael Howard and Peter Paret (Princeton, NJ: Princeton University Press, 1976); Theodore Reed Fehrenbach, *This Kind of War: A Study in Unpreparedness* (New York: Macmillan 1963); Colin S. Gray, *Fighting Talk: Forty Maxims on War, Peace, and Strategy* (Westport, CT: Greenwood, 2007).

26. Dale Shrader and Shanna Shrader, and Steve Fowler, interviews, January 31, 2017, and December 7, 2017, respectively.

27. Eliot A. Cohen, *Supreme Command: Soldiers, Statesmen and Leadership in Wartime* (New York: Simon & Schuster, 2012).

28. Joshua Bolten, interview, SMU-CPH, May 15, 2015, https://vimeo.com/128817283; Ricks, *The Gamble*; Peter Baker, *Days of Fire: Bush and Cheney in the White House* (New York: Anchor Books, 2013); Paula Broadwell and Vernon Loeb, *All In: The Education of General David Petraeus* (London: Penguin, 2012).

29. Eric Victor Larson, *Casualties and Consensus: The Historical Role of Casualties in Domestic Support for US Military Operations* (Santa Monica, CA: RAND, 1996), 67–71, 94–95; Peter Feaver, *Armed Servants: Agency, Oversight, and Civil-Military Relations* (Cambridge, MA: Harvard University Press, 2003), 247; Peter D. Feaver and Christopher Gelpi, *Choosing Your Battles: American Civil-Military Relations and the Use of Force* (Princeton, NJ: Princeton University Press, 2004), 135.

30. Williamson Murray, *Military Adaptation in War: With Fear of Change* (Cambridge: Cambridge University Press, 2011), 6.

31. Frank G. Hoffman and G. Alexander Crowther, "Strategic Assessment and Adaptation: The Surges in Iraq and Afghanistan," in Hooker Jr. and Collins, *Lessons Encountered*, 146–47.

32. John Hannah, interview, SMU-CPH, April 27, 2015, https://vimeo.com/131666291.

33. Baker, "George W. Bush," 306–307.

34. Cohen argued that presidents who actively led their generals were right to do so and produced better wartime results. Cohen, *Supreme Command*; Baker, *Days of Fire*, 516; Bob Woodward, *The War Within: A Secret White House History 2006–2008* (New York: Simon & Schuster, 2008), 84.

35. Baker, *Days of Fire*, 516; Alexander George, "A Case for Multiple Advocacy in Making Foreign Policy," *American Political Science Review* 66, no. 3 (1972): 751–85.

36. Secretary of State Rice indicated that major war policy reviews and change almost never happen early on because the costs to change are so great. Moreover, she argued that a slower reassessment process is more effective in the end. Condoleezza Rice, interview, SMU-CPH, July 20, 2015, https://vimeo.com/134265433.

37. Baker, *Days of Fire*, 516.

38. Bolten, interview SMU-CPH.

39. O'Sullivan, interview, SMU-CPH.

40. Jack Keane, interview, SMU-CPH, August 18, 2015, https://vimeo.com/137792537.

41. Robert Powell, "War as a Commitment Problem," *International Organization* 60, no. 1 (2006): 169–203 (emphasis added).

42. Clausewitz, *On War*, 92.

43. Chad C. Serena, *A Revolution in Military Adaptation: The US Army in the Iraq War* (Washington, DC: Georgetown University Press, 2011), 153.

44. George, "A Case for Multiple Advocacy in Making Foreign Policy."

45. Brent Scowcroft, email, September 13, 2016; Bush and Scowcroft, *A World Transformed*, 1998.

46. Report of the DOD Commission on Beirut International Airport Terrorist Act, October 23, 1983: December 20, 1983, US Government Printing Office, 1984, 43.

47. Clinton, *My Life*, 554.

48. Panetta and Newton, *Worthy Fights*, 290.

49. Ibid.; Hillary Rodham Clinton, *Hard Choices* (New York: Simon & Schuster, 2014).

50. Doug Lute, interview, SMU-CPH, May 28, 2015, https://vimeo.com/131253237.

51. William Clinton, Letter to Congress, October 13, 1993; Clinton, "Address to the Nation on Somalia."

52. Robert ("Bud") McFarlane, phone interview, April 4, 2016; Feaver, interview.

53. Eliot A. Cohen and John Gooch, *Military Misfortunes: The Anatomy of Failure in War* (New York: Free Press, 1991).

54. Albright and Woodward, *Madam Secretary*, 146–48; Clinton, *My Life*, 551–55.

55. Dempsey in Hooker Jr. and Collins, *Lessons Encountered*, 257.

56. Richard Smoke, *Controlling Escalation* (Cambridge, MA: Harvard University Press, 1977), 266, 277, 294–95.

57. Herman Kahn, *On Escalation: Metaphors and Scenarios* (Westport, CT: Praeger, 1965); Samuel B. Bacharach and Edward J. Lawler, *Bargaining: Power, Tactics and Outcomes*

(San Francisco: Jossey-Bass, 1981), 93–94; James D. Fearon, "Domestic Political Audiences and the Escalation of International Disputes," *American Political Science Review* 88, no. 3 (1994): 577–92; James D. Fearon, "Rationalist Explanations for War," *International Organization* 49, no. 3 (1995): 379–414; Thomas C. Schelling, *Micromotives and Macrobehavior* (New York: W. W. Norton, 2006); Forrest E. Morgan et al., *Dangerous Thresholds: Managing Escalation in the 21st Century* (Santa Monica, CA: RAND, 2008), 165–66.

58. Graham T. Allison and Philip Zelikow, *Essence of Decision: Explaining the Cuban Missile Crisis* (Boston: Little Brown, 1999).

59. Christopher Gelpi and Peter D. Feaver, "Speak Softly and Carry a Big Stick? Veterans in the Political Elite and the American Use of Force," *American Political Science Review* 96, no. 4 (2002): 779–93; Feaver and Gelpi, *Choosing Your Battles.*

60. Shawn T. Cochran, "The Civil–Military Divide in Protracted Small War: An Alternative View of Military Leadership Preferences and War Termination," *Armed Forces & Society* 40, no. 1 (2014): 79; Shawn T. Cochran, "Civil-Military Balance of Resolve: The Domestic Politics of Withdrawal from Protracted Small War" (PhD diss., University of Chicago, 2012).

61. Bryan Groves, "Principal-Agent Problems: Why War Strategy Doesn't Always Match Policy Aims," *International Journal of Political Science and Development* 3, no. 2 (February 7, 2015): 63–78.

62. Vikram Singh, phone interview, September 10, 2016.

63. Bryan Groves, "The Importance of Presidential Decision Making: Broader Lessons Derived from the Cuban Missile Crisis," Strategy Bridge: Policy, Strategy, and National Security, February 9, 2014, https://thestrategybridge.org/the-bridge/2014/2/9/the-importance-of-presidential-decision-making.

64. Zalmay Khalilzad, *The Envoy* (New York: St. Martin's, 2016), 283.

65. "1984 Election," *American Presidency Project*, accessed February 11, 2018, http://www.presidency.ucsb.edu/showelection.php?year=1984.

66. Clinton's 1996 reelection, following his sunk cost trap withdrawal, provides another such example.

67. Osama bin Laden, Fatwa Declaring War on the United States, 1998; Tim Naftali, *Blind Spot: The Secret History of American Counterterrorism* (New York: Basic Books, 2009).

68. Timothy J. Geraghty, *Peacekeepers at War: Beirut 1983—The Marine Commander Tells His Story* (Washington, DC: Potomac Books, 2009), xvii; Naftali, *Blind Spot*, chap. 6; Caspar W. Weinberger, *Fighting for Peace: Seven Critical Years in the Pentagon* (New York: Warner Books, 1990).

69. Osama bin Laden, "Fatwa Declaring War on the United States," 1996, 10, https://safe.menlosecurity.com/doc/docview/viewer/docN699C3E71548Dc8a8cb0d6f72d74047e89365155e2f2d32bbb414aff88d9fa4817d3f5c033214.

70. Thomas H. Kean, chair, National Commission on Terrorist Attacks Upon the United States, accessed October 13, 2015, http://www.9-11commission.gov/report/911Report_Ch2.htm; *Milestone Documents in World History: Exploring the Documents That Shaped the World—Osama bin Laden's Declaration of Jihad against Americans* (Ipswich, MA: Salem, 1996), http://webcache.googleusercontent.com/search?q=cache:DMa6U5xmBUwJ:salempress.com/store/pdfs/bin_laden.pdf+&cd=4&hl=en&ct=clnk&gl=us; "Osama bin Laden, Over the Years," CNN, May 2, 2011, http://www.cnn.com/2011/WORLD/asiapcf/05/02/osama.timeline/; Colonel (Ret.) Kenneth Allard, interview, PBS, October 26, 2001.

71. Clinton, Letter to Congress; Clinton, "Address to the Nation on Somalia."

72. Bin Laden, Fatwa Declaring War on the United States.

73. Barack Obama, "Way Forward in Afghanistan," speech at West Point, NY, December 1, 2009.

74. Gerhard Peters and John T. Woolley, "Statement on the Situation in Lebanon," February 7, 1984, online by Gerhard Peters and John T. Woolley, *The American Presidency Project*, accessed April 30, 2016, http://www.presidency.ucsb.edu/ws/?pid=39433; "Documents 256 and 258: Announcements regarding the Redeployment of Marines to Ships off the Coast of Lebanon, American Foreign Policy Current Documents"(Washington, DC: Dept. of State, February 7, 1984).

75. Clausewitz, *On War*.

76. Colin Powell, phone interview, August 8, 2016.

77. Robert Jervis, "Understanding the Bush Doctrine: Preventive Wars and Regime Change," *Political Science Quarterly* 131, no. 2 (2016): 285–311. Leo Blanken and Stephen Rodriguez, "The Strategic Logic of a Forever War," Foreign Policy, September 8, 2021, https://foreignpolicy.com/2021/09/08/afghanistan-biden-sunk-costs-forever-war/; John Harwood, "Why Biden's Afghanistan Exit Wasn't about Good Politics," CNN, August 22, 2021, https://www.cnn.com/2021/08/22/politics/biden-afghanistan-politics-and-polling/index.html; Michael Hirsh, "Is Biden Haunted by Vietnam? Should He Be?: The President Said This Withdrawal Will Be Nothing Like What Happened in 1975, but There Are Some Striking Parallels," Foreign Policy, July 9, 2021, https://foreignpolicy.com/2021/07/09/is-biden-haunted-by-vietnam-should-he-be/; Nahal Toosi and Andrew Desiderio, "A 'Saigon Moment': Biden Feels Political Heat as Chaos Looms in Afghanistan," June 24, 2021, https://www.politico.com/news/2021/06/24/biden-afghanistan-withdraw-troops-white-house-visit-496009; Amber Phillips, "Why No American President Followed through on Promises to End the Afghanistan War—Until Now," *Washington Post*, August 18, 2021, https://www.washingtonpost.com/politics/2021/08/18/why-no-american-president-followed-through-promises-end-afghanistan-war-until-now/; Jonathan Schroden, "Lessons from the Collapse of Afghanistan's Security Forces," *Sentinel* 14, no. 8 (October 2021), https://ctc.usma.edu/lessons-from-the-collapse-of-afghanistans-security-forces/; Nick Turse, "Biden Should Do What Trump Never Could: End America's Forever Wars," *Nation*, January 11, 2021, https://www.thenation.com/article/world/biden-trump-endless-war/.

78. Brose, *The Kill Chain*, 1–20; McMaster and Cassam, *Battlegrounds*, 1–20; Melissa Quinn and Kathryn Watson, "Biden Forcefully Defends Afghanistan Exit and Decision to End War," CBS News, September 1, 2021, https://www.cbsnews.com/news/biden-speech-afghanistan-war-withdrawal-decision/.

79. Office of the Secretary of Defense (OSD), Military and Security Developments Involving the People's Republic of China 2021, Annual Report to Congress, accessed January 13, 2025, https://media.defense.gov/2021/nov/03/2002885874/-1/-1/0/2021-cmpr-final.pdf.

80. John J. Mearsheimer and Glenn Alterman, *The Tragedy of Great Power Politics* (New York: W. W. Norton), 2001.

81. Graham T. Allison, *Destined for War: Can America and China Escape Thucydides' Trap?* (Boston: Houghton Mifflin Harcourt), 2017.

82. Hal Brands and Charles Edel, *The Lessons of Tragedy* (New Haven, CT: Yale University Press, 2019).

83. Joseph Biden, "President Biden: What America Will and Will Not Do in Ukraine," *New York Times*, May 31, 2022.

84. Caroline de Gruyter, "Putin's War Is Europe's 9/11: The Continent Has Finally Woken Up to the Necessity of Hard Power," *Foreign Policy*, February 28, 2022.

85. Hoffman, "One Decade Later," 66–71.

86. Weinberger, "The Uses of Military Power"; Hooker Jr. and Collins, *Lessons Encountered.*

87. Weinberger, "The Uses of Military Power."

88. William J. Clinton, "Presidential Decision Directive (PDD) 25: Reforming Multilateral Peace Operations," May 3, 1994.

89. David Petraeus, emails to author, August 28 and September 8, 2016.

90. Fredric Smoler, "Fighting the Last War—and the Next," *American Heritage* 52, no. 8 (November/December 2001), https://www.americanheritage.com/fighting-last-war-and-next.

91. Hirsh, "Is Biden Haunted by Vietnam?"

92. Woodward, *Obama's Wars*, 324–28.

93. Joseph Biden, "Remarks by President Biden on the Drawdown of U.S. Forces in Afghanistan," July 8, 2021, https://www.whitehouse.gov/briefing-room/speeches-remarks/2021/07/08/remarks-by-president-biden-on-the-drawdown-of-u-s-forces-in-afghanistan/.

94. Daniel Ellsberg, *Secrets: A Memoir of Vietnam and the Pentagon Papers* (London: Penguin, 2003).

95. Philip Zelikow, "The Nature of History's Lessons," in *The Power of the Past: History and Statecraft*, ed. Hal Brands and Jeremi Suri (Washington, DC: Brookings Institution, 2015), 286.

96. Turse, "Biden Should Do What Trump Never Could."

97. Bonnie Kristian, "Turmoil and Taliban Gains in Afghanistan Prove that a US Victory Will Never Be Possible," *USA Today*, July 13, 2021, https://news.yahoo.com/turmoil-taliban-gains-afghanistan-prove-071507059.html, with Andrew Bacevich's 2016 *Foreign Affairs* quote embedded.

98. "Foreign Threats to the 2020 U.S. Federal Elections: Intelligence Community Assessment," declassified version of classified report, National Intelligence Council, March 10, 2021; David E. Sanger and Nicole Perlroth, "Pipeline Attack Yields Urgent Lessons about U.S. Cybersecurity: The Hack Underscored How Vulnerable Government and Industry Are to Even Basic Assaults on Computer Networks," *New York Times*, May 14, 2021, https://www.nytimes.com/2021/05/14/us/politics/pipeline-hack.html; Fabiana Batista, Michael Hirtzer, and Mike Dorning, "All of JBS' U.S. Beef Plants Were Forced Shut by Cyberattack," *Bloomberg*, accessed July 10, 2021, https://www.bloomberg.com/news/articles/2021-05-31/meat-is-latest-cyber-victim-as-hackers-hit-top-supplier-jbs.

99. Bush and Scowcroft, *A World Transformed*, 488–89.

Index

About the Author

Bryan N. Groves is an Army Strategist with a Special Forces background. He has served in South Korea, Germany, Iraq, Bosnia, and Afghanistan in various capacities. Bryan has a PhD in US national security policy from Duke University and a master's degree in international relations from Yale University. He has been a Council on Foreign Relations Term member and taught at his alma mater, West Point. He has worked at the State Department and had assignments across the special operations and conventional communities. While serving on the Joint Staff (J-5), Bryan led the development of strategic documents, including the *President's Unified Command Plan*, the *Chairman's Risk Assessment*, and the *2022 National Military Strategy*. Bryan and his esteemed wife, Richelle, have three wonderful children.